Abuse and Neglect

Institute of Judicial Administration

American Bar Association

Juvenile Justice Standards Project

STANDARDS RELATING TO

Abuse and Neglect

Recommended by the
IJA-ABA JOINT COMMISSION ON JUVENILE JUSTICE STANDARDS

Hon. Irving R. Kaufman, *Chairman*
William S. White and
Margaret K. Rosenheim, *Chairmen of Drafting Committee I*
Robert Burt, *Reporter*
Michael Wald, *Reporter*
Leon Chestang, *Consultant*
Martin Guggenheim, *Special Editor*

Ballinger Publishing Company ● Cambridge, Massachusetts
A Subsidiary of Harper & Row, Publishers, Inc.

DRAFTING COMMITTEE I—INTERVENTION IN THE LIVES OF CHILDREN

This document was prepared for the Juvenile Justice Standards Project of the Institute of Judicial Administration and the American Bar Association. The project is supported by grants prepared under Grant Numbers 71-NI-99-0014; 72-NI-99-0032; 74-NI-99-0043; and 75-NI-99-0101 from the National Institute of Criminal Justice and Law Enforcement, and 76-JN-99-0018; 78-JN-AX-0002; and 79-JN-AX-0025 from the National Institute of Juvenile Justice and Delinquency Prevention, Office of Juvenile Justice and Delinquency Prevention, Law Enforcement Assistance Administration, U.S. Department of Justice, the American Bar Endowment, the Andrew W. Mellon Foundation, the Vincent Astor Foundation, and the Herman Goldman Foundation. The views expressed in this draft do not represent positions taken by the funding sources. Votes on the standards were unanimous in most but not all cases. Specific objections by individual members of the IJA-ABA Joint Commission have been noted in formal dissents printed in the volumes concerned.

Copyright © 1981, Ballinger Publishing Company

Preface

The standards and commentary in this volume are part of a series designed to cover the spectrum of problems pertaining to the laws affecting children. They examine the juvenile justice system and its relationship to the rights and responsibilities of juveniles. The series was prepared under the supervision of a Joint Commission on Juvenile Justice Standards appointed by the Institute of Judicial Administration and the American Bar Association. Twenty volumes in the series have been approved by the House of Delegates of the American Bar Association.

The standards are intended to serve as guidelines for action by legislators, judges, administrators, public and private agencies, local civic groups, and others responsible for or concerned with the treatment of youths at local, state, and federal levels. The twenty-three volumes issued by the joint commission cover the entire field of juvenile justice administration, including the jurisdiction and organization of trial and appellate courts hearing matters concerning juveniles; the transfer of jurisdiction to adult criminal courts; and the functions performed by law enforcement officers and court intake, probation, and corrections personnel. Standards for attorneys representing the state, for juveniles and their families, and for the procedures to be followed at the preadjudication, adjudication, disposition, and postdisposition stages are included. One volume in this series sets forth standards for the statutory classification of delinquent acts and the rules governing the sanctions to be imposed. Other volumes deal with problems affecting nondelinquent youth, including recommendations concerning the permissible range of intervention by the state in cases of abuse or neglect, status offenses (such as truancy and running away), and contractual, medical, educational, and employment rights of minors.

The history of the Juvenile Justice Standards Project illustrates the breadth and scope of its task. In 1971, the Institute of Judicial Administration, a private, nonprofit research and educational organization located at New York University School of Law, began planning the Juvenile Justice Standards Project. At that time, the Project on Standards for Criminal Justice of the ABA, initiated by IJA seven years earlier, was completing the last of twelve volumes of recommendations for the adult criminal justice system. However, those standards were not designed to address the issues confronted by the separate courts handling juvenile matters. The Juvenile Justice Standards Project was created to consider those issues.

A planning committee chaired by then Judge and now Chief Judge Irving R. Kaufman of the United States Court of Appeals for the Second Circuit met in October 1971. That winter, reporters who would be responsible for drafting the volumes met with six planning subcommittees to identify and analyze the important issues in the juvenile justice field. Based on material developed by them, the planning committee charted the areas to be covered.

In February 1973, the ABA became a co-sponsor of the project. IJA continued to serve as the secretariat of the project. The IJA-ABA Joint Commission on Juvenile Justice Standards was then created to serve as the project's governing body. The joint commission, chaired by Chief Judge Kaufman, consists of twenty-nine members, approximately half of whom are lawyers and judges, the balance representing nonlegal disciplines such as psychology and sociology. The chairpersons of the four drafting committees also serve on the joint commission. The perspective of minority groups was introduced by a Minority Group Advisory Committee established in 1973, members of which subsequently joined the commission and the drafting committees. David Gilman has been the director of the project since July 1976.

The task of writing standards and accompanying commentary was undertaken by more than thirty scholars, each of whom was assigned a topic within the jurisdiction of one of the four advisory drafting committees: Committee I, Intervention in the Lives of Children; Committee II, Court Roles and Procedures; Committee III, Treatment and Correction; and Committee IV, Administration. The committees were composed of more than 100 members chosen for their background and experience not only in legal issues affecting youth, but also in related fields such as psychiatry, psychology, sociology, social work, education, corrections, and police work. The standards and commentary produced by the reporters and drafting committees were presented to the IJA-ABA Joint Commission on Juvenile Justice Standards for consideration. The deliberations of the joint commission led to revisions in the standards and commentary presented to them, culminating in the published tentative drafts.

The published tentative drafts were distributed widely to members of the legal community, juvenile justice specialists, and organizations directly concerned with the juvenile justice system for study and comment. The ABA assigned the task of reviewing individual volumes to ABA sections whose members are expert in the specific areas covered by those volumes. Especially helpful during this review period were the comments, observations, and guidance provided by Professor Livingston Hall, Chairperson, Committee on Juvenile Justice of the Section of Criminal Justice, and Marjorie M. Childs, Chairperson of the Juvenile Justice Standards Review Committee of the Section of Family Law of the ABA. The recommendations submitted to the project by the professional groups, attorneys, judges, and ABA sections were presented to an executive committee of the joint commission, to whom the responsibility of responding had been delegated by the full commission. The executive committee consisted of the following members of the joint commission:

Chief Judge Irving R. Kaufman, *Chairman*
Hon. William S. Fort, *Vice Chairman*
Prof. Charles Z. Smith, *Vice Chairman*
Dr. Eli Bower
Allen Breed
William T. Gossett, Esq.
Robert W. Meserve, Esq.
Milton G. Rector
Daniel L. Skoler, Esq.
Hon. William S. White
Hon. Patricia M. Wald, *Special Consultant*

The executive committee met in 1977, 1978, and 1979 to discuss the proposed changes in the published standards and commentary. Minutes issued after the meetings reflecting the decisions by the executive committee were circulated to the members of the joint commission and the ABA House of Delegates, as well as to those who had transmitted comments to the project.

In February 1979, the ABA House of Delegates approved seventeen of the twenty-three published volumes. It was understood that the approved volumes would be revised to conform to the changes described in the minutes of the 1977 and 1978 executive committee meetings. The *Schools and Education* volume was not presented to the House. Of the five remaining volumes, *Court Organization and Administration, Juvenile Delinquency and Sanctions,* and *The Juvenile Probation Function* were approved by the House in February

1980, subject to the changes adopted by the executive committee. *Abuse and Neglect* and *Noncriminal Misbehavior* were held over for final consideration at a future meeting of the House.

Among the agreed-upon changes in the standards was the decision to bracket all numbers limiting time periods and sizes of facilities in order to distinguish precatory from mandatory standards and thereby allow for variations imposed by differences among jurisdictions. In some cases, numerical limitations concerning a juvenile's age also are bracketed.

The tentative drafts of the twenty volumes approved by the ABA House of Delegates, revised as agreed, are now ready for consideration and implementation by the components of the juvenile justice system in the various states and localities.

Much time has elapsed from the start of the project to the present date and significant changes have taken place both in the law and the social climate affecting juvenile justice in this country. Some of the changes are directly traceable to these standards and the intense national interest surrounding their promulgation. Other major changes are the indirect result of the standards; still others derive from independent local influences, such as increases in reported crime rates.

The volumes could not be revised to reflect legal and social developments subsequent to the drafting and release of the tentative drafts in 1975 and 1976 without distorting the context in which they were written and adopted. Therefore, changes in the standards or commentary dictated by the decisions of the executive committee subsequent to the publication of the tentative drafts are indicated in a special notation at the front of each volume.

In addition, the series will be brought up to date in the revised version of the summary volume, *Standards for Juvenile Justice: A Summary and Analysis*, which will describe current history, major trends, and the observable impact of the proposed standards on the juvenile justice system from their earliest dissemination. Far from being outdated, the published standards have become guideposts to the future of juvenile law.

The planning phase of the project was supported by a grant from the National Institute of Law Enforcement and Criminal Justice of the Law Enforcement Assistance Administration. The National Institute also supported the drafting phase of the project, with additional support from grants from the American Bar Endowment, and the Andrew Mellon, Vincent Astor, and Herman Goldman foundations. Both the National Institute and the American Bar Endowment funded the final revision phase of the project.

An account of the history and accomplishment of the project would not be complete without acknowledging the work of some of the people who, although no longer with the project, contributed immeasurably to its achievements. Orison Marden, a former president of the ABA, was co-chairman of the commission from 1974 until his death in August 1975. Paul Nejelski was director of the project during its planning phase from 1971 to 1973. Lawrence Schultz, who was research director from the inception of the project, was director from 1973 until 1974. From 1974 to 1975, Delmar Karlen served as vice-chairman of the commission and as chairman of its executive committee, and Wayne Mucci was director of the project. Barbara Flicker was director of the project from 1975 to 1976. Justice Tom C. Clark was chairman for ABA liaison from 1975 to 1977.

Legal editors included Jo Rena Adams, Paula Ryan, and Ken Taymor. Other valued staff members were Fred Cohen, Pat Pickrell, Peter Garlock, and Oscar Garcia-Rivera. Mary Anne O'Dea and Susan J. Sandler also served as editors. Amy Berlin and Kathy Kolar were research associates. Jennifer K. Schweickart and Ramelle Cochrane Pulitzer were editorial assistants.

It should be noted that the positions adopted by the joint commission and stated in these volumes do not represent the official policies or views of the organizations with which the members of the joint commission and the drafting committees are associated.

This volume is part of the series of standards and commentary prepared under the supervision of Drafting Committee I, which also includes the following volumes:

RIGHTS OF MINORS
JUVENILE DELINQUENCY AND SANCTIONS
NONCRIMINAL MISBEHAVIOR
YOUTH SERVICE AGENCIES
SCHOOLS AND EDUCATION
POLICE HANDLING OF JUVENILE PROBLEMS

Contents

Introduction

Each year approximately 150,000 child "neglect" proceedings are heard by juvenile courts throughout the country. These proceedings are instituted to protect children who presumably are not being cared for adequately by their parents. Upon finding a child "neglected," a court can order that the parents accept supervision and therapy as a condition of continued custody, or can order that the child be removed from his/her home and placed in a foster home, group home, residential treatment center, or institution. The best available data indicate that as many as 50 percent of neglect proceedings result in removal of the child from the natural parents' home.

While most commentators support restricting juvenile court activities in the areas of delinquency and noncriminal misbehavior (see the *Juvenile Delinquency and Sanctions* and *Noncriminal Misbehavior* volumes), there is considerably more controversy regarding the appropriate direction for state policy on behalf of "abused" or "neglected" children. Many commentators advocate expanding, not contracting, state activities in these areas. For example, efforts to overcome poverty have resulted in concern over the "disadvantaged" child. The apparent inability of public schools to decrease performance differences between "advantaged" and "disadvantaged" children led experts from many disciplines to focus on family failures as the cause of "disadvantage" and to support state intervention earlier in life in order to help overcome these disadvantages. In addition, publicity about the extent of physical abuse of children, prompted by the identification of the "battered child syndrome" in 1962, led directly to new legislation establishing reporting schemes to improve the state's ability to find abusing parents.

There is little question that many children in our society grow up in less than "ideal" environments. As a society, we have been unwilling to make the commitments necessary to insure that all children receive adequate schooling, housing, or medical care. However, the

1

fact that many children are denied an "optimal" environment does not clearly lead to the conclusion that we should be expanding coercive state intervention on behalf of children. Determining the appropriate scope of coercive intervention entails evaluating the efficacy of such intervention and examining the costs and benefits of using court proceedings to try to protect children.

In fact, a review of the current system of intervention must make one dubious about the efficacy of expanded intervention. For the past twenty years, experts from many disciplines have been pointing out major defects in the system of intervention. Criticism has focused especially on three aspects of the system: the fact that courts often remove children from their homes without an adequate effort to protect them in their own homes; the fact that children in foster care remain there for long periods of time and are subjected to multiple placements; and the fact that children who cannot be returned home are not provided with new homes, either through adoption, guardianship, or placement in a permanent foster home. Because of these defects and the evidence that coercive intervention may harm, as well as help children, these commentators would severely restrict current intervention efforts.

Closely related to the question of the appropriate scope of intervention is the issue of the amount of discretion that should be given decisionmakers as to when and how to intervene. Proponents of broad intervention often insist that broad, vague laws are essential if we are to protect all children needing help. These commentators would leave it largely to the discretion and presumed expertise of judges and social workers to decide when and how to intervene. See S. Katz, *When Parents Fail* 64–65 (1971). Again, this view is disputed by other experts who see broad, vague laws as ultimately leading to intervention harmful to children. See Mnookin, "Child Custody Adjudication: Judicial Functions in the Face of Indeterminacy," 39 *Law and Contemp. Probs.* 226 (1976).

Recognizing that many children need state protection, but that coercive intervention can harm, as well as help children, we attempt in this volume to provide a sound basis for coercive state intervention on behalf of children that reflects both the needs of children and the limits of coercive intervention. The volume focuses on both substantive standards and the process of intervention.

A central premise of the standards is that the entire intervention process must be viewed as a whole—from the scope of mandatory reporting laws to the termination of parental rights. New laws and administrative procedures are needed that reflect a consistent and integrated set of goals and policies for the entire system.

To provide for an integrated system, the volume proposes standards for each of the major substantive decisions that must be made: the scope of mandatory reporting laws, the basis for coercive court intervention, the grounds for removing children from their homes, both pre- and postadjudication, the grounds for returning children to their parents, and the basis for termination of parental rights. It also proposes procedural standards for making each of these decisions and establishes mechanisms for insuring the quality of all institutional decisionmakers. Finally, standards are proposed to regulate the process of "voluntary placement" of children into foster care without court intervention, since this process is closely connected with the coercive intervention system.

The standards establish a system far different from that presently found in any state, although the best practices found in various states have been adopted. The proposed system is designed to achieve four major goals: to allow intervention only where there is reason to believe that coercive intervention will in fact benefit the child, given the knowledge available about children's needs and the means of helping children, and taking into consideration the resources likely to be available to help children; to insure that when intervention occurs, every effort is made to keep children with their parents, or if this is impossible, to provide them with a stable living situation conducive to their well-being; to insure that procedures are followed which facilitate making appropriate decisions; and to insure that all decisionmakers are held accountable for their actions. This last goal merits special emphasis. One of the most difficult problems we faced in drafting these standards was the absence of data about how the current system works and about the efficacy of various types of intervention. Therefore, the standards provide for a number of monitoring and testing procedures designed to permit continual evaluation of the entire intervention process. Implementation of these mechanisms is critical to the utility of the proposed system.

The standards are based on the initial premise that the proposed goals can best be accomplished if the grounds for state intervention are carefully and narrowly defined and procedural protections are afforded all parties, including the child. A basic tenet of the volume is that great deference should be given to "family autonomy." This tenet is adopted because it is most likely to lead to decisions that help children.

Therefore, the standards propose a new statutory definition of the grounds for intervention. See Part II. The terms "neglect," "abuse," and "dependency" have been abandoned. In their place, we use a new term, "endangered child," and Part II specifies the conditions which constitute "endangerment." In general, coercive intervention is limited to situations where the child has suffered, or is likely to suffer, serious harm. The standards also reject expansion of mandatory reporting laws beyond cases of physical abuse. See Part III. Mandatory reporting is limited to physical abuse since reporting laws are most effective and most likely to be properly used only in dealing with physical abuse.

These statutory bases for coercive intervention are of critical importance to the entire system proposed in this volume. They represent detailed, carefully considered judgments as to those situations in which intervention will likely improve the child's situation. Moreover, because they focus on those cases where the risks of nonintervention are greatest, they should help assure that the limited resources available for helping children are concentrated where the needs are greatest.

In recognition of the seriousness of an intervention decision, from both the parents' and the child's viewpoint, the standards prescribe a number of procedural safeguards for the adjudication process. In line with recent judicial and legislative decisions, these include the right to counsel for parents and child, the right to a formal hearing, and a "clear and convincing" evidence standard for the finding of "endangerment." See Part V.

The standards also provide guidelines for the decisions that must be made following intervention. To a large degree the failure of the present system is not so much in its goals as in the implementation of these goals. Therefore, the standards governing dispositions and post-dispositional monitoring of the endangered child are of particular importance.

Because children removed from their homes and placed in "temporary" foster care often remain there for many years, frequently until their majority, and as a result, often suffer serious psychological damage, the standards are designed to limit the possibility of unwarranted removal. First, they require that preadjudication removal occur only to protect the child from serious physical harm and that any pretrial removal be judicially reviewed within twenty-four hours. See Part IV. With regard to posttrial removal, the standards reject the broad, ill-defined "best interests of the child" formula now used in most states as the criterion for removal, and in its place substitute a more particularized inquiry as to whether removal is necessary to protect the child from the specific harm which precipitated the intervention. Parallel changes are suggested in the criteria for determining whether a child who has been removed from the home should be returned to the natural parents. See Part VI.

In order to avoid the problem of consigning children to long-term, impermanent foster care, the standards develop a set of procedures for monitoring the status of children under court supervision, in order to terminate supervision as expeditiously as possible, and if a child is in foster care, to get the child returned home or placed in another permanent home within a reasonable period of time from the child's perspective.

The main elements of the monitoring procedure are the requirements of specific plans designed to accomplish the goals of intervention, periodic court reviews, and establishment of a grievance mechanism for parental and child complaints about inadequate services. Moreover, the standards require the court and agency to facilitate maximum parent-child contact when a child is in foster care. See Part VII.

Part VIII provides standards for termination of parental rights. It must be recognized that many children who enter foster care cannot be returned to their parents. Their parents may not want them or may be unable to care for them regardless of the services offered. Under present law termination is relatively rare, haphazard, and based on parental fault. In place of this, the standards propose that termination be based on length of time in care. If a child cannot be returned within a reasonable time from the child's perspective—and the time varies with the child's age—then termination would be ordered if it can be shown by clear and convincing evidence that facts sufficient to warrant termination exist, unless termination would be detrimental to the child or it is unlikely that the child can be provided a permanent home, and therefore termination would leave the child without parents.

The standards also restrict the voluntary placement process. Regulations are proposed designed to insure that parents do not place children into foster care unnecessarily. Moreover, if a child remains in care longer than six months, court jurisdiction is invoked to determine whether continued placement is necessary. See Part X.

In general, the standards proposed are much more rule-oriented than the present process. Current laws are extremely vague, giving social agencies and courts enormous discretion about when and how to intervene. The proposed standards are designed to limit this discretion. Moreover, unlike existing laws, the standards require decisionmakers to specifically justify and monitor the impact of every decision they make.

Specified guidelines are proposed because we are convinced that the needs of most children are best protected through such guidelines. In addition, specific standards are more likely to be applied evenhandedly and without economic or cultural discrimination. Carefully drawn, specific standards also can present issues within a court's competence to decide. Current laws not only presume expertise that courts often lack, they also call upon courts to decide issues that cannot be easily adjudicated, such as what is a child's "best interest." Finally, vague standards require judges to make value judgments that are appropriately made only by legislators. The proposed standards place the responsibility of making value judgments at the legislative level, while leaving courts the still very difficult task of applying the standards in a given case.

It is undoubtedly true that, in some cases, the proposed standards will not produce the best result for a given child. They do restrict the options available to judges and social workers. They are designed to protect the interests of *most* children who come under state supervision, as well as to promote other values like fairness. It is believed that through these standards, the interests of most children will be protected by limiting, rather than promoting, the decisionmaker's discretion.

It must be stressed, moreover, that the standards regulate only coercive intervention. It is unquestionably true that much more state support and services for children and families is needed. Unless services, such as day care, income maintenance, and health insurance are provided to all families, many thousands of children will grow up under extremely adverse conditions. The cost of this state neglect of children is enormous, to the children and to society.

In recommending that the scope of coercive intervention be restricted, not expanded, we are expressing doubt about the limits of coercive intervention, not about the need for services. We simply lack the knowledge and institutional capability to improve the lives of large numbers of children through coercive means. Moreover, in a democratic society every effort should be made to enable families to adequately care for their children before resorting to coercive programs.

In developing the proposed standards, we have attempted to base each standard on the best available data about children's needs and the likely impact of any given policy. The data on which we have relied are discussed in the commentaries and in even greater detail in two articles written by one of the co-reporters. See Wald, "State Intervention on Behalf of 'Neglected' Children: A Search for Realistic Standards," 27 *Stan. L. Rev.* 985 (1975); Wald, "State Intervention on Behalf of 'Neglected' Children: Standards for Removal of Children from Their Homes, Monitoring the Status of Children in Foster Care, and Termination of Parental Rights," 28 *Stan. L. Rev.*

623 (1976). However, it must be recognized that the "science" of child development is still in its infancy, at least with regard to the issues directly related to endangered children. Only in the last ten years have studies been conducted on the impact of different intervention policies. There is still substantial disagreement among experts about the appropriate direction for state policy. In addition, it is impossible to foresee how the proposed standards will actually be implemented in practice and how they will affect court and agency behavior.

Therefore, the standards should not be viewed as a final model. It may well be that in operation some of them do not promote the goals they were designed to accomplish. Moreover, as more data become available about children and about the efficacy of different means of intervention, changes in the statutory definition or in other standards may be appropriate. Therefore, if these standards are adopted, there should be an ongoing evaluation of their effect and periodic legislative review of the entire system.

Finally, it must be stressed that the entire process of state intervention must be viewed as a whole, and that laws and regulations regarding each aspect of the system must be drafted in terms of, and be related to, laws and regulations pertaining to the other parts of the system. Thus, each of the proposed standards should be considered not only singly, but as it relates to each of the other standards. We would not necessarily recommend any of the specific standards if other aspects of the proposed system were not adopted.

Addendum
of
Revisions in the 1977 Tentative Draft

As discussed in the Preface, the published tentative drafts were distributed to the appropriate ABA sections and other interested individuals and organizations. Comments and suggestions concerning the volumes were solicited by the executive committee of the IJA-ABA Joint Commission. The executive committee then reviewed the standards and commentary within the context of the recommendations received and adopted certain modifications. The specific changes affecting this volume are set forth below. Corrections in form, spelling, or punctuation are not included in this enumeration.

1. The Introduction was revised slightly to show the change in emphasis, which now mandates retaining parental rights and restoring custody unless the court finds the child would be harmed, rather than the original version authorizing termination or removal unless it would be detrimental to the child.

2. Standard 2.1 D. was amended to add to the definition of sexual abuse situations in which the parents knew or should have known the child was being sexually abused by another and failed to take appropriate action.

Commentary was revised to include a reference to the federal Child Abuse Prevention and Treatment and Adoption Reform Act, barring the commercial use and exploitation of children.

3. Standard 2.2 was amended by changing the phrase "to assume jurisdiction" to "to justify intervention."

4. Standard 3.3 was amended by deleting the portions pertaining to procedures in Part V, which have been revised substantially. See Items 7 to 11 below. The standard was amended further by adding a provision that a warrant must be obtained if the report recipient agency wishes to interview or investigate the parents or custodians

or take custody of the child against the wishes of the parents or custodians.

Commentary was revised accordingly.

5. Standard 3.5 was amended to make hearings challenging reports of abuse nonpublic unless interested persons show they should be public.

6. Standard 4.3 on court review of emergency temporary custody was amended to conform to revisions in Part V on court proceedings. Provision for court-approved investigation prior to the filing of a petition was eliminated.

Commentary was revised accordingly.

7. Standard 5.1 was amended to incorporate the procedures for intake review of complaints in *The Juvenile Probation Function* volume and eliminate inconsistent or duplicative provisions.

The standard was amended further by adding new preadjudication proceedings derived from the *Pretrial Court Procedures* and *Adjudication* volumes. New standards barring access to social and investigative reports prior to an adjudication of endangerment, as in delinquency proceedings, and abrogating certain privileged communications also were added.

Commentary was revised accordingly.

8. Standard 5.2, providing for a preadjudication investigation of the petition, was amended by moving it from Part V to Part VI, thereby transforming the process into a predisposition investigation and report, as in delinquency proceedings. See Item 12 below.

Commentary was revised accordingly.

9. Standard 5.3 on postinvestigation proceedings was amended by deleting the references to the preadjudication investigation and post-investigation hearing and combining the remaining provisions with new Standard 5.2 on preadjudication proceedings.

New Standard 5.3 was drafted to include standards for both contested and uncontested proceedings. The new procedures for hearings on uncontested petitions were based on the standards for judicial scrutiny of admissions in delinquency proceedings in the *Adjudication* volume. Standards for recording proceedings and for preserving and expunging records also were added.

Commentary was revised accordingly.

10. New Standard 5.4 on findings of law and fact following the hearing was added.

11. New Standard 5.5 on appeals was added.

12. New Standard 6.1 on predisposition investigation and reports was added. Standard 6.1 A. provides for an investigation by the probation department after an adjudication of endangerment. Stan-

dard 6.1 B. stipulates the information to be included in the predisposition report. Standard 6.1 C. requires that the report be distributed to the court and to all parties to the proceeding. Standards 6.1 B. and C. derive from former Standards 5.2 F. 1. and 2.

13. Standard 6.1 was changed to Standard 6.2 and amended to specify time limitations for the dispositional hearing, differentiated according to whether the child is in custody or at home.

14. Standard 6.2 was amended and combined with former Standard 6.1 to constitute new Standard 6.2.

15. Standard 6.3. was amended by changing subsection A. 5 from "placement" of a homemaker in the home to ordering the state or parents to employ a homemaker. New subsection C. was added to express the state's responsibility to provide an adequate level of services.

Commentary was revised accordingly.

16. Standard 6.4 was amended by adding to the general goal for all dispositions the principle of least restrictive alternative and deleting a condition to the prohibition against removal where the environment is beyond the parents' control.

17. Standard 6.5 A. was amended to eliminate references to a plan for services when a child is left in the home to be submitted *after* the dispositional hearing.

18. Standard 6.5 B. 3. was amended by adding a preference for placement with the child's relatives.

19. Standard 6.6 was amended by adding custodians to the caption, deleting termination of parental rights as a disposition following an adjudication of endangerment, and adding a new subsection D. barring removal from foster parents in certain situations.

20. Standard 7.1 was amended by adding grievance officers to those authorized to request court review prior to the six-month review. All time periods *except* the six-month review were bracketed.

21. Standard 7.5 D. was amended to change the warning to parents that termination may occur at the next review hearing to a warning of possible termination in a proceeding under Part VIII.

Commentary was revised accordingly.

22. New Standard 8.1 was added to provide for separate court proceedings as a prerequisite to termination of parental rights.

23. New Standard 8.2 was added to cover voluntary termination or relinquishment of parental rights. The standard is based in large part on the Model Act to Free Children for Permanent Placement (hereinafter, Model Act), Section 3.

24. New Standard 8.3 on involuntary termination was added. The procedures are essentially the same as the procedures for endanger-

ment proceedings. The bases for termination in subsection C. were derived in part from the Model Act, Section 4, as modified by general principles underlying the standards in this and other volumes in the series.

25. Former Standards 8.1, 8.2, and 8.3 were deleted.

26. Standard 8.4 was amended by deleting the reference to former Standard 8.2.

27. New Standard 8.5 on dispositional proceedings was added. Subsection A., providing for the information to be included in the predispositional report, was based on the Model Act Section 13(c).

28. New Standard 8.6 was added to provide for an interlocutory order for termination of parental rights. Voluntary termination also was covered by this standard.

29. Former Standard 8.5 was changed to Standard 8.7. Standard 8.7 B. was amended by adding the concept of making the original interlocutory order final when adoption or guardianship has been effected and by adding the alternative orders of extending the duration of the interlocutory order or returning custody and parental rights to the parents if no permanent placement has been found.

30. Standard 10.4 G. was amended by changing one year as the period of placement that precedes possible termination of parental rights to eighteen months *if* the parents have failed to maintain contact for three years. See new Standard 8.3 C. 6.

31. Standard 10.5 was amended to add a preference for placement as chosen by the parents and child, in the absence of good cause to the contrary.

Commentary was revised accordingly.

32. Commentary to Standard 2.1 A. was revised by adding the comment that "serious" is used in the standard to connote "significant" physical injury.

33. Commentary to Standard 2.1 C. was revised to note that significant clinically demonstrable emotional harm caused by parental action or neglect could be grounds for official intervention.

34. Commentary to Standard 3.2 C. was revised by adding a reference to abuses by foster care agencies with respect to improper or overlong placements of reported children.

35. Commentary to Standard 4.1 A. was revised to require agencies that take custody of a child to act immediately to safeguard the child and report to the court.

36. Commentary to Parts V, VI, and VIII was revised and expanded to cover the amendments, deletions, and additions to the standards in those parts.

37. Commentary to Standard 6.3 C. was amended further by adding a discussion of placement in a residential treatment center as a disposition for an endangered child, with cautionary observations on the child's right to the least restrictive placement and to refuse nonemergency services. Purchase of services also was discussed.

38. Commentary to Standard 6.5 was revised to add the stricture that an agency's financial considerations should not be permitted to prolong placements. A further recommendation was that the agency's plan include training for foster parents.

39. Commentary to Standard 10.4 C. was revised to provide that the agency should refer cases to the juvenile court in which parents exercise their right to resume custody of their children more than twice within a thirty-day period.

40. Commentary to Standard 10.8 was revised to reflect the changes in the standards for termination of parental rights in Part VIII and in the underlying principles of that part.

Standards

PART I: GENERAL PRINCIPLES

1.1 Family autonomy.

Laws structuring a system of coercive intervention on behalf of endangered children should be based on a strong presumption for parental autonomy in child rearing. Coercive state intervention should occur only when a child is suffering specific harms as defined in Standard 2.1. Active state involvement in child care or extensive monitoring of each child's development should be available only on a truly voluntary basis, except in the situations described by these standards.

1.2 Purpose of intervention.

Coercive state intervention should be premised upon specific harms that a child has suffered or is likely to suffer.

1.3 Statutory guidelines.

The statutory grounds for coercive intervention on behalf of endangered children:

A. should be defined as specifically as possible;

B. should authorize intervention only where the child is suffering, or there is a substantial likelihood that the child will imminently suffer, serious harm;

C. should permit coercive intervention only for categories of harm where intervention will, in most cases, do more good than harm.

1.4 Protecting cultural differences.

Standards for coercive intervention should take into account cultural differences in childrearing. All decisionmakers should examine the child's needs in light of the child's cultural background and values.

1.5 Child's interests paramount.

State intervention should promote family autonomy and strength-

15

en family life whenever possible. However, in cases where a child's needs as defined in these standards conflict with his/her parents' interests, the child's needs should have priority.

1.6 Continuity and stability.

When state intervention is necessary, the entire system of intervention should be designed to promote a child's need for a continuous, stable living environment.

1.7 Recognizing developmental differences.

Laws aimed at protecting children should reflect developmental differences among children of different ages.

1.8 Accountability.

The system of coercive state intervention should be designed to insure that all agencies, including courts, participating in the intervention process are held accountable for all of their actions.

PART II: STATUTORY GROUNDS FOR INTERVENTION

2.1 Statutory grounds for intervention.

Courts should be authorized to assume jurisdiction in order to condition continued parental custody upon the parents' accepting supervision or to remove a child from his/her home only when a child is endangered in a manner specified in subsections A.-F.:

A. a child has suffered, or there is a substantial risk that a child will imminently suffer, a physical harm, inflicted nonaccidentally upon him/her by his/her parents, which causes, or creates a substantial risk of causing disfigurement, impairment of bodily functioning, or other serious physical injury;

B. a child has suffered, or there is a substantial risk that the child will imminently suffer, physical harm causing disfigurement, impairment of bodily functioning, or other serious physical injury as a result of conditions created by his/her parents or by the failure of the parents to adequately supervise or protect him/her;

C. a child is suffering serious emotional damage, evidenced by severe anxiety, depression, or withdrawal, or untoward aggressive behavior toward self or others, and the child's parents are not willing to provide treatment for him/her;

D. a child has been sexually abused by his/her parent, or a member of his/her household, or by another person where the parent knew or should have known and failed to take appropriate action (alternative: a child has been sexually abused by his/her parent or a member of his/her household, and is seriously harmed physically or emotionally thereby);

E. a child is in need of medical treatment to cure, alleviate, or prevent him/her from suffering serious physical harm which may result in death, disfigurement, or substantial impairment of bodily functions, and his/her parents are unwilling to provide or consent to the medical treatment;

F. a child is committing delinquent acts as a result of parental encouragement, guidance, or approval.

2.2 Need for intervention in specific case.

The fact that a child is endangered in a manner specified in Standard 2.1 A.-F. should be a necessary but not sufficient condition for a court to intervene. To justify intervention, a court should also have to find that intervention is necessary to protect the child from being endangered in the future. This decision should be made in accordance with the standards proposed in Part VI.

PART III: REPORTING OF ABUSED CHILDREN

3.1 Required reports.

A. Any physician, nurse, dentist, optometrist, medical examiner, or coroner, or any other medical or mental health professional, Christian Science practitioner, religious healer, schoolteacher and other pupil personnel, social or public assistance worker, child care worker in any day care center or child caring institution, police or law enforcement officer who has reasonable cause to suspect that a child, coming before him/her in his/her official or professional capacity, is an abused child as defined by Standard 3.1 B. should be required to make a report to any report recipient agency listed for that geographic locality pursuant to Standard 3.2.

B. An "abused child," for purposes of Standard 3.1 A., is a child who has suffered physical harm, inflicted nonaccidentally upon him/her by his/her parent(s) or person(s) exercising essentially equivalent custody and control over the child, which injury causes or creates a substantial risk of causing death, disfigurement, impairment of bodily functioning, or other serious physical injury.

C. Any person making a report or participating in any subsequent proceedings regarding such report pursuant to this Part should be immune from any civil or criminal liability as a result of such actions, provided that such person was acting in good faith in such actions. In any proceeding regarding such liability, good faith should be presumed.

D. The privileged character of communication between husband

and wife and between any professional person and his/her patient or client, except privilege between attorney and client, should be abrogated regarding matters subject to this Part, and should not justify failure to report or the exclusion of evidence in any proceeding resulting from a report pursuant to this Part.

E. Any person who knowingly fails to make a report required pursuant to this Part should be guilty of a misdemeanor (and/or should be liable, regarding any injuries proximately caused by such failure, for compensatory and/or punitive damages in civil litigation maintained on behalf of the child or his/her estate).

3.2 Recipients and format of report.

A. The state department of social services (or equivalent state agency) should be required to issue a list of qualified report recipient agencies (which may be public or private agencies), and to designate geographic localities within the state within which each such recipient agency would be authorized to receive reports made pursuant to Standard 3.1 A. The state department should ensure that there be at least one qualified report recipient agency for every designated geographic locality within the state.

B. An agency should be eligible for listing as a qualified report recipient agency if it demonstrates, to the satisfaction of the state department, that it has adequate capacity to provide, or obtain provision of, protection to children who may be the subject of reports pursuant to this Part. The state department should be required to promulgate regulations setting standards for such adequate capacity which specify requisite staff personnel (which may include, without limitation, pediatric physicians and other medical care personnel, mental health professionals and paraprofessionals, and attorneys and legal paraprofessionals), requisite agency organizational structure, and any other matters relevant to adequate child-protective capacities.

C. The state department should review, at least every two years, whether an agency listed as a qualified report recipient agency continues to meet the requirements for listing pursuant to Standard 3.2 B. For purposes of such review, the state department should examine the agency's disposition of and efficacy in cases reported to it pursuant to this Part. Each agency should maintain records, in a format prescribed by regulations of the state department, to facilitate such review. Such regulations should provide safeguards against any use of such records that would disclose the identity, except where specifically authorized by this Part, or otherwise work to the detriment of persons who have been named in reports made pursuant to this Part.

D. The format of the reports to the report recipient agencies, in satisfaction of the requirements of Standard 3.1 A., should be specified by regulation of the state department. Such regulations should provide that initial reports pursuant to Standard 3.1 A. be made by telephone to a report recipient agency, and that telephonic and any written reports contain such information as the state department may specify.

3.3 Action by report recipient agency.

A. A report recipient agency receiving a report submitted pursuant to Standard 3.1 A. should be required to immediately undertake investigation of the report and to determine *inter alia* whether there is reason to believe the child subject of the report is an abused child, as defined in Standard 3.1 B., and whether protection of the child requires filing of a petition pursuant to Part V, and/or taking emergency temporary custody of the child pursuant to Part IV.

B. 1. If the agency determines, upon initial receipt of the report or at any subsequent time after its initial contact with the child that filing of a petition pursuant to Part V or emergency temporary custody pursuant to Part IV is necessary for the protection of the child, it should promptly take such action, except that the agency has no authority to examine or take custody of the child or to interview the parents or custodians or visit the child's home, against the wishes of the child's parents or custodians named in the report, except as specifically authorized by a court as provided in subsections 2.-5., or as specifically authorized by Part IV regarding emergency temporary custody of the child.

2. If the agency wishes to examine or take custody of the child, to interview the parents or custodians, or to visit the child's home against the wishes of the child's parents or custodians named in the report, it must obtain a warrant to search, duly ordered by the court authorizing the agency to make such investigation. Such an order may be obtained *ex parte.*

3. A warrant should not be granted except upon a finding by the court of probable cause to believe that the child comes within the jurisdiction of the court pursuant to the standards set out in Part II.

4. The warrant should set forth with particularity the places to be investigated, the persons to be interviewed, and the basis for the finding of probable cause. The warrant should state that refusal to allow an investigation may lead to the sanctions provided in subsection 5.

5. a. If the parents or custodians named in the report refuse to

allow access to the child after being served with a copy of the warrant ordering such access, the investigating agency may take custody of the child for a time no longer than reasonably necessary for investigative purposes, but in no event should custody of the child be taken for a longer consecutive period than eight hours, nor should custody be maintained between 8:00 P.M. and 8:00 A.M.

b. Where access to other information has been refused after a copy of the warrant ordering such access was served, the court may subject the person having custody of the information to civil contempt penalties until it is provided to the investigating agency.

C. Identifying characteristics in all unsubstantiated reports (including names, addresses, and any other such identifying characteristics of persons named in a report) should be expunged from the files of the report recipient agency immediately following completion of the agency's listing review pursuant to Standard 3.2 C., within two years of the report's receipt. In any event, identifying characteristics in all reports should be expunged from the files of the report recipient agency within seven years of the report's receipt.

3.4 Central register of child abuse.

A. The state department of social services (or equivalent state agency) should be required to maintain a central register of child abuse. Upon receipt of a report made pursuant to Standard 3.1 A., the report recipient agency should immediately notify the central register by telephone and transmit a copy of any written report to the central register for recordation.

B. Within sixty days of its initial notification of a report for recordation, the report recipient agency should be required to indicate its action pursuant to Standard 3.3, and to indicate any subsequent action regarding such report at intervals no later than sixty days thereafter until the agency has terminated contact with the persons named in the report. If at any time the report recipient agency indicates that the report (including names, addresses, and any other such identifying characteristics of persons named in the report) should be expunged, the central register should immediately effect such expungement. In any event, all reports (including names, addresses, and any other such identifying characteristics of persons named in the report) should be expunged from the central register seven years from the date the report was initially received by the report recipient agency.

C. The central register, and any employee or agent thereof, should not make available recordation and any information regarding reports to any person or agency except to the following, upon their request:

1. a report recipient agency within this state, listed pursuant to Standard 3.2, or a child protective agency in another state deemed equivalent, under regulations promulgated by the state department of social services (or equivalent state agency), to such report recipient agency within this state;

2. any person (including both child and parent(s) and alleged abuser [if other than parent(s)]) who is named in a report (or another, such as an attorney, acting in that person's behalf), except that such person should not be informed of the name, address, occupation, or other identifying characteristics of the person who submitted the report to the report recipient agency;

3. a court authorized to conduct proceedings pursuant to Part V;

4. a person engaged in bona fide research, with written permission of the director of the state department (except that no information regarding the names, addresses or any other such identifying characteristics of persons named in the report should be made available to this person). Any person who violates the provisions of this standard by disseminating or knowingly permitting the dissemination of recordation and any information regarding reports in the central register to any other person or agency should be guilty of a misdemeanor (and/or should be liable for compensatory and/or punitive damages in civil litigation by or on behalf of person(s) named in a report).

3.5 Action by central register.

The central register should be required to notify by registered mail, immediately upon recordation of a report, any person (including child and parents and alleged abuser [if other than parent]) who is named in a report recorded in the central register, and to subsequently notify such person of any further recordation or information (including any expungement of the report) regarding such report submitted to the register pursuant to Standard 3.4, except as provided in Standard 3.4 C. 2. Any such person should have the right, and be so informed, to inspect the report and to challenge whether its entire contents, or any part thereof, should be altered or wholly expunged. Proceedings, including nonpublic hearings, except where an interested person can show they should be public, and other procedural matters regarding any such challenge should be governed by the administrative procedures act of this state.

PART IV: EMERGENCY TEMPORARY CUSTODY
OF AN ENDANGERED CHILD

4.1 Authorized emergency custody of endangered child.

A. Any physician, police or law enforcement official, or agent or employee of an agency designated pursuant to Standard 4.1 C. should be authorized to take physical custody of a child, notwithstanding the wishes of the child's parents or other such caretakers, if the physician, official, or agent or employee has probable cause to believe such custody is necessary to prevent the child's imminent death or serious bodily injury and that the child's parents or other such caretakers are unable or unwilling to protect the child from such imminent death or injury; provided that where risk to the child appears created solely because the child has been left unattended at home, such physician, official, or agent or employee should be authorized only to provide an emergency caretaker to attend the child at home until the child's parents return or sufficient time elapses to indicate that the parents do not intend to return home; and provided further that no such physician, official, or agent or employee is authorized to take physical custody of a child unless risk to the child is so imminent that there is no time to secure such court approval. Any physician or police or law enforcement official who takes custody of a child pursuant to this standard should immediately contact an agency designated pursuant to Standard 4.1 C., which should thereupon take custody of the child for such disposition as indicated in Standard 4.2.

B. Any physician, police or law enforcement official, or agent or employee of an agency who takes custody or care of a child pursuant to Standard 4.1 A. should be immune from any civil or criminal liability as a consequence of such action, provided that such person was acting in good faith in such action. In any proceeding regarding such liability, good faith should be presumed.

C. The state department of social services (or equivalent state agency) should be required to designate at least one agency within each geographic locality within the state, of those agencies listed as qualified report recipient agencies pursuant to Standard 3.2, whose agents or employees would be authorized to take custody of children pursuant to Standard 4.1. To qualify for such designation, an agency must demonstrate to the satisfaction of the state department that it has adequate capacity to safeguard the physical and emotional well-being of children requiring emergency temporary custody pursuant to this Part. The state department should be required to promulgate regulations specifying standards for personnel qualification, custodial facilities, and other aspects of temporary custodial care which an agency must provide, or have access to, regarding children subject to this Part. Each agency designated should thereafter be required to demonstrate, in conjunction with review proceedings pursuant to Standard 3.2 C., that it continues to meet the requirements for designation pursuant to this standard, in view of its efficacy in safeguarding the well-being of children subject to this Part.

4.2 Agency disposition of children in emergency temporary custody.

A. An agency taking custody of a child pursuant to Standard 4.1 should place the child in a nonsecure setting which will adequately safeguard his/her physical and emotional well-being. Such agency should be authorized to provide immediately, or secure the provision of, emergency medical care if necessary to prevent the child's imminent death or serious bodily injury, notwithstanding the wishes of the child's parents or other such persons. The agency should ensure that the child's parents or other such caretakers have opportunity to visit with the child, at least every day for the duration of custody pursuant to this Part (including without limitation the provision of transportation for the parents or other such persons) unless such visits, even if supervised, would be seriously harmful to the child (due account being given, among other considerations, to the child's wishes regarding visits).

B. No later than the first business day after taking custody of a child pursuant to Standard 4.1, the agency should be required to report such action to the court authorized to conduct proceedings by Part V and to explain the specific circumstances justifying the taking of custody and the specific measures implemented to safeguard the physical and emotional well-being of the child. The agency should, at the same time, submit a petition without prior screening by the intake processing agency, under Standard 5.1 B., except that if the agency decides against such submission, it should immediately return the child to the custody of his/her parents or other such caretakers.

4.3 Court review regarding children in emergency temporary custody.

A. Immediately upon receipt of a petition submitted pursuant to Standard 4.2, the court should direct notification pursuant to Standard 5.1 C., appointment of counsel for the child pursuant to Standard 5.1 D., and referral of the petition for prosecution pursuant to Standard 5.1 B. On the same business day if at all practicable, and no later than the next business day, the court should convene a hearing to determine whether emergency temporary custody of the child should be continued.

B. The court should be authorized to continue emergency temporary custody of the child, pursuant to Standard 4.1, if it determines:

1. custody of the child with his/her parents or other such caretakers named in the petition would create an imminent substantial risk of death or serious bodily injury to the child, and no provision of services or other arrangement is available which would adequately safeguard the child in such custody against such risk;

2. the conditions of custody away from the child's parents or other such caretakers are adequate to safeguard his/her physical and emotional well-being (including without limitation direction by the court to provide emergency medical care to the child if necessary to prevent the risk found pursuant to subsection 1.); and

3. the child's parents or other such persons named in the petition would be provided opportunity to visit with the child at least every day for the duration of custody pursuant to this Part (including without limitation the provision of transportation for the parents or other such caretakers unless such visits, even if supervised, would be seriously harmful to the child (due account being given, among other considerations, to the child's wishes regarding visits).

4.4 Custody during pendency of proceeding.

Upon motion of any party to a proceeding pursuant to Part V, at any time during the pendency of the proceeding, the court may, following a hearing, authorize emergency temporary custody of a child with an agency designated pursuant to Standard 4.1 C., if the court determines such custody is justified pursuant to the criteria specified in Standard 4.3 B.

PART V: COURT PROCEEDINGS*

5.1 Complaint and petition.

A. Submission of complaint.

1. Any person may submit a complaint to the juvenile court alleging and specifying reasons why the juvenile court should find a child within the jurisdiction of the court, pursuant to the standards set out in Part II. Any complaint that serves as the basis for a filed petition of endangerment should be sworn to

*Robert Burt and Michael Wald were not the reporters for this revised edition. Martin Guggenheim was the special editor.

and signed by a person who has personal knowledge of the facts or is informed of them and believes that they are true.

2. Any person submitting a complaint or any person providing information upon which a complaint or petition might be based should be immune from any civil or criminal liability as a result of such action or as a result of participating in any subsequent proceedings regarding such action, provided that such person was acting in good faith in such action. In any proceeding regarding such liability good faith should be presumed.

B. Intake review of complaints.

1. Upon receipt of a complaint, an intake officer of the juvenile probation agency should promptly determine whether the allegations, on their face, are sufficiently specific and, if proven, would constitute grounds for court jurisdiction pursuant to the standards set out in Part II. If the intake officer determines that the allegations, on their face, are not sufficiently specific, or, if proven, would not constitute grounds for court intervention, the intake officer should dismiss the complaint. If the legal sufficiency of the complaint is unclear, the intake officer should ask the appropriate prosecuting official for a determination of its sufficiency. If the intake officer determines that the complaint is sufficient, the officer should determine a disposition of the complaint. The following are permissible dispositions at intake:

a. Unconditional dismissal of a complaint.

Unconditional dismissal of a complaint is the termination of all proceedings arising out of the complaint.

b. Judicial disposition of a complaint.

Judicial disposition of a complaint is the initiation of formal judicial proceedings through the filing of a petition.

c. Referral to a community agency.

Referral to a community agency is the referral of the child and his/her parents to an agency, including a child protective services agency, for further consideration.

2. In determining a disposition of a complaint at intake, the intake officer should:

a. determine whether coercive intervention appears authorized as provided in Standard 2.1 A.-F.;

b. determine whether judicial intervention appears necessary to protect the child from being endangered in the future, as provided in Standard 2.2; and

c. consider the resources available both within and without the juvenile justice system.

3. The standards for intake procedures set out in Section IV of *The Juvenile Probation Function: Intake and Predisposition In-*

vestigative Services should apply to intake review of complaints of endangerment, except that the privilege against self-incrimination at intake should apply to the parent or other custodian who is the subject of the complaint pursuant to the standards in Part II of this volume, and a right to assistance of counsel should be available to that parent or other adult custodian as a waivable right. The standards incorporated by reference are *Juvenile Probation Function* Standards 2.9 Necessity for and desirability of written guidelines and rules; 2.10 Initiation of intake proceedings and receipt of complaint by intake officer; 2.11 Intake investigation; 2.12 Juvenile's privilege against self-incrimination at intake; 2.13 Juvenile's right to assistance of counsel at intake; 2.14 Intake interviews and dispositional conferences; and 2.15 Length of intake process. In addition, *Juvenile Probation Function* Standard 2.16, Role of intake officer and prosecutor in filing of petition: right of complainant to file a petition, also should apply to the intake review of complaints of endangerment, except that the references to a petition in those cases in which the conduct charged "would constitute a crime if committed by an adult" should be deemed to refer to a petition of endangerment in this volume.

C. Parties.

The following should be parties to all proceedings regarding a child alleged to be or adjudicated endangered:

    1. the child;

    2. the child's parents, guardians, and, if relevant, any other adults having substantial ties to the child who have been performing the caretaking role; and

    3. the petitioner.

5.2 Preadjudication proceedings.

    A. Written petition.

Each jurisdiction should provide by law that the filing of a written petition, sworn to and signed by a person who has personal knowledge of the facts or is informed of them and believes they are true, giving the parents adequate notice of the charges is a requisite for endangerment proceedings to begin. If appropriate challenge is made to the legal sufficiency of the petition, the judge of the juvenile court should rule on that challenge before calling upon the parents to plead.

    B. Filing and signing of the petition.

Petitions alleging endangerment should be prepared, filed, and signed by the juvenile prosecutor to certify that he or she has read the petition and that to the best of his or her knowledge, information, and belief there is good ground to support it.

C. Notification of filing, service, and initial appearance.

Upon filing of the petition, the court should issue a summons directing the parties to appear at a specified time and place and serve the summons, with a copy of the petition attached, at least twenty-four hours in advance of the first appearance, upon the parents of the child alleged to be endangered. If, after reasonable effort, personal service is not made, the court should order substituted service. The initial appearance before the court should occur within [one] week of the filing of the petition, except if a child is in emergency temporary custody pursuant to the standards in Part IV, the first appearance should occur on the same business day, if possible, and no later than the next business day. At the first appearance, the court should:

1. notify the parents that such petition has been filed;

2. provide the parents with a copy of such petition, including identification by name of the person submitting such petition;

3. inform the parents of the nature and possible consequences of the proceedings and that they have a right to representation by counsel at all stages of the proceedings regarding such petition;

4. inform the parents that if they are unable to afford counsel, the court will appoint counsel at public expense, provided that, if a conflict of interest appears likely between parents named in the petition, the court may in its discretion appoint separate counsel for each parent; and

5. inform the parents of their right to confront and cross-examine witnesses and to request a probable cause hearing.

D. Appointment of counsel for child.

Upon filing, the court should be required to appoint counsel at public expense to represent the child identified in the petition, as a party to the proceedings. No reimbursement should be sought from the parents or the child for the cost of such counsel, regardless of the parents' or child's financial resources.

E. Attendance at all proceedings.

In all proceedings regarding the petition, the parents of the child should be entitled to attend, except that the proceeding may go forward without such presence if the parents fail to appear after reasonable notification (including without limitation efforts by court-designated persons to contact the parents by telephone and by visitation to the parents' last known address of residence within the jurisdiction of the court). The child identified in such petition should attend such proceedings unless the court finds, on motion of any party, that such attendance would be detrimental to the child. If the parents or custodians named in the petition fail to attend, the court may proceed to the hearing only if the child is represented by counsel. If the parents or custodians named in the petition were not present at the hearing and appear thereafter and move the court for a rehearing, the court should grant the motion unless it finds that they willfully refused to appear at the hearing or that the rehearing would be unjust because of the lapse of time since the hearing was held.

F. Evidence at all proceedings.

In all proceedings regarding the petition, sworn testimony and other competent and relevant evidence may be admitted pursuant to the principles governing evidence in civil matters in the courts of general jurisdiction in the state. The court may admit testimony by the child who is the subject of the petition or by any other children whose testimony might be relevant regarding the petition if, upon motion of the party wishing to proffer the testimony of such child, the court determines that the child is sufficiently mature to provide competent evidence and that testifying will not be detrimental to the child. In making such determination regarding the child's proffered testimony, the court may direct psychological or other examinations and impose appropriate conditions for taking any testimony to safeguard the child from detriment. However, the court should not have access to any investigational or social history report prior to adjudication unless it has been admitted into evidence. The privileged character of communications between husband and wife and between any professional person and his or her patient or client, except the privilege between attorney and client, should not be a ground for excluding evidence that would otherwise be admissible.

G. Temporary custody.

If the child remains in emergency temporary custody pursuant to Standard 4.3, no later than [two] working days following the filing of the petition, the court should convene a hearing to determine whether emergency temporary custody should be continued.

Once the parents have been informed of the proceeding and counsel has been assigned or retained, the court should hold a second detention hearing upon the request of the parents. At this hearing, the burden should be on the petitioner to show by relevant, material, and competent evidence, subject to cross-examination, that continued emergency temporary custody is necessary, pursuant to the standards set out in Standard 4.3 B.

H. Appointment of independent experts.

Any party to the proceeding may petition the court for appointment of experts, at public expense, for independent evaluation of the matter before the court. The court should grant such petition, unless it finds the expert unnecessary.

I. Discovery.

The standards governing disclosure of matters in connection with proceedings to determine whether the petition should be granted, disposition of granted petitions (Part VI), or review proceedings (Part VII) should be the same for the child and the parents as for the respondent in delinquency cases set out in the *Pretrial Court Proceedings* volume.

J. Subpoenas.

Upon request of any party, a subpoena should be issued by the court (or its clerk) commanding the attendance and testimony of any person at any proceeding conducted pursuant to this Part or commanding the production of documents for use in any such proceeding, except that the attendance and testimony of any children (including the child subject of the petition) should be governed by Standard 5.2 E. and F. Failure by any person without adequate excuse to obey a subpoena served upon him/her may be deemed a contempt of the court subject to civil contempt penalties.

K. Interpreters at all proceedings.

The court should appoint an interpreter or otherwise ensure that language barriers do not deprive the parents, child, witnesses, or other participants of the ability to understand and participate effectively in all stages of the proceedings.

5.3 Adjudication proceedings.

A. Proceedings to determine contested petition.

In any proceeding to determine whether the petition should be granted, the following should apply:

1. Upon request of the child or the parents, the sole trier of fact should be a jury whose verdict must be unanimous, and which may consist of as few as six persons. In the absence of such request from either such party, the trier of fact should be the court. Under no circumstances should the trier of fact, or the judge prior to adjudication, have access to any investigational or social history report, unless it has been duly admitted into evidence at the hearing, as provided in Standard 5.2 F.

2. The burden should rest on the prosecutor of the petition to prove by clear and convincing evidence allegations sufficient to support the petition.

3. Proof that access has been refused to sources of or means for obtaining information, or that the parents have refused to attend

or to testify without adequate excuse, or regarding conduct of the parents toward another child should be admissible, if the court determines such proof relevant to the allegations in the petition; except that proof of either such matter, standing alone, should not be sufficient to sustain the granting of the petition.

4. Time for hearing. A hearing regarding a child who has remained in emergency temporary custody should take place no later than [twenty-five] days after the filing of the petition. If, within [twenty-five] days, the petitioner is not ready to go forward with the hearing, the court must order the child returned to his or her parents and dismiss the petition with prejudice unless there is good cause shown for the delay. In the event such cause is shown, the court must continue to find that conditions exist, pursuant to Standard 4.3, justifying the continuation of the child in emergency temporary custody. In no event should a delay beyond [twenty-five] days be authorized for longer than [seven] additional days.

For all other cases under this part, a hearing should be held within [sixty] days of the filing of the petition. If at the end of this time the petition is not ready to proceed, the court should dismiss the petition with prejudice.

B. Uncontested petitions.

If the parents wish to admit to all or any part of the allegations in the petition, sufficient to give the court authority to order a disposi- of the proceeding other than dismissal as set out in Part VI, the court should convene a hearing at which testimony should be taken regarding the voluntariness and validity of the parents' decision. The judge should not accept a plea admitting an allegation of the petition without first addressing the parents personally, in language calculated to communicate effectively with them, to:

1. Determine that the parents understand the nature of the allegations;

2. Inform the parents of the right to a hearing at which the petitioner must confront respondent with witnesses and prove the allegations by clear and convincing competent evidence and at which the parents' attorney will be permitted to cross-examine the witnesses called by the petitioner and to call witnesses on the parents' behalf;

3. Inform the parents of the right to remain silent with respect to the allegations of the petition as well as of the right to testify if desired;

4. Inform the parents of the right to appeal from the decision reached in the trial;

5. Inform the parents of the right to a trial by jury;

6. Inform the parents that one gives up those rights by a plea admitting an allegation of the petition;

7. Inform the parents that if the court accepts the plea, the court can enter any final order of disposition set forth in Part VI;

8. Determine that the plea is voluntary; and

9. Determine that the parents were given the effective assistance of an attorney, if the parents were represented by counsel.

The court should allow the parents to withdraw a plea admitting an allegation of the petition whenever the parents prove that withdrawal is necessary to correct a manifest injustice. If the court accepts an admission, it should enter an order finding that the child is endangered.

C. Recording proceedings.

1. A verbatim record should be made and preserved of all proceedings, whether or not the allegations in the petition are contested.

2. The record should be preserved and, with any exhibits, kept confidential.

3. The requirement of preservation should be subordinated to any order for expungement of the record and the requirement of confidentiality should be subordinated to court orders on behalf of the parents, child, or petitioner for a verbatim transcript of the record for use in subsequent legal proceedings.

5.4 Findings.

A. The trier of fact should record its findings specifically. Findings of fact and law should be articulated separately on the record. If the trier of fact determines that facts sufficient to sustain the petition have been established, the court should enter an order finding that the child is endangered. If the trier of fact determines that facts sufficient to sustain the petition have not been established, the court should dismiss the petition.

B. Each jurisdiction should provide by law that a finding by juvenile court that a child is endangered should only be used for the purpose of providing the court with the authority to order an appropriate disposition for the child pursuant to Standard 6.3.

5.5 Appeals.

Appeals from a finding that a child is endangered should not be allowed as of right. Interlocutory appeals from such orders may be allowed only in the discretion of the appellate court. Appeals as of right exist only from a final order of disposition. The standards governing appeals from proceedings under this Part should be the same as those set out in the *Appeals and Collateral Review* standards, except that the parties entitled to take an appeal under *Appeals and Collateral Review* Standard 2.2 also should include the petitioner pursuant to Standard 5.1 C. above.

PART VI: DISPOSITIONS

6.1 Predisposition investigation and reports.

A. Predisposition investigation.

After the court has entered a finding pursuant to Standard 5.4 F. that a child is endangered, it should authorize an investigation to be conducted by the probation department to supply the necessary information for an order of disposition.

B. Predisposition report.

The predisposition report should include the following information:

1. a description of the specific programs and/or placements, for both the parents and the child, which will be needed in order to prevent further harm to the child, the reasons why such programs and/or placements are likely to be useful, the availability of any proposed services, and the agency's plans for ensuring that the services will be delivered;

2. a statement of the indications (*e.g.*, specific changes in parental behavior) that will be used to determine that the family no longer needs supervision or that placement is no longer necessary;

3. an estimate of the time in which the goals of intervention should be achieved or in which it will be known they cannot be achieved.

4. In any case where removal from parental custody is recommended, the report should contain:

a. a full description of the reasons why the child cannot be adequately protected in the home, including a description of any previous efforts to work with the parents with the child in the home, the "in-home treatment programs," *e.g.*, homemakers, which have been considered and rejected, and the parents' attitude toward placement of the child;

b. a statement of the likely harms the child will suffer as a result of removal (this section should include an exploration of the nature of the parent-child attachment and the anticipated effect of separation and loss to both the parents and the child);

c. a description of the steps that will be taken to minimize harm to the child that may result if separation occurs.

5. If no removal from parental custody is recommended, the report should indicate what services or custodial arrangements, if any, have been offered to and/or accepted by the parents of the child.

C. The investigating agency should be required to provide its report to the court and the court should provide copies of such report to all parties to the proceedings.

6.2 Proceeding to determine disposition.

Following a finding pursuant to Standard 5.4 that a child is endangered, the court should, as soon as practicable, but no later than [forty-five] days thereafter, convene a hearing to determine the disposition of the petition. If the child is in emergency temporary custody, the court should be required to convene the hearing no later than [twenty] working days following the finding that the child is endangered. All parties to the proceeding should participate in the hearing, and all matters relevant to the court's determination should be presented in evidence at the hearing. In deciding the appropriate disposition, the court should have available and should consider the dispositional report prepared by the investigating agency pursuant to Standard 6.1 B.

6.3 Available dispositions.

A. A court should have at least the following dispositional alternatives and resources:

1. dismissal of the case;

2. wardship with informal supervision;

3. ordering the parents to accept social work supervision;

4. ordering the parents and/or the child to accept individual or family therapy or medical treatment;

5. ordering the state or parents to employ a homemaker in the home;

6. placement of the child in a day care program;

7. placement of the child with a relative, in a foster family or group home, or in a residential treatment center.

B. A court should have authority to order that the parent accept, and that the state provide, any of the above services.

C. It should be the state's responsibility to provide an adequate level of services.

6.4 Standards for choosing a disposition.

A. General goal.

The goal of all dispositions should be to protect the child from the harm justifying intervention in the least restrictive manner available to the court.

B. Dispositions other than removal of the child.

In ordering a disposition other than removal of the child from his/her home, the court should choose a program designed to alleviate the immediate danger to the child, to mitigate or cure any damage the child has already suffered, and to aid the parents so that the child will not be endangered in the future. In selecting a program, the court should choose those services which least interfere with family autonomy, provided that the services are adequate to protect the child.

C. Removal.

1. A child should not be removed from his/her home unless the court finds that:

a. the child has been physically abused as defined in Standard 2.1 A., and there is a preponderance of evidence that the child cannot be protected from further physical abuse without being removed from his/her home; or

b. the child has been endangered in one of the other ways specified by statute and there is clear and convincing evidence that the child cannot be protected from further harm of the type justifying intervention unless removed from his/her home.

2. Even if a court finds subsections 1. a. or b. applicable, before any child is removed from his/her home, the court must find that there is a placement in fact available in which the child will not be endangered.

3. The court should not be authorized to remove a child when the child is endangered solely due to environmental conditions beyond the control of the parents, which the parents would be willing to remedy if they were able to do so.

4. Those advocating removal should bear the burden of proof on all these issues.

6.5 Initial plans.

A. Children left in their own home.

Whenever a child is left in his/her own home, the agency should develop with the parent a specific plan detailing any changes in parental behavior or home conditions that must be made in order for the child not to be endangered. The plan should also specify the services that will be provided to the parent and/or the child to insure that the child will not be endangered. If there is a dispute regarding any aspect of the plan, final resolution should be by the court.

B. Children removed from their homes.

Before a child is ordered removed from his/her home, the agency charged with his/her care should provide the court with a specific plan as to where the child will be placed, what steps will be taken to return the child home, and what actions the agency will take to maintain parent-child ties. Whenever possible, this plan should be developed in consultation with the parent, who should be encouraged to help in the placement. If there is a dispute regarding any aspect of the plan, final resolution should be by the court.

1. The plan should specify what services the parents will receive in order to enable them to resume custody and what actions the parents must take in order to resume custody.

2. The plan should provide for the maximum parent-child contact possible, unless the court finds that visitation should be limited because it will be seriously detrimental to the child.

3. A child generally should be placed as close to home as possible, preferably in his/her own neighborhood, unless the court finds that placement at a greater distance is necessary to promote the child's well-being. In the absence of good cause to the contrary, preference should be given to a placement with the child's relatives.

6.6 Rights of parents, custodians, and children following removal.

A. All placements are for a temporary period. Every effort should be made to facilitate the return of the child as quickly as possible.

B. When a child is removed from his/her home, his/her parents should retain the right to consent to major medical decisions, to the child's marriage, or to the child's joining the armed services, unless parental consent is not generally required for any of these decisions or the court finds that the parents' refusal to consent would be seriously detrimental to the child.

C. Depending on the child's age and maturity, the agency should also solicit and consider the child's participation in decisions regarding his/her care while in placement.

D. Unless a child is being returned to his/her parents, the child should not be removed from a foster home in which he/she has resided for at least one year without providing the foster parents with notice and an opportunity to be heard before a court. If the foster parents object to the removal and wish to continue to care for the child, the child should not be removed when the removal would be detrimental to the child's emotional well-being.

PART VII: MONITORING OF CHILDREN UNDER
COURT SUPERVISION AND TERMINATION OF SUPERVISION

7.1 Periodic court reviews.

The status of all children under court supervision should be reviewed by the court in a formal hearing held at least once every six months following the initial dispositional hearing. The court may also review a case, upon request of the grievance officer or any party, at any time prior to the six-month review. At least [fourteen] days prior to a review hearing, the agency workers in charge of providing services to the child and parents should submit to the court a supplemental report indicating the services offered to the parents and child, the impact of such services, and should make a dispositional recommendation. Copies of this report should go to all parties and their counsel. The parents, unless they are physically unable to do so, and a representative of the supervising agency, should be required to attend each six-month review hearing. The court may also require or permit the attendance of any other necessary persons.

7.2 Interim reports.

The agency charged with supervising a child in placement should be responsible for ensuring that all ordered services are provided. It should report to the court if it is unable to provide such services, for whatever reason. The agency may perform services other than those ordered, as necessitated by the case situation.

7.3 Grievance officers.

There should be available in every community, either within the agency supervising a child found endangered or in a separate agency, a position of grievance officer. This person should be available to receive complaints from any parent or child who feels he/she is not receiving the services ordered by the court. The court should inform the parents and child or child's counsel of the name of such officer, how to contact him/her, and the services the grievance officer can provide.

7.4 Standard for termination of services when child not removed from home.

A. At each six-month review hearing of a case where the child has not been removed from his/her home, the court should establish on record whether the conditions still exist that required initial intervention. If not, the court should terminate jurisdiction.

B. If the conditions that require continued supervision still exist, the court should establish:

1. what services have been provided to or offered to the parents;

2. whether the parents are satisfied with the delivery of services;

3. whether the agency is satisfied with the cooperation given to it by the parents;

4. whether additional services should be ordered and when termination of supervision can be expected.

C. Court jurisdiction should terminate automatically eighteen months after the initial finding of jurisdiction, unless, pursuant to motion by any party, the court finds, following a formal hearing, that there is clear and convincing evidence that the child is still endangered or would be endangered if services are withdrawn.

7.5 Standard for return of children in placement.

A. Whenever a child is in foster care, the court should determine at each six-month review hearing whether the child can be returned home, and if not, whether parental rights should be terminated under the standards in Part VIII.

B. A child should be returned home unless the court finds by a preponderance of the evidence that the child will be endangered, in the manner specified in Part II, if returned home. When a child is returned, casework supervision should continue for a period of six months, at which point there should be a hearing on the need for continued intervention as specified in Standard 7.4 A.

C. At each review hearing where the child is not returned home and parental rights are not terminated, the court should establish on the record:

1. what services have been provided to or offered to the parents to facilitate reunion;

2. whether the parents are satisfied with the services offered;

3. the extent to which the parents have visited the child and any reasons why visitation has not occurred or been infrequent;

4. whether the agency is satisfied with the cooperation given to it by the parents;

5. whether additional services are needed to facilitate the return of the child to his/her parents or guardian; if so, the court should order such services;

6. when return of the child can be expected.

D. If a child is not returned to his/her parents at such review hearing, and parental rights are not terminated, the court should advise the parents that termination of parental rights may occur at a proceeding initiated under the standards in Part VIII.

PART VIII: TERMINATIONS OF PARENTAL RIGHTS*

8.1 Court proceedings.

Each jurisdiction should provide by law that the filing of a written petition giving the parents and the child adequate notice of the basis upon which termination of parental rights is sought is a requisite to a proceeding to terminate parental rights.

8.2 Voluntary termination (relinquishment).

A. The court may terminate parental rights based on the consent of the parents upon a petition duly presented. The petitioner may be either the parents or an agency that has custody of the child. Such a petition may not be filed until at least seventy-two hours after the child's birth.

B. The court should accept a relinquishment or voluntary consent to termination of parental rights only if:

1. The parents appear personally before the court in a hearing that should be recorded pursuant to Standard 5.3 C. The court should address the parents and determine that the parents' consent to the termination of parental rights is the product of a voluntary decision. The court should address the parents in language calculated to communicate effectively with the parents and determine:

a. that the parents understand that they have the right to the custody of the child;

b. that the parents may lose the right to the custody of the child only in accordance with procedures set forth in Standard 8.3;

c. that relinquishment will result in the permanent termination of all legal relationship and control over the child; or

2. If the court finds that the parents are unable to appear in person at the hearing, the court may accept the written consent or relinquishment given before a judge of any court of record, accompanied by the judge's signed findings. These findings should recite that the judge questioned the parents and found that the consent was informed and voluntary.

C. If the court is satisfied that the parents voluntarily wish to terminate parental rights, the court should enter an interlocutory order of termination. Such order should not become final for at least thirty days, during which time the parents may, for any reason, revoke the consent. After thirty days, the provisions for an inter-

---

*Robert Burt and Michael Wald were not the reporters for this revised edition. Martin Guggenheim was the special editor.

locutory order for termination of parental rights set forth in Standard 8.5 should apply.

D. Once an order has been made final, it should be reconsidered only upon a motion by or on behalf of the parents alleging that the parents' consent was obtained through fraud or duress. Such a motion should be filed no later than two years after a final order terminating parental rights has been issued by the court.

E. Regardless of the provisions of Standard 8.2 B. 1.–2., a court should not be authorized to order termination if any of the exceptions in Standard 8.4 are applicable.

8.3 Involuntary termination.

A. Court proceedings to terminate parental rights involuntarily.

No court should terminate parental rights without the consent of the parents except upon instituting a separate proceeding in juvenile court in accordance with the provisions set forth in this Part.

B. Procedure.

1. Written petition. The grounds for termination should be stated with specificity in the petition in accordance with the standards set forth in subsection C.

2. Petitioner. The following persons are eligible to file a petition under this Part:

   a. an agency that has custody of a child;

   b. either parent seeking termination with respect to the other parent;

   c. a foster parent or guardian who has had continuous custody for at least eighteen months who alleges abandonment pursuant to Standard 8.3 C. 1. c. or a foster parent or guardian who has had continuous custody for at least three years who alleges any other basis for termination;

   d. a guardian of the child's person, legal custodian, or the child's guardian ad litem appointed in a prior proceeding.

3. Prosecutor. Upon receipt of the petition, the appropriate prosecution official should examine it to determine its legal sufficiency. If the prosecutor determines that the petition is legally sufficient, it should be filed and signed by a person who has personal knowledge of the facts or is informed of them and believes that they are true. All petitions should be countersigned and filed by the prosecutor. The prosecutor may refuse to file a petition only on the grounds of legal insufficiency.

4. Parties. The following should be parties to all proceedings to terminate parental rights:

    a. the child;

    b. the child's parents, guardians, custodian, and, if relevant, any other adults having substantial ties to the child who have been assuming the duties of the caretaking role;

    c. the petitioner.

    5. Service of summons and petition. Upon the filing of a petition, the clerk should issue a summons. The summons should direct the parties to appear before the court at a specified time and place for an initial appearance on the petition. A copy of the petition should be attached to the summons. Service of the summons with the petition should be made promptly upon the parents of the child. The summons should advise the parents of the purpose of the proceedings and of their right to counsel. Service of the summons and petition, if made personally, should be made at least twenty-four hours in advance of the first appearance. If, after reasonable effort, personal service is not made, the court may make an order providing for substituted service in the manner provided for substituted service in civil courts of record.

    6. First appearance. At the first appearance, the court should provide the parents with a copy of the petition, including identification by name and association of the person submitting such petition, and inform the parents on the record of the following:

    a. the nature and possible consequences of the proceedings;

    b. the parents' and the child's right to representation by counsel at all stages of the proceeding regarding such petition, and their right to appointed counsel at public expense if they are unable to afford counsel;

    c. their right to confront and cross-examine witnesses; and

    d. their right to remain silent.

    7. Appointment of counsel for child. Counsel should also be appointed at public expense to represent the child identified in the petition, as a party to the proceedings. No reimbursement should be sought from the parents or the child for the cost of such counsel, regardless of their financial resources.

    8. Attendance at all proceedings. In all proceedings regarding the petition, the presence of the parents should be required, except that the proceedings may go forward without such presence if the parents fail to appear after reasonable notification (including, without limitation, efforts by court-designated persons to contact the parents by telephone and visitation to the parents' last known address within the jurisdiction of the court). The child identified in such petition should attend such proceedings unless the court finds on motion of any party that the attendance of a

child under the age of twelve years would be detrimental to the child.

If the parents or custodians named in the petition fail to attend, the court may proceed to the termination hearing. If counsel for the parent has already been assigned by the court or has entered a notice of appearance, he or she should participate in the hearing. If the parents or custodians named in the petition were not present at the hearing and appear thereafter and move the court for a rehearing, the court should grant the motion unless it finds that they willfully refused to appear at the hearing or that the rehearing would be unjust because of the lapse of time since the hearing was held.

9. Interpreters. The court should appoint an interpreter or otherwise ensure that language barriers do not deprive the parents, child, witnesses, or other participants of the ability to understand and participate effectively in all stages of the proceedings.

10. Discovery. General civil rules of procedure, including discovery and pretrial practice, should be applicable to termination proceedings, provided, however, that after the filing of a petition, the court may cause any person within its jurisdiction, including the child and the parents, to be examined by a physician, psychiatrist, or psychologist when it appears that such examination will be relevant to a proper determination of the charges. A party's willful and unexcused failure to comply with a lawful discovery order may be dealt with pursuant to the general civil rules of discovery, including the power of contempt. Except as otherwise provided, the standards governing disclosure of matters in connection with proceedings under this Part should be the same for the child and the parents as for the respondent in delinquency cases, as set out in the *Pretrial Court Proceedings* volume.

11. Appointment of independent experts. Any party to the proceeding may petition the court for appointment of experts, at public expense, for independent evaluation of the matter before the court. The court should grant such petition unless it finds the expert is unnecessary.

12. Subpoenas. Upon request of any party, a subpoena should be issued by the court (or its clerk), commanding the attendance and testimony of any person at any proceeding conducted pursuant to this Part, or commanding the production of documents for use in any such proceeding.

13. Public access to adjudication proceedings. The court should honor any request by the parents or child that specified members of the public be permitted to observe the hearing.

14. Burden of proof. The burden should rest on the petitioner to prove by clear and convincing evidence allegations sufficient to support the petition.

15. Evidence. Only legally relevant material and competent evidence, subject to cross-examination by all parties, may be admissible to the hearing, pursuant to the principles governing evidence in civil matters in the courts of general jurisdiction in the state.

16. Findings. If the trier of fact, after a hearing, determines that facts exist sufficient to terminate parental rights pursuant to the standards set out in Standard 8.3 C., the court should convene a dispositional hearing in accordance with Standard 8.5.

If the finder of fact determines that facts sufficient to terminate parental rights have not been established, the court should dismiss the petition.

C. Basis for involuntary termination.

Before entering an interlocutory order of termination of parental rights, a court, after a hearing, must find one or more of the following facts:

1. The child has been abandoned. For the purposes of this Part, a child has been abandoned when:

a. his/her parents have not cared for or contacted him/her, although the parents are physically able to do so, for a period of [sixty] days, and the parents have failed to secure a living arrangement for the child that assures the child protection from harm that would authorize a judicial declaration of endangerment pursuant to Standard 2.1;

b. he/she has been found to be endangered pursuant to Part V and has been in placement, and the parents for a period of more than one year have failed to maintain contact with the child although physically able to do so, notwithstanding the diligent efforts of the agency to encourage and strengthen the parental relationship; or

c. he/she has been in the custody of a third party without court order, or by court order pursuant to Standard 10.7, for a period of eighteen months, and the parents for a period of more than eighteen months have failed to maintain contact with the child although physically able and not prevented from doing so by the custodian.

2. The child has been removed from the parents previously under the test established in Standard 6.4 C., has been returned to his/her parents, has been found to be endangered a second time, requiring removal, has been out of the home for at least six months, and there is a substantial likelihood that sufficient legal

justification to keep the child from being returned home, as specified in Standard 6.4 C., will continue to exist in the foreseeable future.

3. The child has been found to be endangered in the manner specified in Standard 2.1 A., more than six months earlier another child in the family had been found endangered under 2.1 A., the child has been out of the home for at least six months, and there is a substantial likelihood that sufficient legal justification to keep the child from being returned home, as specified in Standard 6.4 C., will continue to exist in the foreseeable future.

4. The child was found to be endangered pursuant to Standard 5.4, the child has been in placement for two or more years if under the age of three, or three or more years if over the age of three, the agency has fulfilled its obligations undertaken pursuant to Standard 6.5 B., and there is a substantial likelihood that sufficient legal justification to keep the child from being returned home, as specified in Standard 6.4 C., will continue to exist in the foreseeable future.

5. The child has been in the custody of a third party without court order, or by court order pursuant to Standard 10.7, for a period of three years, the third party wishes to adopt the child, and

    a. the parents do not want or are unable to accept custody at the present time;

    b. return of the child to the parents will cause the child to suffer serious and sustained emotional harm; or

    c. the child is twelve years or older and wants to be adopted.

6. The child has been in voluntary placement by court order pursuant to Standard 10.7 for a period of three years and

    a. the parents do not want or are unable to accept custody at the present time;

    b. return of the child to the parents will cause the child to suffer serious and sustained emotional harm; or

    c. the child is twelve years or older and wants to be adopted.

8.4 Situations in which termination should not be ordered.

Even if a child comes within the provisions of Standard 8.2 or 8.3, a court should not order termination if it finds by clear and convincing evidence that any of the following are applicable:

A. because of the closeness of the parent-child relationship, it would be detrimental to the child to terminate parental rights;

B. the child is placed with a relative who does not wish to adopt the child;

C. because of the nature of the child's problems, the child is placed in a residential treatment facility, and continuation of parental rights will not prevent finding the child a permanent family placement if the parents cannot resume custody when residential care is no longer needed;

D. the child cannot be placed permanently in a family environment and failure to terminate will not impair the child's opportunity for a permanent placement in a family setting;

E. a child over age ten objects to termination.

8.5 Dispositional proceedings.

A. Predisposition report.

Upon a finding that facts exist sufficient to terminate parental rights, the court should order a complete predisposition report prepared by the probation department for the dispositional hearing. A copy of the report should be provided to each of the parties to the proceeding. The report should include:

1. the present physical, mental, and emotional conditions of the child and his/her parents, including the results of all medical, psychiatric, or psychological examinations of the child or of any parent whose relationship to the child is subject to termination;

2. the nature of all past and existing relationships among the child, his/her siblings, and his/her parents;

3. the proposed plan for the child;

4. the child's own preferences; and

5. any other facts pertinent to determining whether parental rights should be terminated.

B. Dispositional hearing.

A dispositional hearing should be held within [forty-five] days of the finding pursuant to Standard 8.3 B. 16. All parties to the proceedings should be able to participate in this hearing, and all matters relevant to the court's determination should be presented in evidence.

8.6 Interlocutory order for termination of parental rights; appeals.

A. If the court after a hearing finds that one or more of the bases exist pursuant to Standard 8.3 C. and that none of the bases in Standard 8.4 C. is applicable, it should enter an interlocutory order terminating parental rights. An interlocutory order terminating parental rights may be made final or vacated in accordance with the provisions in Standard 8.7 B.

B. Appeals. An appeal may be taken as of right from a court order entered pursuant to Standard 8.3 B. 16., 8.6, or 8.7. The standards governing appeals from proceedings under this Part should be the same as those set out in the *Appeals and Collateral Review* standards, except that the parties entitled to take an appeal under *Appeals and Collateral Review* Standard 2.2 should include the petitioner, pursuant to Standard 8.3 B. 2. and 4. above.

8.7 Actions following termination.

A. When parental rights are terminated, a court should order the child placed for adoption, placed with legal guardians, or left in long-term foster care. Where possible, adoption is preferable. However, a child should not be removed from a foster home if the foster parents are unwilling or unable to adopt the child, but are willing to provide, and are capable of providing, the child with a permanent home, and the removal of the child from the physical custody of the foster parents would be detrimental to his/her emotional well-being because the child has substantial psychological ties to the foster parents.

B. When an adoption or guardianship has been perfected, the court should make its interlocutory order final and terminate its jurisdiction over the child. If some other long-term placement for the child has been made, the court should continue the hearing to a specific future date not more than one year after the date of the order of continued jurisdiction. After the hearing, the court should extend the interlocutory order to a specified date to permit further efforts to provide a permanent placement, or vacate the interlocutory order and restore parental rights to the child's parents.

PART IX: CRIMINAL LIABILITY FOR PARENTAL CONDUCT

9.1 Limiting criminal prosecutions.

Criminal prosecution for conduct that is the subject of a petition for court jurisdiction filed pursuant to these standards should be authorized only if the court in which such petition has been filed certifies that such prosecution will not unduly harm the interests of the child named in the petition.

PART X: VOLUNTARY PLACEMENT

10.1 Definition.

For purposes of this Part, "voluntary placement" is any placement of a child under twelve years of age into foster care when the placement is made at the request of the child's parents and is made through a public or state supported private agency without any court involvement. This Part does not apply to placements in a state mental hospital or other residential facility for mentally ill or retarded children.

10.2 Need for statutory regulation.

All states should adopt a statutory structure regulating voluntary placements.

10.3 Preplacement inquiries.

Prior to accepting a child for voluntary placement, the agency worker should:

A. Explore fully with the parents the need for placement and the alternatives to placement of the child.

B. Prepare a social study on the need for placement; the study should explore alternatives to placement and elaborate the reasons why placement is necessary. However, a child may be placed prior to completion of the social study if the child would be endangered if left at home or the parents cannot care for the child at home even if provided with services.

C. Review with an agency supervisor the decision to place the child.

D. Determine that an adequate placement is in fact available for the child.

10.4 Placement agreements.

When a child is accepted for placement, the agency should enter into a formal agreement with the parents specifying the rights and obligations of each party. The agreement should contain at least the following provisions:

A. a statement by the parents that the placement is completely voluntary on their part and not made under any threats or pressure from an agency;

B. a statement by the parents that they have discussed the need for placement, and alternatives to placement, with the agency worker and have concluded that they cannot care for their child at home;

C. notice that the parents may resume custody of their child within forty-eight hours of notifying the agency of their desire to do so;

D. a statement by the parents that they will maintain contact with the child while he/she is in placement;

E. a statement by the agency that it will provide the parents with services to enable them to resume custody of their child;

F. notification to the parents of the specific worker in charge of helping them resume custody and an agreement that the agency will inform the parents immediately if there is a change in workers assigned to them;

G. a statement that if the child remains in placement longer than six months, the case will automatically be reviewed by the juvenile court, and that termination of parental rights might occur if the child remains in placement for eighteen months if the parents have failed to maintain contact or three years even if the parents have maintained contact.

10.5 Parental involvement in placement.

The agency should involve the parents and the child in the placement process to the maximum extent possible, including consulting with the parents and the child, if he/she is of sufficient maturity, in the choice of an appropriate placement, and should request the parents to participate in bringing the child to the new home or facility. Preference should be given to the placement of choice of the parents and the child, in the absence of good cause to the contrary.

10.6 Written plans.

Within two weeks of accepting a child for placement, the agency and parents should develop a written plan describing the steps that will be taken by each to facilitate the quickest possible return of the child and to maximize parent-child contact during placement. The plan should contain at least the following elements:

A. provisions for maximum possible visitation;

B. a description of the specific services that will be provided by the agency to aid the parents;

C. a description of the specific changes in parental condition or home environment that are necessary in order for the parents to resume custody; and

D. provisions for helping the parents participate in the care of the child while he/she is in placement.

10.7 Juvenile court supervision.

No child should remain in placement longer than six months unless the child is made a ward of the juvenile court, and the court, at a hearing in which both the parents and child are represented by counsel, finds that continued placement is necessary.

10.8 Termination of parental rights.

If a child is brought under court supervision, the standards for termination of parental rights contained in Part VIII should apply.

Standards with Commentary

PART I: GENERAL PRINCIPLES

1.1 Family autonomy.

Laws structuring a system of coercive intervention on behalf of endangered children should be based on a strong presumption for parental autonomy in child rearing. Coercive state intervention should occur only when a child is suffering specific harms as defined in Standard 2.1. Active state involvement in child care or extensive monitoring of each child's development should be available only on a truly voluntary basis except in situations described by these standards.

Commentary

This section specifies the basic value preference underlying the proposed standards, that childrearing should be left to the discretion of parents unless they fail to protect a child from certain harms, specified by statute. This preference is consistent not only with our historic policy of giving substantial deference to parental decision-making with regard to childrearing, but also with the great majority of statutory enactments and judicial decisions in this country. See, *e.g.*, Mass. Gen. Law, ch. 119, S1 (1969); *Wisconsin v. Yoder*, 406 U.S. 205, 232 (1972); *Stanley v. Illinois*, 405 U.S. 645, 651 (1972).

Coercive state intervention should be limited for a number of reasons. Our political commitments to individual freedom and privacy, diversity of views and lifestyles, and free exercise of religious beliefs are all promoted by allowing families to raise children in a wide variety of living situations and diverse childrearing patterns. Extensive intervention carries a substantial risk of intervening to "save" children of poor parents and/or minority cultures.

49

Moreover, a presumption in favor of parental autonomy comports with our limited knowledge regarding childrearing and ways to effect long-term change in a given child's development. See I. S. White, *Federal Programs for Young Children: Review and Recommendations* 130-367 (1973); J. Goldstein, A. Freud and A. Solnit, *Beyond the Best Interests of the Child* 51-52 (1973). We have no agreed upon values about the "proper" way to raise a child. The best we can do is establish certain basic harms from which all children should be protected.

In addition, there is substantial evidence that, except in cases involving very seriously harmed children, we are unable to improve a child's situation through coercive intervention. See, *e.g.*, G. Brown, *The Multi-Problem Dilemma: A Social Research Demonstration with Multi-Problem Families* (1968). In fact intervention may worsen the child's situation. See commentary to Standard 1.3, *infra*.

Adopting this preference does not mean that children will be left unprotected. The standards proposed herein define a level of minimum care that a parent must provide. Moreover, Standard 1.1 stipulates that a variety of child care services should be available to families on a genuinely voluntary basis. There is much that can and should be done to better the situation of children and families, without coercive intervention.

1.2 Purpose of intervention.

Coercive state intervention should be premised upon specific harms that a child has suffered or is likely to suffer.

Commentary

This standard specifies that the statutory definition of endangerment should be drafted in terms of specific harms from which children are to be protected, rather than in terms of parental conduct.

It is generally accepted that the purpose of intervention is to protect children from harm, not to punish parents for "undesirable" conduct or home conditions unrelated to the child's wellbeing. See Paulsen, "The Delinquency, Neglect and Dependency Jurisdiction of the Juvenile Court," in M. Rosenheim, *Justice for the Child* (1962). However, most state statutes define the grounds for intervention in terms of parental behavior or home conditions without requiring any showing that the child is being harmed by the behavior of the parent or conditions in the home. The statutes appear to assume that we can tell whether a child is endangered, and intervention is appropriate, solely on the basis of parental conduct.

This assumption is contrary to the available social science evidence which indicates that it is very difficult or impossible to correlate parental behavior to specific detriment to the child, especially if one is trying to predict long-term harm to the child's development. See, *e.g.*, J. Goldstein, A. Freud and A. Solnit, *Beyond the Best Interests of the Child* 51–52 (1973). Studies have amply demonstrated that even our most sophisticated techniques of predicting long-range harm to children on the basis of particular parental behavior are woefully inadequate. Summarizing the findings of his recently completed comprehensive review of existing studies, Harvard psychologist Sheldon White states:

> Neither theory nor research has specified the exact mechanisms by which a child's development and his family functioning are linked. While speculation abounds, there is little agreement about how these family functions produce variations in measures of health, learning and affect. Nor do we know the relative importance of internal (individual and family) versus external (social and economic) factors. White, *Federal Programs for Young Children: Review and Recommendations* 240 (1973).

Since prediction is so difficult, the danger of overintervention, i.e., intervention harmful to the child (see commentary to Standard 1.3), is increased by focusing solely on parental behavior. Moreover, there is substantial evidence that intervention often occurs in situations where there is no demonstrable harm to the child and no strong likelihood of harm occurring. A review of appellate cases indicates that courts still intervene, and even remove children from their homes, because they disapprove of the parents' lifestyles or childrearing practices. See, *e.g.*, *In re Raya*, 255 Cal. App. 2d 260, 63 Cal. Rptr. 252 (3d Dist. 1967) (parents not legally married); *In re Yardley*, 260 Iowa 259, 149 N.W.2d 162 (1967) (mother "frequented taverns"); *In re Anonymous*, 37 Misc. 2d 411, 238 N.Y.2d 422 (Fam. Ct. 1962) (mother had men visitors overnight); *In re Watson*, 95 N.Y.S.2d 798 (Dom. Rel. Ct. 1950) (parent adhered to "extreme" religious practices); *In re Cager*, 251 Md. 473, 248 A.2d 384 (1968) (parent was the mother of an illegitimate child). None of these cases contained evidence of harm to the children. Such intervention often harms, rather than protects children. See J. Bowlby, *Child Care and the Growth of Love* 85 (1965).

If the purpose of intervention is to protect children from specific harms, the most reliable way of insuring that intervention takes place only when appropriate is to define the bases for intervention in terms of those harms we wish to prevent. See Standard 2.1.

1.3 Statutory guidelines.

The statutory grounds for coercive intervention on behalf of endangered children:

A. should be defined as specifically as possible;

B. should authorize intervention only where the child is suffering, or there is a substantial likelihood that the child will imminently suffer, serious harm;

C. should permit coercive intervention only for categories of harm where intervention will, in most cases, do more good than harm.

Commentary

These principles are closely related to the judgment that the grounds for intervention should be defined in terms of specific harms to the child. Together they establish the basic value premises and set forth a general philosophy regarding the appropriate scope of coercive intervention.

These standards provide that the grounds for intervention be defined specifically and that intervention be permissible only in cases of serious harm. Moreover, in determining whether intervention should be permissible for any given harm, the legislature should determine that, in general, coercive intervention on this basis will benefit more children than it will harm.

For purposes of this standard, "substantial likelihood" means real and considerable probability; "imminently" means that the harm will occur within days or weeks, not months or years. The specific harms justifying intervention are contained in Standard 2.1 *infra*.

Vagueness. At present, all state statutes define the grounds for intervention in extremely broad and vague language. Typically, they permit intervention whenever the child is in an "unsuitable" home or when a parent fails to provide for the child's "physical," "mental," or "medical" needs. See, *e.g.*, Cal. Welf. & Inst'ns Code § 600 (West 1972).

It is claimed that vague laws are necessary because the types of "neglectful" behavior vary widely and broad statutes enable judges to examine each situation on its own facts. See, *e.g.*, S. Katz, *When Parents Fail* 64 (1971); Gill, "The Legal Nature of Neglect" 6 *N.P.P.A. J.* 1, 5-6 (1960). It is assumed that judges, without legislative guidance, will make appropriate decisions on a case-by-case basis.

The present resort to vague, general statutes is unacceptable for a number of reasons. Most importantly, by failing to identify the specific harms which justify intervention, such laws increase the likelihood that decisions will be made to intervene in situations where the child will be harmed by intervention. It has become increasingly clear in recent years that coercive intervention can be harmful to children as well as helpful. See J. Bowlby, *Child Care and the Growth of Love* (1965); Mnookin, "Foster Care: In Whose Best Interest," 43 *Harv. Ed. Rev.* 599 (1973); Areen, "Intervention Between Parent and Child: A Reappraisal of the State's Role in Child Neglect and Abuse Cases," 63 *Geo. L. Rev.* 887 (1975). This is especially true when intervention leads to removal of the child from the home. See H. Stone, *Foster Care in Question* (1970). See commentary to Standard 6.5 B. below. Therefore, it is necessary to provide specific guidelines to courts and social work agencies regarding those types of harms which justify intervention and that define the situations in which intervention is likely to be beneficial to the child.

Moreover, vague laws facilitate arbitrary, and even discriminatory, intervention. Unless the bases for intervention are clearly defined, each social worker and judge can make his/her own value judgments about those harms which justify intervention. There is substantial evidence that such decisions sometimes involve imposing middle class values upon poor families without taking into account different cultural patterns of child rearing. Vague laws also result in unequal treatment of similarly situated persons. Again, it must be recognized that such arbitrary intervention not only is violative of basic values in our society, it may also be quite harmful to the children who are being "protected."

In addition, specific legislative definition of the grounds for intervention should compel courts to specify in each case the harm being prevented by intervention. This should increase the chances of appropriate dispositions in each case. Making sound decisions about the appropriate disposition, even in a case where intervention is justified, requires weighing the harms to be prevented or alleviated against the harms likely to result from that disposition. See Standards 6.1–6.4 and commentary *infra*. This cannot be done where the harms to be prevented are not specified, as often happens under vague statutes. Unless the basis for intervention is specifically noted by the court, it is impossible for the decisionmaker or others to later evaluate the efficacy of such intervention, since the appropriate criteria to measure success or failure are unknown.

Finally, all intervention involves value judgments about appropriate childrearing practices and value choices about where and how a child should grow up. Considering the seriousness of the decision to intervene, intervention should be permissible only where there is a clear-cut decision, openly and deliberately made by responsible political bodies, that that type of harm involved justifies intervention. Such value judgments should not be left to the individual tastes of hundreds of nonaccountable decisionmakers.

Seriousness of Harm. Merely defining harm specifically will not insure appropriate intervention, however. A ground for intervention might be stated quite specifically, yet intervention may not be beneficial to most children. This standard reflects the judgment that coercive intervention is not appropriate merely because a child is being "harmed," regardless of the nature of the harm. It is further a rejection of the claim that the goal of state intervention should be to protect a child from a home environment which is not "optimal" for the child. Instead it calls for a statutory definition which limits intervention to situations involving "serious" harm. Basically these are defined as situations where a child is suffering or is likely to imminently suffer severe physical or emotional damage. See Standard 2.1 *infra.*

There are a number of reasons for limiting intervention to situations involving actual or potential serious harm to children. First, this limitation is consistent with the presumption of family autonomy stated in Standard 1.1. State intervention necessarily interferes with family autonomy, often to the extent of removing a child from the family. Given the magnitude of the intrusion, it should be resorted to only in cases where the child is likely to be seriously harmed absent intervention.

It cannot be assumed, moreover, that coercive intervention is generally desirable. This is especially true if intervention leads to removal of a child from his/her home. There is substantial evidence that continuity of relationships is extremely important to children. See J. Goldstein, A. Freud and A. Solnit, *Beyond the Best Interests of the Child* 31-34 (1973). Removing a child from his/her family may cause serious psychological damage—damage more serious than the harm intervention is supposed to prevent. *Id.* at 19-20; J. Bowlby, *Child Care and the Growth of Love* 13-30 (2d ed. 1965). Moreover, we often lack the ability to insure that a child is placed in a setting superior to his/her own home. The shortcomings of foster care are now well documented. See Mnookin, "Foster Care: In Whose Best Interest," 43 *Harv. Ed. Rev.* 599 (1973); Maluccio, "Foster Family Care Revisited: Problems and Prospects," 31 *Public Welfare* 12 (1973); H. Stone, *Foster Care in Question* (1970).

Coercive action not involving removal may also be emotionally disruptive and prove harmful to the child. The presence of "outsiders" can prove threatening to the parent-child relationship. See, *e.g.*, J. Goldstein, A. Freud and A. Solnit, *supra* at 52; J. Handler, *The Coercive Social Worker* (1973). Moreover there is evidence that, except in cases involving very seriously harmed children, we are unable to improve a child's situation through coercive state intervention. See, *e.g.*, White, *Federal Programs for Young Children: Review and Recommendations* 238-287 (1973); Fischer, "Is Casework Effective? A Review," *Social Work* 5 (January 1973). This is particularly true in cases involving unwilling clients. See, *e.g.*, G. Brown, *The Multi-Problem Dilemma: A Social Research Demonstration with Multi-Problem Families* (1968). In part this is due to factors such as inadequate resources, poorly trained personnel, and high turnover among caseworkers. See Levine, "Caveat Parens: A Demystification of the Child Protection System," 35 *U. Pitt. L. Rev.* 1, 13-15 (1973); Paulsen, "Juvenile Courts, Family Courts and the Poor Man," 54 *Cal. L. Rev.* 694, 710-711 (1966). Moreover, it must be recognized that to a large degree we face a problem of lack of knowledge as well as lack of funds.

Therefore, it is preferable to utilize coercive intervention cautiously. By limiting intervention to situations where the harm is serious, we can assume that intervention will generally do more good than harm. Furthermore, this limitation would result in a more rational use of our limited resources, by channeling the finite resources available for helping children to those children in the most danger. It is tempting to intervene more broadly, since many children and families could use more services such as day care or homemakers. Additional services clearly should be available on a voluntary basis. However, services forced upon families are less effective and more likely to harm, rather than help, children.

Finally, limiting coercive intervention to situations where there is serious harm minimizes the danger of imposing middle class values on all families and ignoring cultural differences in childrearing.

Imminence of Harm. The standard also provides that intervention should be limited to situations where the harm has already occurred or where there is a substantial likelihood of its imminent occurrence. Intervention based on prediction of future harm should not be permissible.

This standard does not reject the value of state policies designed to prevent neglect and abuse or to respond when neglect or abuse has occurred. However, because our limited knowledge of childrearing practices and child development renders predictions of future harm a very difficult endeavor, coercive intervention should be restricted to situations where harm has occurred or is imminent. See J. Goldstein, A. Freud and A. Solnit, *supra* at 49-52; White, *supra* at 130-260. "In the absence of scientific certainty it must be borne in mind that the farther back from the point of imminent danger the law draws the safety line of police regulation, so much greater is the possibility that legislative interference is unwarranted." E. Freund, *Standards of American Legislation* 83 (1917).

This standard does not require waiting until a child has actually been injured, however. If a substantial danger of imminent harm can be demonstrated, intervention would be authorized. Examples of such situations are discussed in the commentary to Standard 2.1 A.-F. *infra*. Again, more social services, available on a voluntary basis, should result in less need for coercive intervention.

1.4 Protecting cultural differences.

Standards for coercive intervention should take into account cultural differences in childrearing. All decisionmakers should examine the child's needs in light of the child's cultural background and values.

Commentary

This standard further develops the value premise established in Standard 1.1 *supra*. Given the cultural pluralism and diversity of childrearing practices in our society, it is essential that any system authorizing coercive state involvement in childrearing fully take those differences into account. Moreover, failure to recognize that children can develop adequately in a range of environments and with different types of parenting may lead to intervention that disturbs a healthful situation for the child.

Thus, for example, in some cultures a major role in childrearing may be assumed by adults other than the natural parent. Sometimes this care will be provided by relatives; in other situations it may be provided by adults living in the same building or block as the parents, although there is no blood relationship involved. Where such adults are providing care intervention would not be justified, even though the parent's care of the child is inadequate in some respects.

Moreover, this standard requires that a child's need for cultural identity and continuity of cultural heritage be recognized whenever intervention is necessary. Every effort should be made to preserve such continuities if a child must be removed from the home or when a family is required to accept casework supervision.

1.5 Child's interests paramount.

State intervention should promote family autonomy and strengthen family life whenever possible. However, in cases where a child's needs, as defined in these standards conflict with his/her parents' interests, the child's needs should have priority.

Commentary

This standard states that the goal of intervention, when it is necessary, should be to preserve families and to strengthen family life. However, when situations arise in which the needs of the child cannot be protected in a manner acceptable to the parents, or when a child cannot be protected while remaining with the parents, this standard provides that the child's needs be given priority.

The goal of preserving families is the prevailing ethic in social work literature, judicial decisions, and legislation. However, in many, if not all, states the child welfare system often contributes to breaking up, rather than preserving family units. Considerably more money is spent at the state and local level on services provided to children removed from their homes than on services providing support to keep families intact. Under these standards every state and agency policy, including financial policy, would be evaluated in terms of its impact on preserving and strengthening families.

Preservation of parental autonomy, or even of family units, is not always possible however. A fundamental tenet of these standards is that the child's needs receive priority. We should protect the child because he/she is a helpless party who needs state protection from a situation being created by his/her parents. Although the parents may not be in any sense morally blameworthy, they should suffer the consequences of their inadequacy rather than the child. Moreover, as Goldstein, Freud and Solnit state, by protecting a child from physical and/or emotional damage, we are increasing the probability that he/she will become an adequate parent. While it is extremely difficult to make predictions in individual cases, clearly many people demonstrate the same inadequacies as parents that their own parents displayed. For example, many abusing parents were abused children. By adopting policies that favor the child's needs, we may be helping future, as well as present, generations of children.

1.6 Continuity and stability.

When state intervention is necessary, the entire system of intervention should be designed to promote a child's need for a continuous, stable living environment.

Commentary

Virtually all experts, from many different professional disciplines, agree that children need and benefit from continuous, stable home environments. See, *e.g.*, J. Goldstein, A. Freud and A. Solnit, *Beyond the Best Interests of the Child* (1973); J. Bowlby, *Attachment and*

Loss, Vol. II *Separation* (1973); M. Rutter, *Maternal Deprivation Reassessed* (1972). Because of the importance of continuity and stability to children, preservation of ongoing relationships should be a major goal of the intervention system.

The "child neglect system" cannot, of course, remove all sources of discontinuity from children's lives. For example, children will continue to be subjected to discontinuities arising out of divorces, death of parents, and illnesses. However, when coercive intervention is necessary, it should be implemented in a manner that preserves stable and continuous relationships whenever this can be done without further endangering the child. Thus, in light of this principle, we should be reluctant to remove children from homes where they have stable relationships. See Standard 6.4 C. *infra.* If a child must be removed, maximum effort should be made to maintain the child's contact with his/her parents. See Standards 6.5, 6.6 *infra.* If a child cannot be returned home, the child care system should provide him/her with another stable environment and not a series of foster homes. See Part VIII *infra.*

Moreover, in considering a child's needs for continuity and stability, it should be recognized that there are many elements to a child's environment: his/her parents, other relatives, parent surrogates, language and culture, ethnic identity. The need for continuity in all these areas should be considered at every decision point.

1.7 Recognizing developmental differences.

Laws aimed at protecting children should reflect developmental differences among children of different ages.

Commentary

At present, the laws regulating state intervention, removal of children from their homes, and termination of parental rights apply the same rules regardless of the age of the child involved. This approach is unrealistic. Children undergo substantial psychological changes as they grow older, and the impact of any given policy is likely to be far different on children of different ages. For example, the impact of termination of parental rights will be far different on a six-month-old child, who is readily adoptable and has not yet formed an attachment to a parent figure, than on a six-year-old who is deeply attached to his/her parents.

Therefore, the standards proposed herein apply different rules depending on the child's age. See, *e.g.,* Standard 8.3 C. *infra.* The categories are broad; we do not have sufficient data to permit finer distinctions. However, agencies and courts should also take into account on a case-by-case basis the child's developmental state in determining whether intervention is appropriate and if so, what type of intervention is most appropriate.

1.8 Accountability.

The system of coercive state intervention should be designed to insure that all agencies, including courts, participating in the intervention process are held accountable for all of their actions.

Commentary

This standard establishes a goal central to the success of all of the other standards. While it may seem unnecessary to state that government agencies and agents should be accountable for their actions, the lack of accountability in our present child welfare systems requires our emphasizing this goal.

At present the intervention process is an extremely low visibility process, with courts and social work agencies having enormous discretionary power to coercively intervene in family situations and to take such drastic steps as removing a child from his/her home. See S. Katz, *When Parents Fail*, ch. 2–3 (1971); Levine, "Caveat Parens: A Demystification of the Child Protection System," 35 *U. Pitt. L. Rev.* 1 (1973). There are very few mechanisms built into the system to review most decisions or to review success or failure of the intervention efforts. In many places, courts have largely abdicated their responsibilities to social work agencies. Yet there are no means of checking on agency performance. Moreover, appeals are relatively few, thereby limiting them as an effective means of holding trial courts accountable.

To a large extent the success of any intervention depends on the availability of sufficient high quality agencies. Unfortunately, such services often are unavailable in many states. Child care agencies are understaffed and must rely on inexperienced, untrained personnel. Caseloads are large; staff turnover is very high. See Campbell, "The Neglected Child: His and His Family's Treatment Under Massachusetts Law and Practice and Their Rights Under the Due Process Clause," *Suff. L. Rev.* 631 (1970); A. Gruber, *Foster Home Care in Massachusetts: A Study of Foster Children, Their Biological and Foster Parents* (1973). In fact, several recent studies show that in at least some states many children brought into the child care system are basically ignored by state agencies, especially if they enter foster care. See A. Gruber, *supra*.

Adequate funding is essential if the purposes of intervention are to be served. However, money alone will not solve the problems of the present system. It is also necessary to insure that each part of the system is, in fact, performing adequately. The standards proposed herein attempt to define specifically the bases for state intervention and to provide guidelines for each of the critical decisions which must be made following intervention, *e.g.*, what disposition to make, how to provide services to children and parents when the child is in foster care, when to terminate parental rights. A variety of mechanisms are provided to insure that each decision is carefully considered and subject to review. See, *e.g.*, Standards 7.1–7.5 *infra*. Implementation of the mechanisms is essential if the substantive standards proposed herein are to work in the best interests of children and families.

PART II: STATUTORY GROUNDS FOR INTERVENTION

2.1 Statutory grounds for intervention.
Courts should be authorized to assume jurisdiction in order to condition continued parental custody upon the parents' accepting supervision or to remove a child from his/her home only when a child is endangered in a manner specified in subsections A.–F.

Commentary

This standard specifies that coercive state intervention may occur only if the child is endangered in a manner specified in subsections A.–F. *infra*. Subsections A.–F. are meant to provide a statutory definition of "endangerment," replacing existing laws on neglect and abuse. The fact that a child comes within one of these categories is not sufficient for a finding of jurisdiction, however. The court must also find, pursuant to Standard 2.2 *infra*, that intervention is necessary to protect the child.

The statutory grounds for intervention are critical to the structure of the entire system proposed in this volume. They provide courts with guidelines as to when they may assume jurisdiction over the family. They also inform investigating agencies when they may investigate an allegation that a child is endangered. Thus, they provide specific limits on the nature and extent of coercive state action.

The specific harms justifying intervention are drafted in accordance with the principles discussed in Standards 1.2 and 1.3 *supra*, *i.e.*, the definitions focus on the child and authorize intervention only for serious harms where, in general, the remedy of coercive intervention will be beneficial to the child. Thus, not every type of harm from which we might wish to protect children constitutes a basis for intervention. For example, we might want all children to grow up in a home where they are "loved." Ideally, each home would provide each child the best available opportunity to fulfill his/her potential in society. See D. Gil, *Violence Against Children* 202 (1973).

However, few families provide children with "ideal" environments. If intervention is permissible because parents are not sufficiently affectionate, because a home is dirty, because the parents are providing less stimulation than desirable, or because the parents are thought to be "immoral," as defined by judges and social workers, intervention would be pervasive. Yet there is every reason to believe that intervention to protect children from such "harms," especially if removal is the only alternative, would more often result in harms greater to the child than the "harm" from which he/she is being protected. We have neither the resources nor the knowledge to protect children against all harms. Finally, the broader the grounds for intervention, the greater the possibility of arbitrary or discriminatory intervention.

The proposed grounds focus primarily on the child's physical well-being, although intervention is permitted, in very limited circumstances, where a child is suffering from "emotional" damage. The standards specifically omit language authorizing intervention because a child is living in an "immoral" home environment, an "unsuitable" home, a "dirty" home, or with parents who are "inadequate." All of these terms allow overintervention, often on an arbitrary basis, without any evidence of harm to the child. As previously stated, see commentary to Standard 1.2, the only way to insure that state intervention truly helps children is to focus on them, not on their parents.

There is also no specific provision in the standard allowing intervention where a child is "abandoned." It is assumed that if a child is *truly* abandoned, *i.e.*, there is no adult caring for or willing to continue caring for the child, the child will fall under one of the other categories provided. Thus if a parent is unwilling to care for a child, it is likely that intervention will be justified to protect the child from physical danger. In other situations where there is an adult caring for the child, *e.g.*, when a child is cared for by members of an "extended" family—whether or not there is a blood relationship—intervention is not authorized.

The proposed grounds for intervention reject the positions of those who advocate limiting intervention solely to cases of physical abuse and those who would support intervention whenever a child is "deprive[d] . . . of equal rights and liberties, and/or [denied] optimal development." See D. Gil, *Violence Against Children* 202 (1973). Those advocating the narrower definition claim that we lack the knowledge and resources to protect any but the most seriously abused children, *i.e.*, those who are "battered" by their parents. They believe that intervention in nonphysical abuse cases will likely be done in a discriminatory manner and without helping the child. Therefore, according to proponents of this view, coercive intervention should not be permitted unless the parent has severely and willfully injured the child.

Commentators supporting broad definitions tend to minimize the lack of resources and to focus on the well documented fact that many children grow up in quite undesirable conditions. They argue that it is unrealistic to single out physical abuse when children can be equally damaged in other ways. To some degree these commentators recognize that the problem does not always lie with the parents, but they are willing to use neglect laws in lieu of social programs to help all families.

The proposed grounds for intervention attempt to strike a middle ground, isolating a number of harms which are considered most serious, regardless of whether they are physical or emotional, but not including so many harms, or harms so broadly defined, that we cannot hope to intervene usefully in all the cases that will be brought. Moreover, a number of procedural protections are established to limit the possibility of unwise, arbitrary, or discriminatory intervention. See Parts IV and V *infra*. These procedures, plus the standards limiting removal of children from their homes, see Standard 6.4 C. *infra*, and providing review mechanisms for all decisions, see Part VII *infra*, should limit the possibility of unwarranted and discriminatory intervention. In seeking a middle ground, inevitably some children will be excluded who need protection, and intervention will occur in some cases where it is unwarranted. However, no system can assure intervention every time it is required, and only when, it is beneficial to a child.

Although each ground for intervention is defined specifically, all of the grounds leave some room for interpretation and expansion. Therefore, it is essential that they be read and administered in light of the central goals established for the entire system, *i.e.*, to recognize family autonomy, to limit intervention to cases where there is substantial reason to believe that intervention is both necessary to protect a child and will in fact benefit the specific child, to preserve family units whenever possible, and to recognize cultural and ethnic differences in childrearing.

It must be kept in mind that each of the grounds *authorizes but does not require a court to intervene.* Moreover, intervention may take many forms, only one of which is removal of the child from the family. The grounds for removal are strictly limited by Standard 6.4 C. *infra.*

A. [Coercive intervention should be authorized when] a child has suffered, or there is a substantial risk that a child will imminently suffer, a physical harm, inflicted nonaccidentally upon him/her by his/her parents, which causes, or creates a substantial risk of causing disfigurement, impairment of bodily functioning, or other serious physical injury.

Commentary

This standard authorizes intervention when a child has been physically abused by his/her parent, *i.e.*, cases where a parent has nonaccidentally injured the child. Unlike present statutes, which usually do not specify the extent of the injury needed to justify intervention, the standard specifies that the harm must be a serious one, generally evidenced by disfigurement or substantial impairment of bodily functioning. As used in this standard, "serious" is intended to mean "significant." Such injury need not have already occurred to justify intervention, however. If a child has been physically harmed by a parent in a manner that might cause serious harm, but did not do so in the particular instance, intervention would still be permissible.

Intervention to protect a child from physical abuse is currently authorized in all states. Clearly, killing, maiming, or severely beating a human being are not acceptable forms of behavior. There is no greater reason to allow such conduct in a family setting than in society-at-large. Yet there are significant gradations in the types of harms which might result from intentionally striking a child. A recent nationwide survey found that more than half of the reported cases of physical abuse of children involved minor bruises or abrasions that did not require treatment. D. Gil, *Violence Against Children* 118–119 (1973).

The proposed definition seeks to distinguish between cases of physical discipline which, even if they result in minor bruises, pose no threat of severe or permanent damage, and cases which do pose such a threat. This does not imply acceptance of corporal punishment as a means of discipline. Rather, it reflects the judgment that even in cases of physical injury, unless the actual or potential injury is serious, the detriment from coercive intervention is likely to be greater than the benefit. A family being investigated for physical abuse is subjected to substantial trauma. The child may be removed from the home and subjected to questioning and court appearances. Other children in the family may become frightened and upset.

These costs are clearly required if the parental conduct results in serious injury or threatens to do so. But they are not warranted solely to prevent physical punishment by the parent unless the manner in which the child was punished or injured is such that we need to be worried about the future safety of the child.

The critical part of the standard is the requirement that the child be injured in a way that causes or creates a substantial risk of causing disfigurement, impairment of bodily functioning, or other serious physical injury. The intent of the standard is to prevent injuries such as broken bones, burns, internal injuries, loss of hearing, sight, etc. It is not intended to cover cases of minor bruises or black and blue marks, unless the child was treated in a way that indicates that more serious injury is likely to occur in the future. In making this decision, a course of parental conduct and the psychological state of the parents may be considered, as well as the injury itself.

The standard allows intervention based on the "substantial risk" that parental action may cause or is "likely to imminently" cause such an injury, as well as on the basis of actual injuries. "Substantial risk" denotes real, genuine, and considerable chance or hazard, and "imminently" refers to that which is impending or is threatening to occur in the near future. The fact that in a given instance a child is not killed, disfigured, or substantially impaired should not preclude intervention if it can be shown that the parental actions in the given case create a substantial likelihood of more serious injury in the future. For example, if a parent throws an infant against a wall, but the infant sustains only minor injuries, we should not wait until the child is again injured more seriously before intervening. However, courts should exercise extra caution in intervening when a child has not actually suffered injury, since there is greater possibility of incorrectly predicting the need for intervention.

In this regard, intervention may be justified, in very limited circumstances, to protect children not actually physically abused if another child in the family has been abused. However, the fact that one child has been abused is not, in and of itself, a sufficient basis for declaring the other children endangered. There is still little data available on what percentage of abusing parents are abusive to more than one child. Therefore, a court should only find the other children endangered if there are facts other than the abuse of one child, such as parental mental illness or addiction related to the abuse, which indicate that the other children are endangered as well.

Finally, it should be noted that intervention does not have to be premised on a conclusive showing that an injury was actually inflicted by a parent. Under Standard 2.1 B., intervention is permissible if the parent fails to protect the child from serious physical injury. This section is intended to cover cases of unexplained injuries if the nature of the injury, or a history of past injuries, makes it likely either that the injuries were inflicted nonaccidentally or through inadequate care or supervision.

B. [Coercive intervention should be authorized when] a child has suffered, or where there is a substantial risk that the child will imminently suffer, physical harm causing disfigurement, impairment of bodily functioning, or other serious physical injury as a result of conditions created by his/her parents or by the failure of the parents to adequately supervise or protect him/her;

Commentary

This standard is an expansion of the grounds provided in Standard 2.1 A. *supra.* It is designed to cover situations where a child is physically endangered, to the same degree as in Standard 2.1 A. but the danger is created by parental failure to adequately protect or supervise the child, or by home conditions so dangerous that they pose an immediate threat to the child, rather than by intentional infliction of injury by the parent.

At present, "inadequate parental care" constitutes one of the most frequent bases for intervention. Under present statutes, however, there is no requirement that the parental inadequacy or poor home conditions be related to a specific harm to the child. Intervention is often premised on the possibility, not likelihood, of harm. This standard provides a considerably more limited basis for intervention. Intervention would not be justified solely because a home is dirty, because a parent leaves a child unattended for a brief period of time, or because a social agency believes that the parent is providing inadequate care or attention to the child. Instead there would have to be a showing that harm had actually occurred or a finding of specific factors that demonstrate that harm is imminently likely. Moreover, coercive intervention would not be appropriate if the parent is willing and able to correct the situation. In such cases state aid may be necessary to help the parents overcome the problem, but this should be provided without coercive intervention.

Several examples give some idea of the types of situations covered by this subsection:

Example No. 1: A five-year-old child is regularly left to wander streets late at night. The parent knows of the problem and takes no action. Intervention is permissible.

Example No. 2: The home of a three-year-old child contains a high voltage wire which is left exposed despite the fact that the parents have been made aware and given the resources to correct the problem if they are financially unable to do so. Intervention is permissible.

Example No. 3: A child is being physically abused, in a manner likely to cause serious injury, by a person other than the parent or guardian (such as a boyfriend or girlfriend of the parent), and the parent is unwilling or unable to protect the child from this third party. Intervention is permissible.

Example No. 4: A small child is severely beaten by a babysitter. The parent dismisses the sitter and takes steps to insure the adequacy of future caretakers. Intervention is not permissible.

Example No. 5: A child is living in a home that is poorly furnished, has some cracks in the plaster, and there is an irregular feeding schedule. The child has not been injured and does not suffer severe malnutrition. Intervention is not permissible.

In general, coercive intervention is not appropriate under this standard if the child is endangered due to "community neglect," where the parents are willing to correct the situation but lack the resources to do so. For example, if a family lives in a very dangerous tenement, but no other housing is available, or if a child is being regularly beaten up by neighborhood children and the parent is trying unsuccessfully to prevent such occurrences; services may be offered to help the family, but these should be on a voluntary basis.

The two examples above illustrate a basic value judgment underlying this standard, *i.e.*, that coercive intervention generally is not justified, even though a child is seriously endangered, if the danger arises from environmental conditions beyond the parents' control. Unfortunately, there are some children who are endangered because of the poverty of their parents and the consequent inability of their parents to provide them basic protection and necessities. It is wrong for society to take coercive action against these parents and children, especially if this means placing the children in foster care. Coercive intervention should not be a way of remedying societal neglect of the poor. We must face the issue of poverty and its associated negative impact on children directly, not by juvenile court actions.

It must be recognized, however, that at present the only way to provide needed services to the family may be by bringing the child under court jurisdiction. A number of statutes restrict financial help unless the child is under court supervision. Such statutes should be changed; but until they are, a court might still take jurisdiction under this standard in order to provide services. In such cases, removal would be barred. See Standard 6.4 C. 4.

This exception is only a limited one and should not be seen as generally incorporating "fault" notions into these standards. Except in this situation, intervention is permissible if a child is endangered regardless of parental fault. Thus, intervention would be appropriate if a very young child is repeatedly left unattended because of a parent's mental illness, alcoholism or drug addiction. Intervention might also be based on unexplained serious injuries, especially if there is a history of such injuries. The fact that these are conditions beyond the parents' control should not limit intervention.

This subsection may also be used to assume court jurisdiction in "failure to thrive" cases, *i.e.*, cases where a very young child is evidencing severe malnutrition, extremely low physical growth rate, delayed bone maturation, and significant retardation of motor development. See R. Patton and L. Gardner, *Growth Failure in Maternal Deprivation* xi, 15, 27–28, 32 (1963). If such a child shows improved growth and eating while under medical care, and the parent refuses continued treatment, intervention would be authorized.

Under this standard, if serious physical injury has actually occurred, intervention is authorized for the same reasons as in physical abuse cases—prediction of harm is not a problem. See commentary to Standard 2.1 A. However, cases where injury has not occurred pose greater difficulty. In such situations the hazards of prediction are substantial and the potential for abuse cannot be dismissed lightly. Standard 2.1 B. attempts to limit the possibility of overprediction by authorizing intervention in the absence of physical harm only in those cases where there is a "substantial risk" that the child will "imminently" suffer disfigurement, impairment of bodily functions, or other serious physical injury as a result of conditions created by the parents or their failure to adequately supervise the child. The explanation of the terms "substantial risk" and "imminently" found in the commentary to Standard 2.1 A. is applicable here.

Again, it must be emphasized that this standard is not intended as a general authorization to intervene to protect a child living in undesirable circumstances—no matter how undesirable—absent a showing of serious injury, actual or imminent. Efforts to improve the lives of children in "bad" environments should come through generally available social programs, not child neglect proceedings.

C. [Coercive intervention should be authorized when] a child is suffering serious emotional damage, evidenced by severe anxiety, depression, or withdrawal, or untoward aggressive behavior toward self or others, and the child's parents are not willing to provide treatment for him/her;

Commentary

Standard 2.1 C. authorizes intervention when a child *is suffering* certain types of serious emotional damage which his/her parents are unwilling to have treated. The standard does not require a showing that the parents' behavior is causally connected to the child's emotional problems.

Whether emotional damage should be a basis for intervention is one of the most controversial issues regarding the grounds for intervention. A number of commentators have criticized the failure of most present statutes to explicitly include emotional neglect among the harms justifying intervention. See, *e.g.*, S. Katz, *When Parents Fail* 62 (1971); Areen, "Intervention Between Parents and Child: A Reappraisal of the State's Role in Child Neglect and Abuse Cases," 63 *Geo. L. J.* 887, 933–34 (1975). It is contended that children can be at least as badly harmed emotionally as physically, and that the long-term consequences of emotional damage may be even greater than those from physical abuse. Therefore, proponents argue that it is unrealistic and extremely detrimental to children to fail to intervene on this basis.

On the other hand, there are substantial arguments against allowing any intervention for purely emotional harms. The major reasons are: A. because of the great difficulty in developing a workable definition of the term "emotional damage," this ground is subject to widely varied interpretation and opens the way to unwarranted intervention. "Emotional neglect" may be used to bring in cases which the standards attempt to exclude, such as "immoral" homes or "poor parenting" cases. B. Even if we could provide a reasonable definition, we lack the knowledge and resources to intervene successfully in a coercive manner. Treatment will generally require parental involvement or cooperation and this can only be obtained voluntarily.

The difficulty of definition is recognized by supporters of intervention. See Katz, *supra* at 68; Areen, *supra* at 933. (See also Idaho Code Ann. § 16-1626 Supp. 1973 for an example of the broad language adopted in those states which specifically permit intervention on this ground.) However, these commentators would rely on the judgment of the court to screen out inappropriate cases.

There is undoubtedly substantial merit to the claims of commentators on both sides of the issue. All commentators recognize the potential harm; they also recognize the substantial possibility of misuse of this ground for intervention. Standard 2.1 C. tries to resolve the problem by defining emotional damage for purposes of authorizing coercive intervention specifically and narrowly, *i.e.*, a child who evidences "severe anxiety, depression, or withdrawal, or untoward aggressive behavior toward self or others," and whose parents are unwilling to provide treatment for him/her, and by requiring that the child *actually* be suffering the harm.

The goal of the definition is to tie intervention to certain specific symptoms, symptoms which have a fairly well defined meaning to mental health professionals. The specific symptoms were selected after a review of the literature on child development and after extensive discussions with pediatricians, psychoanalysts, psychiatrists, psychologists, and social workers. Although other symptoms could undoubtedly be selected in lieu of or in addition to those specified, it is felt that these criteria afford a viable operational definition of emotional damage without providing an open-ended basis for intervention. The application of the standard will entail heavy reliance on mental health professionals. It is hoped that such testimony will take into account developmental and cultural differences in children, as well as the appropriateness of any behavior to the child's environment. For example, a child in an inadequate school or dangerous neighborhood might be quite appropriately anxious, depressed, or even hostile.

The definition should place sufficient constraints on expert testimony and judicial decisionmaking so that it will not be based solely on individual views regarding proper child development. It is possible that in practice this definition will prove either too broad or too narrow. These standards should not be considered frozen. Periodic review to see how they are working and to incorporate new knowledge is essential.

The standard limits intervention to situations where the child is actually evidencing the symptoms. Intervention may not be premised on the prediction of harm. Without actual damage it is extremely difficult both to predict the likely future development of the child and to assess the impact of intervention. See commentary to Standard 1.2. Moreover, given the limited resources available to help those children suffering emotional damage whose parents request help, it is extremely unwise to permit intervention where the damage is speculative and the services probably unavailable.

The standard does not require that emotional damage be caused by parental conduct. If a child evidences serious damage and the parent is unwilling to provide help, intervention is justified regardless of the cause of the harm. Intervention should occur only when the parents are unwilling to provide treatment necessary to help the child. In general, the parents should determine what treatment is appropriate. However, if a court finds that the treatment being provided by the parents is clearly inadequate, this would constitute failure to provide treatment. On the other hand, if the parents are not providing treatment because they are financially unable to do so, they should be provided with the necessary services without coercive intervention. Nevertheless, significant clinically demonstrable emotional harm could be grounds for intervention when caused by parents' acts or neglect.

D. [Coercive intervention should be authorized when] a child has been sexually abused by his/her parent, or a member of his/her household, or by another person where the parent knew or should have known and failed to take appropriate action (alternative: a child has been sexually abused by his/her parent or a member of his/her household, and is seriously harmed physically or emotionally thereby);

Commentary

Perhaps the most universally condemned behavior of a parent or other family or household member toward a child involves sexual conduct with the child. Thus it may seem apparent that "sexual abuse" clearly ought to be a basis for intervention.

Yet, the available studies come to diverse findings regarding the negative impact of sexual "abuse." See, *e.g.*, Y. Tormes, *Child Victims of Incest* 7–8 (1968); V. De Francis, *Protecting the Child Victim of Sex Crimes Committed by Adults* (1969). While some studies find significant harm, see J. Benward and J. Densen-Gerber, *Incest as a Causative Factor in Anti-Social Behavior: An Exploratory Study* (1975), other commentators concluded that the children studied suffered no significant short or long-term negative effects. See S. Weinberg, *Incest Behavior* 75, 147–153 (1955); Bender and Blau, "The Reaction of Children to Sexual Relations With Adults," 7 *Am. J. Orthopsych.* 500 (1937); Yorukoglu and Kemph, "Children Not Severely Damaged by Incest With a Parent," 5 *J. Am. Acad. Child Psych.* 3 (1966). Moreover, the process of intervention may be more disturbing to the child than the sexual activity. Even the limited public exposure may be traumatic for the child, especially if relatives, friends, or teachers are made aware of the situation. More importantly, the process of proof, requiring repeated interviews of, and possible court testimony by, the child can create great anxiety or other emotional harm. Finally, there is little evidence of the efficacy of treatment programs following intervention which might justify the added trauma. Neither is there evidence that the activity, once discovered, will be continued.

While these factors militate against including sexual abuse among the harms justifying intervention *unless* there is evidence of emotional damage (see alternative), there are several considerations unique to sexual abuse cases that support the broader basis for intervention adopted by these standards. First, according to several studies, sexual abuse is usually only one of several negative factors operative in families where this conduct occurs. The studies report that the father often has physically beaten the children or created an atmosphere of terror in the house. See Y. Tormes, *supra* at 27–31; S. Weinberg, *supra* at 55–171. Even though the home situation might not justify intervention if there were no sexual abuse, the added problems caused by the charges of sexual abuse might justify singling out these families for special attention.

Second, while the behavior may have been condoned by both parents and acquiesced in by the child prior to the time it became public knowledge, the fact that the sexual conduct has been reported undoubtedly drastically alters the family situation. The child is now likely to feel guilt or shame. Therefore, it may be essential to intervene in order to assess the impact of the discovery on the child and to insure that the conduct is discontinued.

Finally, sexual abuse cases involve a factor not generally prevalent in neglect situations: the likelihood of a criminal prosecution against the parent. While most criminal child neglect statutes cover conduct other than sexual abuse, the little available evidence indicates that criminal charges are most frequently brought in sexual abuse cases. Criminal proceedings can be extremely harmful to the child. The child must undergo the trauma of interviews and testifying. In many cases additional pressure is created by the parents who encourage the child not to cooperate with the prosecuting authorities.

Moreover, criminal prosecution often results in the father's imprisonment. Splitting up the family and imprisoning the father may add to the child's problems. Meaningful treatment for the child may require treatment of the entire family. In addition, the child may suffer guilt feelings over the parent's imprisonment.

While endangerment proceedings may necessitate questioning the child both in and out of court, the chances are greater that the negative effects can be avoided or minimized in a juvenile court hearing. Interviews can be conducted by social workers, accustomed to dealing with children, rather than by prosecutors. Without the threat of criminal sanctions, the parent may choose not to contest the charges. If a hearing is necessary, the lower standard of proof may make it unnecessary for the child to testify. In any case, the hearing is generally private rather than before a jury, and the testimony can be taken in chambers. Finally, the juvenile court is concerned solely with the wellbeing of the child and open to a greater range of dispositions than the criminal court. These proceedings will likely be less punitive and more treatment oriented than criminal proceedings.

Therefore, criminal proceedings should be utilized sparingly, if at all. See Part IX *infra*. But this requires having available endangerment proceedings through which the child can be protected. For this reason, as well as those previously noted, coercive intervention should be permissible when a parent or other family member or member of the household in which the child lives has "sexually abused" the child.

The standard does not define "sexual abuse." It is intended that intervention be authorized where the subject action would be a violation of the relevant state penal law (or would have been a violation if the laws are repealed). As a factual matter, it may be difficult to distinguish between appropriate displays of affection and fondling or other behavior possibly disturbing or damaging to the child. Although relying on penal laws may, in some cases, result in definitional vagueness, it should suffice since only the most severe types of behavior are ordinarily reported.

The commercial use of children also may be a basis for intervention under this standard. See Child Abuse Prevention and Treatment and Adoption Reform Act, 42 U.S.C. 5104, in which sexual abuse includes the obscene or pornographic photographing, filming, or depiction of children for commercial use or other forms of sexual exploitation.

E. [Coercive intervention should be authorized when] a child is in need of medical treatment to cure, alleviate, or prevent him/her from suffering serious physical harm which may result in death, disfigurement, or substantial impairment of bodily functions, and his/her parents are unwilling to provide or consent to the medical treatment;

Commentary

Standard 2.1 E. authorizes intervention to secure medical treatment when such care is required to cure, alleviate, or prevent the child's suffering serious physical harm, and his/her parents refuse to provide the needed treatment. The standard differs from previous grounds in that the harm is neither intentionally inflicted on the child, nor a result of parental failure to adequately protect or supervise the child. These cases involve medical problems related to disease, accidental injury, or physical defects. As in the case of emotional damage, the standard does not apply in cases when parental inaction is due to financial inability to provide the care. In such cases the services should be provided without coercive intervention.

The cases arising on this basis generally involve issues quite dissimilar from those involved in cases arising under 2.1 A. and B. Often the parents' refusal to provide treatment rests on constitutional claims or on the claim that the proposed medical treatment is too dangerous. Because of the unique nature of the issues to be decided, a separate statutory category is provided to alert the court to the special nature of the problem.

At present, many states authorize court intervention when a parent fails to provide a child with "adequate medical care." See, e.g., Ala. Stat. § 47.17070(5) (1969); Ga. Code tit. 26, § 7185-02(h) (1966); and "Guides to the Judge in Medical Orders Affecting Children," 14 Crime & Delinq. 107 (1968). Typically, these statutes provide little guidance as to when intervention is justified, usually referring only to the general obligation to provide necessary medical treatment.

Under such statutes courts virtually always intervene if there is a serious risk of death to the child absent treatment. See, e.g., State v. Perricone, 37 N.J. 463, 181 A.2d 751, cert. denied, 371 U.S. 890 (1962); but compare In re Hudson, 13 Wash. 2d 673, 126 P.2d 765 (1942). However, when the proposed treatment is necessary to alleviate some lesser impairment, such as a serious deformity or a disabling disease, courts have adopted divergent positions. Compare, e.g., In re Green, 448 Pa. 338, 292 A.2d 387 (1972), remanding to final court, 452 Pa. 373, 307 A.2d 279 (1973), aff'd final court decision on remand, with In re D., 70 Misc. 2d 953, 335 N.Y.S.2d 638 (Fam. Ct. 1972).

The proposed ground reflects the judgment that courts should abstain from intervention unless the possible harm is very serious. However, the standard does not require the court to abstain until the child is threatened with death. Any injury which may result in disfigurement or substantial impairment of bodily functioning would justify intervention.

Many cases arising under this standard will involve parents refusing medical treatment on religious grounds. In cases where the child is threatened with death, courts have overruled the constitutional objections. See Jehovah's Witness v. Kings County Hosp., 278 F. Supp. 488 (W.D. Wash. 1967); State v. Perricone, 37 N.J.463, 181 A.2d 751, cert. denied, 371 U.S. 890 (1967). Although the case law is not definitive, it is likely that the constitutional objections are also inapplicable in cases involving serious harm to the child. See Note, "State Intrusions Into Family Affairs: Justifications and Limitations," 26 *Stan. L. Rev.* 1383, 1394–1401 (1974).

Nonetheless, the basis of the parents' objection, whether religious or premised on a concern that the operation is too dangerous, should not be ignored by courts in deciding whether intervention is appropriate. In every case the court must weigh the risk involved to the child both by intervening and by not intervening. Moreover, the court should consider the fact that parents in such cases usually have a strong interest in the well-being of their children. Therefore, the parents' judgment, based on their knowledge of their child, should be accorded substantial deference. The court should be especially deferential when the proposed intervention involves a prolonged treatment process, since parental cooperation will often be essential to the success of any on-going treatment.

Finally, the court should consider the child's views in all cases except those involving children under age three. If, as may often be the case, the child shares the parents' views of medical treatment, this may lessen the chances of successful treatment and increase the child's emotional trauma.

The standard applies only in cases of physical harm. If the child is evidencing emotional damage, intervention is justified only under the conditions specified in 2.1 C.

F. [Coercive intervention should be authorized when] a child is committing delinquent acts as a result of parental encouragement, guidance, or approval.

Commentary

Standard 2.1 F. provides a very limited basis for intervention; it applies only in those cases where a child is committing delinquent acts as a direct result of parental encouragement, guidance, or approval. The subsection is not meant to cover situations where it is thought that the child's delinquent behavior is related to poor home conditions if there is no evidence that the parents either encouraged or approved of the child's actions. At present, neglect allegations are sometimes used as a "lesser charge" to delinquency allegations in order to minimize the harshness of a delinquency adjudication. This practice is ill-considered. Unless the parents directly encouraged or participated in the delinquent act, it is virtually impossible to show that a minor committed a given offense because the parents were "neglecting" him/her.

This standard does not preclude bringing a delinquency charge against the child. It only provides an alternative to such charges. It is also possible, in some cases, that the parent as well as the child will be charged with criminal conduct.

However, it is intended that endangerment proceedings should be the primary means of intervention in such situations. Endangerment proceedings are particularly appropriate in cases involving younger children (under age ten), or when it appears that the child's conduct was so directly the result of parental influence that it is unfair to stigmatize the child by labeling him/her delinquent. In addition, under some statutes the juvenile court has fewer dispositional alternatives after a finding of delinquency than after a neglect finding. See, *e.g.*, Cal. Welf. & Inst'ns Code § § 506, 725, 726, 727 (West 1972).

2.2 Need for intervention in specific case.

The fact that a child is endangered in a manner specified in Standard 2.1 A.-F. should be a necessary but not sufficient condition for a court to intervene. To justify intervention, a court should also have to find that intervention is necessary to protect the child from being endangered in the future. This decision should be made in accordance with the standards proposed in Part VI.

Commentary

The purpose of all coercive intervention should be to protect the child from future harm, not to punish parents or to provide ongoing supervision of families where the child is not endangered. A child who has been harmed, or is in imminent danger of being harmed in a manner specified in 2.1, usually will need some type of protection from a state agency in order to insure that the child will not be harmed in the future. However, intervention is not appropriate every time a court finds a child has been harmed in a manner specified by statute.

A court should not order coercive intervention unless such intervention is needed to protect the child from future harm. Moreover, as discussed in Standard 6.4 A. and B. *infra*, the court should not order intervention more extensive than is needed to protect the child from the specific harm justifying intervention.

There are at least three types of situations where intervention would not be appropriate although a finding has been made that the child comes within the provisions of Standard 2.1. First, there may be some cases where the child was injured by a parent, but the evidence indicates there is little danger of future harm. For example, a child may be physically injured by a parent in a moment of anger, but all evidence indicates that this was a one-time event and supervision is unnecessary to protect the child.

Second, coercive intervention may be inappropriate in cases where the parents' and child's situation has changed from the time the court petition was initially filed. For example, a very young child may not have been adequately protected because his/her parent worked and left the child without a caretaker. However, since the filing of the petition, the child has been placed in a day care center and now is adequately protected.

Third, there may be some cases where intervention will place the child in a more detrimental position. For example, in some medical care cases the court may find the proposed medical treatment too risky or the child unwilling to accept the treatment. In sexual abuse cases there may be no resources available for providing counseling to the family, and the child and parents may function best without any state supervision. If the family is dealing with the situation adequately, and there is no basis for concluding that future abuse is likely, intervention should not be ordered.

These categories are not meant to be inclusive. The basic purpose of this standard is to provide a test which requires each decisionmaker to carefully evaluate the need for intervention and to determine whether there are resources available to make intervention useful. All coercive intervention has detrimental, as well as beneficial, aspects. State supervision may be traumatic to the child as well as the parent. It may alter family relations in negative, as well as positive, ways. It is costly. Therefore, it is essential that the costs, as well as the benefits, be weighed on a case by case basis before intervention is ordered.

When intervention is needed, there are a range of intervention strategies. Standards for choosing among these strategies are presented in Part VI *infra*.

PART III: REPORTING OF ABUSED CHILDREN

3.1 Required reports.

A. Any physician, nurse, dentist, optometrist, medical examiner, or coroner, or any other medical or mental health professional, Christian Science practitioner, religious healer, schoolteacher and other pupil personnel, social or public assistance worker, child care worker in any day care center or child caring institution, police or law enforcement officer who has reasonable cause to suspect that a child, coming before him/her in his/her official or professional capacity, is an abused child as defined by Standard 3.1 B. should be required to make a report to any report recipient agency listed for that geographic locality pursuant to Standard 3.2.

Commentary

Since 1966, every state has enacted mandatory child abuse reporting laws requiring professionals to report to some state authority any child who appears to be intentionally physically abused by his/her parent. Physicians are the principle target group for current reporting legislation and are designated in all but six states as a class of professionals with reporting responsibility. Reporting is mandatory for members of each of the other professional groups mentioned in this subsection in at least one or more states. In five states, however, a legal obligation to report is imposed upon *any person* who has "knowledge" (Tennessee), "reason to believe" (Indiana), "cause to believe" (Texas and Utah), or "cause to suspect" (New Hampshire) that injury has been inflicted on a child, rather than upon any particular target group. Another seventeen states supplement requirements placed upon certain classes of professionals with a statutory duty to report placed on "any other person" who becomes aware of a child injured by nonaccidental means. See V. DeFrancis and C. Lucht, *Child Abuse Legislation in the 1970's* 10 (1974). The laws of six states further provide that reporting is permissible rather than mandatory with respect to persons other than the cited professionals. See Chart in DeFrancis and Lucht, *supra*, at 22-23. This latter approach is implicitly adopted here. This subsection is essentially the same as the comparable provision proposed in A. Sussman, *Reporting Child Abuse and Neglect: Guidelines for Legislation* 18-23 (1975).

B. An "abused child," for purposes of Standard 3.1 A., is a child who has suffered physical harm, inflicted nonaccidentally upon him/her by his/her parent(s) or person(s) exercising essentially equivalent custody and control over the child, which injury causes or creates a substantial risk of causing death, disfigurement, impairment of bodily functioning, or other serious physical injury.

Commentary

The definition of "abused child" in subsection B. is typical of current state laws. In recent years, a considerable number of state legislatures (some forty-three, according to recent research, see Katz et al., "Child Neglect Laws in America," 9 *Fam. L. Q.* 40-41, 1975) have expanded mandatory reporting laws to cover some form of child neglect as well as physical abuse. This standard rejects that expansion, and mandates reporting only of "abused" rather than all "endangered" children for the following reasons:

1. Experience under existing mandatory abuse reporting laws indicates that the great bulk of reports point to poor and poor/black families. See D. Gil, *Violence Against Children* (1973). It seems likely (though it cannot be conclusively demonstrated) that child abuse is not in fact limited to poor and poor/black families, but rather that the predominance of such reported cases is an artifact of the reporting system. The fact that the reporting system may be systematically biased is not necessarily a reason for abandoning abuse reports since seriously abused children need protection whatever their socioeconomic or racial status. But the likelihood of systematic bias in the reporting system is a strong argument against applying that system beyond physical injuries to matters such as "neglect," "emotional neglect" or even "sexual abuse" which are much more open-ended and subject to vast social and cultural biases in their definitions. (By middle class norms, for example, it would be "sexually abusive" for children regularly to witness sexual intercourse by their parents, but these norms are regularly disregarded in other groups in this society and there is no substantial reason to believe that these children are thereby harmed.) Laws prescribing mandatory reports beyond physical abuse have led to greatly increased reporting and, accordingly, to increased interventions into families. Though there is no systematic study yet available of the operation of these new reporting laws, it is likely that their impact is the same as the prior abuse reporting laws, and that an added wave of reports and interventions into poor and poor/black families has taken place. There is thus substantial reason to believe that these new interventions express only cultural bias and severely harm the children who purportedly are "rescued."

2. Current responses to child abuse and neglect reports give little confidence that the current trend toward expanding the numbers and kinds of cases brought to official attention beyond physical abuse will in fact assist the additionally identified children. It appears that substantial numbers of allegedly and actually abused or neglected children are removed from their parents and remain in foster or institutional placement for substantial periods of time. See Mnookin, "Foster Care—In Whose Best Interest?" 43 *Harv. Educ. Rev.* 599 (1973). Many children are ultimately returned to their parents without any adequate services having been provided to the parents to ensure against repetition of the previous abusive conduct. Other children remain for indefinite periods in "limbo statuses" of foster or institutional care without any assured lasting familial ties, since termination of parental rights is relatively infrequent even when children are not returned to their parents during long terms. Some few

centers in the country claim greater therapeutic finesse and success in pursuing the true psychological interests of abused children. Even if these claims can be substantially documented, it is clear that society has not yet been able to replicate the services provided in these few programs for the great bulk of children now reported as abused.

The haphazard interventions we now provide for physically abused children are probably justified on the ground that, though our intervention techniques cannot assure against grave psychological injury to the children separated from their parents, the risks to their physical wellbeing urgently require intervention. But to require reports, and likely interventions, beyond those for physical injuries—to harms whose injury is more rooted in adverse psychological consequences from parental practices—is absurd unless we can have some reasonable assurance that our intervention techniques in fact safeguard the child's psychological wellbeing.

3. Mandating reports even of child abuse can, in some cases, interfere with efforts to provide effective therapy to the abusing family. Particularly if criminal prosecution follows from such reports, effective therapy in the interests of child and parent both is typically stymied. Though criminal prosecution is relatively infrequent, it apparently occurs in haphazard fashion in response to the fortuities of newspaper coverage. See Part IX and commentary. But even if criminal prosecution does not result, psychotherapy with many families is compromised because the therapist is forced to divulge confidential communications. Forcing such breach of confidence can be justified when the child's physical life is at stake. But it is much harder to justify such interferences with the prospect of successful psychotherapy for suspected "neglecting" or "sexually abusing" families. For many such families, mandatory reporting will not only fail to bring benefits to the child; such reporting will actively hurt the child by interfering with the prospects of successful psychotherapy for the child and his/her family. Discretion to report, when the therapist has reason to believe the child cannot adequately be protected in the processes of therapy, provides a more helpful legal response to this problem.

4. Enactment of expanded mandatory reporting will encourage legislators who pass such a statute to believe that they are "doing something"—something that is truly constructive and helpful—for children mistreated by their parents, without spending any state funds. Child abuse reporting laws have enormous political seductiveness since they create the appearance of action without any extraordinary financial burden involved in legislative mandates for truly effective action. Existing child abuse reporting laws are essentially

fictitious because there is no state commitment for effective service response behind those laws. It would endorse that harmful fiction by now pressing for expansion of such laws, thus implicitly labelling them as successful enterprises in the interests of children.

C. Any person making a report or participating in any subsequent proceedings regarding such report pursuant to this Part should be immune from any civil or criminal liability as a result of such actions, provided that such person was acting in good faith in such actions. In any proceeding regarding such liability, good faith should be presumed.

Commentary

The purpose of this subsection is to protect child abuse reporters from inappropriate retaliation in response to their reports, particularly from angered parents who were the subject of reports. Absolute immunity is not, however, provided; the majority of current state statutes agree with this position, providing immunity only for good faith reports. See V. DeFrancis and C. Lucht, *Child Abuse Legislation in the 1970's* 12 (1974). In some states, good faith is statutorily presumed. See A. Sussman, *Reporting Child Abuse and Neglect: Guidelines for Legislation* 33 (1975). This presumption is explicitly provided here.

D. The privileged character of communication between husband and wife and between any professional person and his/her patient or client, except privilege between attorney and client, should be abrogated regarding matters subject to this Part, and should not justify failure to report or the exclusion of evidence in any proceeding resulting from a report pursuant to this Part.

Commentary

A clause waiving certain privileges is a standard part of current reporting legislation. The privileged nature of communications between doctor and patient is abrogated in thirty-nine states as well as in Washington, D.C., Guam, and the Virgin Islands. Waiver of the husband-wife privilege occurs in the laws of thirty-three jurisdictions, and is inferred in the statutory language of another ten (*i.e.*, with a waiver of doctor-patient and "similar" privileges). The attorney-client privilege is generally preserved, except in the reporting statutes of Alabama, Massachusetts, and Nevada. V. DeFrancis and C. Lucht, *Child Abuse Legislation in the 1970's* 12, chart at 21–22 (1974).

See commentary on a similar proposed provision in A. Sussman, *Reporting Child Abuse and Neglect: Guidelines for Legislation* 35–36 (1975).

E. Any person who knowingly fails to make a report required pursuant to this Part should be guilty of a misdemeanor (and/or should be liable, regarding any injuries proximately caused by such failure, for compensatory and/or punitive damages in civil litigation maintained on behalf of the child or his/her estate).

Commentary

The reporting statutes of twenty-nine states and the Virgin Islands provide misdemeanor penalties for failure to report. See also the proposed provision in A. Sussman, *Reporting Child Abuse and Neglect: Guidelines for Legislation* 33–34 (1975). This criminal penalty has, however, rarely been enforced in any state. It may be that the threat of civil liability, to reimburse the child or his/her estate, for harm coming from failure to report would be a more effective spur toward reporting. Initiative for such litigation would, however, rest with private parties and thus there is no great likelihood of its frequent or aggressive invocation. The question of choice between civil or criminal liability, or conjoining both, thus appears quite close, and the proposed standard reflects that conclusion.

3.2 Recipients and format of report.
  A. The state department of social services (or equivalent state agency) should be required to issue a list of qualified report recipient agencies (which may be public or private agencies), and to designate geographic localities within the state within which each such recipient agency would be authorized to receive reports made pursuant to Standard 3.1 A. The state department should ensure that there be at least one qualified report recipient agency for every designated geographic locality within the state.
  B. An agency should be eligible for listing as a qualified report recipient agency if it demonstrates, to the satisfaction of the state department, that it has adequate capacity to provide, or obtain provision of, protection to children who may be the subject of reports pursuant to this Part. The state department should be required to promulgate regulations indicating standards for such adequate capacity, which specify requisite staff personnel (which may include, without limitation, pediatric physicians and other medical care personnel, mental health professionals and paraprofessionals, and attor-

neys and legal paraprofessionals), requisite agency organizational structure, and any other matters relevant to adequate child-protective capacities.

C. The state department should review, at least every two years, whether an agency listed as a qualified report recipient agency continues to meet the requirements for listing pursuant to Standard 3.2 B. For purposes of such review, the state department should examine the agency's disposition of and efficacy in cases reported to it pursuant to this Part. Each agency should maintain records, in a format prescribed by regulations of the state department, to facilitate such review. Such regulations should provide safeguards against any use of such records that would disclose the identity, except where specifically authorized by this Part, or otherwise work to the detriment of persons who have been named in reports made pursuant to this Part.

D. The format of the reports to the report recipient agencies, in satisfaction of the requirements of Standard 3.1 A., should be specified by regulation of the state department. Such regulations should provide that initial reports pursuant to Standard 3.1 A. be made by telephone to a report recipient agency, and that telephonic and any written reports contain such information as the state department may specify.

Commentary

This standard is designed to serve two goals: first, to sponsor continuing investigation of the efficacy of interventions brought by reporting and, second, to permit some discretion in reporting where preserving confidential relations between the parent and professional person would aid a therapeutic relationship in the child's interests. Both of these goals are ignored under existing laws. Currently, the law's goal is the report itself; there is no mechanism structured into the reporting laws that provides some check on the efficacy of reporting. Further, under current laws only a narrow range of state agencies qualify as report recipients. At present, twenty-three jurisdictions designate a single agency to receive reports. In seventeen, the receiver agency is a state or county department of welfare. In only five states is a law enforcement agency designated as the sole recipient; and in one state the juvenile court receives all reports. In other states, reports must be made to one of two or more specified agencies or to two or more of the designated receivers. In forty-three states, a report to the department of social services at the state or local level is required—either exclusively or among other reports. See

V. DeFrancis and C. Lucht, *Child Abuse Legislation in the 1970's* 11, 177-178, chart at 24-25 (1974).

These two goals—testing efficacy and fostering discretion in reporting—can be better served without altering the first step in the basic format of existing abuse reporting laws. That is, the law can continue to mandate reports from a wide range of professional persons likely to have contact with young children—school personnel, physicians, and other medical personnel and the like. But, unlike the current law, this obligation should be satisfied by reports to a potentially extensive list of public and private community agencies that specialize in responding to the problems of abusing families. The professional would be required to report to *some* qualified agency, but would have discretion to choose *which* agency.

A statewide agency—the State Department of Social Services or its equivalent—should be charged with compiling a list of acceptable report recipients in each community. The standard provides that this list should be revised every two years. It is here, in the compilation and continued revision of this list, that "quality control" and "efficacy investigation" should take place. The statewide listing agency, that is, should permit a public or private community agency to remain listed as an acceptable abuse report recipient only if that agency can demonstrate from records of the cases it has handled that it has capacity to respond helpfully in the best interests of suspected abused children.

The process of statewide agency listing review would be the mechanism for intensive inquiry into the efficacy of the entire range of interventions into alleged and actual abusing families which, as discussed above, is critically lacking and essential for justification of any state sponsored external interventions into family life in the interests of children. The state listing agency would apply general criteria of competence to the various agencies, elaborated by specific staffing and programmatic standards. In some small or rural communities, it may be that the only authorized report recipient agency qualifying as competent for responding to abusing families would be the court-related county or state child protective services agency. In larger communities, it may be that both private and public agencies would qualify as report recipients thus giving an option to report originators to choose among various recipient agencies.

Many professionals now involved in operating special programs for abusing families are advocating a "multi-disciplinary team" for each community composed of psychiatrists, pediatric physicians, social workers, attorneys and others. The state listing agency could mandate such a team concept for all, or for selected, communities within the state. Similarly, the state listing agency could require that abuse reports be purposely diverted, in the first instance, away from court and court-related agencies. But in view of the many untested empirical propositions about efficacy of differing intervention techniques, it is inadvisable to provide for a single pattern of service program organization for every state. Rather, as noted earlier, the goal for nationally applicable model legislation should be to design institutional structures which are likely to work toward answering the critical open and untested questions in this field.

The constitutional doctrine, which still has vitality in state courts, regarding delegation of legislative authority to private parties is not in conflict with the recommendation here that private as well as public agencies should be licensed as report recipient agencies. Professor Davis, in his exhaustive treatise on administrative law, has stated that state courts have invalidated legislative delegations which fail to provide "either adequate standards or adequate safeguards" to guide the exercise of delegated powers. *Administrative Law Treatise*, § 2.17 at 77 (1970 Supp.). The extensive supervision by the state licensing agency over the actions of both private and public report recipient agencies envisioned by these standards would clearly obviate any constitutional doubts. Further, in matters of child welfare there is a strong state tradition of legislative reliance on private agencies. Particularly regarding adoptive placements, private agencies have traditionally exercised extensive roles both in placement itself and in investigating prospective adoptive families in connection with judicial adoption proceedings. See Clark, *The Law of Domestic Relations* 638-44 (1968). There is growing recognition that the authority exercised by such private agencies is "state action" and must be consistent with constitutional norms regarding, for example, religious or racial criteria for adoptive placement and adequately fair procedures. See *id.* at 644-51. But the legitimacy of such delegated authority as such in this critically important child welfare matter is widely accepted.

Although the recipient agency may itself be a foster agency, there have been many abuses in states by recipient agencies which improperly place children in foster care or keep them there for too long a period of time. The primary purpose of this standard, however, is to prescribe and standardize the duties of an agency in receipt of a report. The purpose is to *limit* investigative powers and to provide a process by which investigations may be carried out in cases in which an emergency removal seems necessary. See Commentary to Standard 3.3.

Subsection D. provides that the state agency should prescribe the formats for reports. Urgency in reporting is emphasized in most of the existing statutes and the requirement of an oral report by telephone or otherwise is fairly standard. The present trend in state laws seems to be in the direction of lessening demands upon report sources. Four states now require written reports only when specifically requested by the recipient agency. Another four states have dispensed entirely with the requirement of a written report. Thirty-one states as well as the District of Columbia, Guam, and the Virgin Islands require that oral reports be followed by written ones within a specified period of time. New Jersey demands a written report only from physicians. Requirements making reporting an onerous task, such as Michigan regulations which require that reports be filled out in quadruplicate and submitted to each of four different agencies, are rare. V. DeFrancis and C. Lucht, *supra*, at 11, 181.

3.3 Action by report recipient agency.

A. A report recipient agency receiving a report submitted pursuant to Standard 3.1 A. should be required to immediately undertake investigation of the report and to determine *inter alia* whether there is reason to believe the child subject of the report is an abused child, as defined in Standard 3.1 B., and whether protection of the child requires filing of a petition pursuant to Part V, and/or taking emergency temporary custody of the child pursuant to Part IV.

B. 1. If the agency determines, upon initial receipt of the report or at any subsequent time after its initial contact with the child that filing of a petition pursuant to Part V or emergency temporary custody pursuant to Part IV is necessary for the protection of the child, it should promptly take such action, except that the agency has no authority to examine or take custody of the child or to interview the parents or custodians or visit the child's home, against the wishes of the child's parents or custodians named in the report, except as specifically authorized by a court as provided in subsections 2.-5., or as specifically authorized by Part IV regarding emergency temporary custody of the child.

2. If the agency wishes to examine or take custody of the child, to interview the parents or custodians, or to visit the child's home against the wishes of the child's parents or custodians named in the report, it must obtain a warrant to search, duly ordered by the court authorizing the agency to make such investigation. Such an order may be obtained *ex parte*.

3. A warrant should not be granted except upon a finding by the court of probable cause to believe that the child comes within the jurisdiction of the court pursuant to the standards set out in Part II.

4. The warrant should set forth with particularity the places to be investigated, the persons to be interviewed, and the basis for the finding of probable cause. The warrant should state that refusal to allow an investigation may lead to the sanctions provided in subsection 5.

5. a. If the parents or custodians named in the report refuse to allow access to the child after being served with a copy of the warrant ordering such access, the investigating agency may take custody of the child for a time no longer than reasonably necessary for investigative purposes, but in no event should custody of the child be taken for a longer consecutive period than eight hours, nor should custody be maintained between 8:00 P.M. and 8:00 A.M.

   b. Where access to other information has been refused after a copy of the warrant ordering such access was served, the court may subject the person having custody of the information to civil contempt penalties until it is provided to the investigating agency.

C. Identifying characteristics in all unsubstantiated reports (including names, addresses, and any other such identifying characteristics of persons named in a report) should be expunged from the files of the report recipient agency immediately following completion of the agency's listing review pursuant to Standard 3.2 C., within two years of the report's receipt. In any event, identifying characteristics in all reports should be expunged from the files of the report recipient agency within seven years of the report's receipt.

Commentary

Under this standard, the authorized report recipient agency is required to investigate every abuse report. The agency is, however, given no authority to override parental wishes in conducting its investigation. Interviews with the child or parent or home visits contrary to parental wishes can only take place with explicit court approval, as indicated in Standard 3.3 B.

The purpose of this standard is to strike a proper balance between the need of the state to investigate allegations of endangerment of children and the privacy interests of the family. If the agency in its view cannot conduct an adequate investigation due to the objection of the parents, the only recourse available to the agency is to seek a search warrant in the court. Children who are in immediate need of removal pursuant to Standard 4.1 may be removed without prior approval. For children who are not endangered to the degree that there exists "probable cause to believe . . . custody is necessary to prevent the child's imminent death or serious bodily injury" (Standard 4.1 A.), however, a warrant is required to investigate the family over its objection.

It is clear that the Fourth Amendment protects more than the accused criminal. *Camara v. Municipal Court*, 387 U.S. 523 (1967); *Marshall v. Barlow's Inc.*, 436 U.S. 307 (1978). The Fourth Amendment, by its terms, guarantees "the right of the people to be secure in their persons, houses, papers, and effects." Although the Supreme Court has upheld visitation to homes of recipients of public assistance under penalty of loss of benefits, without the issuance of a search warrant, the court noted that such visitation "is not forced or compelled. . . . If consent to the visitation is withheld, no visitation takes place." *Wyman v. James*, 400 U.S. 309, 317–318 (1971). The purely investigative function contemplated in this standard justifies Fourth Amendment protection against unjustified intervention. For a complete discussion of the reasons for a warrant requirement, see Levine, "Caveat Parens: A Demystification of the Child Protection System," 35 *U. Pitt. L. Rev.* 1, 45–48 (1973); and Burt, "Forcing Protection on Children and Their Parents: The Impact of *Wyman v. James*," 69 *Mich. L. Rev.* 1259 (1971).

Once the warrant has been issued, the investigation may be carried forward over the objection of the parents. If it is necessary to take physical custody of the child for investigative purposes, this should be carried out in the least disruptive and potentially damaging way possible. Standard 3.3 B. 5. a. limits the agency's options.

The agency's investigation before any court recourse would be limited to such matters as contacting the person reporting the suspected abuse and the parents, and soliciting parental consent for interviews with them and the child, in order to verify the reported abuse. If, for example, the agency found, after these investigative contacts, that the report came from a physician who had directly observed serious bruises on the child and the parents refused to permit agency employees to see the child either at their home or on agency premises, then as provided in Standard 3.3 A. there would be clear "reason to believe [that] the child subject of the report is an abused child . . . [and that] protection of the child requires filing of a petition" in court, and perhaps even taking of temporary emergency custody. In many reported cases, however, invocation of the court or emergency custody would not be required to protect the child even if there was some evidence that the parents had been physically abusive toward the child. If, for example, the child's injuries were slight, the parents welcomed the agency contact with some obvious relief and the problems which had led to the child abuse were both readily apparent to the agency and easily correctable, then court referral would be both unnecessary and possibly counterproductive for the ultimate protection and welfare of the child.

The critical innovation of these standards is that, following its investigation, the report recipient agency would have discretion as to whether it would in turn report the child to a court for invocation of forced intervention into the family. Through existence of this discretion, the agency could make an individualized judgment about the family's need for and capacity to respond to an intervention without direct invocation of legal coercion. This therapeutic relationship would not, of course, fit precisely into the traditional mental health model in which the patient wholly controls what information the therapist is authorized to release to third parties. Here, instead, the therapist would control whether third parties would be involved— whether, that is, state power would be invoked in order to protect the child. This hybrid version of existing reporting laws and the traditional mental health relationship paradigm appears particularly suited to the special problems of abusing families as described in current professional literature: that while they need sympathetic assistance in resolving the underlying psychological dynamic conflicts that find expression in child abuse, they and their abused child also need firm and visible control to protect them and their child from their "worst selves." If an agency with demonstrated capacity to provide effective, sympathetic assistance is given discretion to invoke external controls, but not obliged to do so invariably and always at the abusing family's first appearance in the agency, greater therapeutic flexibility and finesse in the long-range best interest of abused children should result.

Not every agency has such capacity. Nor indeed does every agency that thinks it has such capacity in fact have the capacity. But one of the tasks of the statewide listing agency, in its periodic reviews of the quality and efficacy of agencies' work with abused families, would be to scrutinize the records of each agency to determine what kinds of cases were not reported for state intervention and the subsequent history of those cases. If it appeared that an agency was misusing this discretion, or failing to maintain adequate follow-up with the families who were not reported because of perceived therapeutic progress, this could be adequate ground for invocation of the basic sanction against the agency—that is, delisting. The sanction of removing a professional agency from the list of specialized abusing family service agencies is both more likely to be invoked, and has greater likely deterrent impact than criminal sanctions for nonreporting as under existing laws. Delisting of an agency is not only a highly visible, deeply felt slur on professional competence; it also removes an agency from important sources of funding, a sanction which will grow in significance as the current trend for federal funding support of services to abusing families gains greater momentum.

3.4 Central register of child abuse.

A. The state department of social services (or equivalent state agency) should be required to maintain a central register of child abuse. Upon receipt of a report made pursuant to Standard 3.1 A., the report recipient agency should immediately notify the central register by telephone and transmit a copy of any written report to the central register for recordation.

B. Within sixty days of its initial notification of a report for recordation, the report recipient agency should be required to indicate its action pursuant to Standard 3.3 and to indicate any subsequent action regarding such report at intervals no later than sixty days thereafter until the agency has terminated contact with the persons named in the report. If at any time the report recipient agency indicates that the report (including names, addresses, and any other such identifying characteristics of persons named in the report) should be expunged, the central register should immediately effect such expungement. In any event, all reports (including names, addresses, and any other such identifying characteristics of persons named in the report) should be expunged from the central register seven years from the date the report was initially received by the report recipient agency.

C. The central register, and any employee or agent thereof, should not make available recordation and any information regarding reports to any person or agency except to the following, upon their request:

1. a report recipient agency within this state, listed pursuant to Standard 3.2, or a child protective agency in another state deemed equivalent, under regulations promulgated by the state department of social services (or equivalent state agency), to such report recipient agency within this state;

2. any person (including both child and parent(s) and alleged abuser [if other than parent]) who is named in a report (or another, such as an attorney, acting in that person's behalf), except that such person should not be informed of the name, address, occupation, or other identifying characteristics of the person who submitted the report to the report recipient agency;

3. a court authorized to conduct proceedings pursuant to Part V;

4. a person engaged in bona fide research, with written permission of the director of the state department (except that no information regarding the names, addresses, or any other such identifying characteristics of persons named in the report should be made available to this person). Any person who violates the provisions of this standard by disseminating or knowingly permitting the dissemination of recordation and any information regarding reports in the central register to any other person or agency should be guilty of a misdemeanor (and/or should be liable for compensatory and/or punitive damages in civil litigation by or on behalf of person(s) named in a report).

3.5 Action by central register.

The central register should be required to notify by registered mail, immediately upon recordation of a report, any person (including child and parents and alleged abuser [if other than parent]) who is named in a report recorded in the central register, and to subsequently notify such person of any further recordation or information (including any expungement of the report) regarding such report submitted to the register pursuant to Standard 3.4, except as provided in Standard 3.4 C. 2. Any such person should have the right, and be so informed, to inspect the report and to challenge whether its entire contents, or any part thereof, should be altered or wholly expunged. Proceedings, including nonpublic hearings, except where an interested person can show they should be public, and other procedural matters regarding any such challenge should be governed by the administrative procedures act of this state.

Commentary

Central registries of some form are maintained in forty-seven jurisdictions. Thirty-three of these registries are mandated by law, while the remaining fourteen are maintained as a matter of administrative policy. The trend seems clearly to be in the direction of increasing recognition of the value of such registries. Between 1970 and 1974, fourteen states added provisions for central registries to their child abuse laws. At least in the majority of states, these central registries are maintained by the state department of social services. V. DeFrancis and C. Lucht, *Child Abuse Legislation in the 1970's* 13, 178 (1974).

Two main functions are intended to be served by the operations of the central registries: A. providing information facilitating the identification of repeated child abusers and the assessment of the probable seriousness of recurring cases; B. gathering data and statistics on the nature and incidence of child abuse. Although both purposes are of undoubted validity and use in dealing with the problem of child abuse in society, nevertheless certain dangers inherent in the central registry system must be considered.

More specifically, the principle dangers of prejudice and stigma must be guarded against to as great an extent as possible in the law. The recording of cases with a central registry must not be allowed to be a factor in jumping to a conclusion of guilt in a subsequent situation of suspected child abuse on the basis of an earlier recorded report. Neither should parents or children be unfairly or unduly stigmatized as a result of an incident of child abuse. It is to be noted that not only may an adult suffer from a continuing label as a child abuser, but, especially in the light of evidence that abused children are more likely to abuse their own children, the child may well be damaged by a continuing label as an "abused child." The provisions in Standards 3.4 and 3.5 controlling access to register reports and mandating expungement (*i.e.*, physical removal) of unsubstantiated and "stale" reports are directed to these purposes. See generally A. Sussman, *Reporting Child Abuse and Neglect: Guidelines for Legislation* 43–53 (1975).

The provision in Standard 3.4 C. 4., suggesting that access to identifying information in the reports be withheld from researchers, would not apply to research conducted by the state department or related governmental agencies. In order to monitor or assess the efficacy of interventions, follow-up studies of individual cases can be critically important and for this purpose access to identifying information would be needed. There is also reason for concern about unregulated handling of reports even by agency personnel. Control of such intra-agency recordkeeping practices, particularly when much information will be computerized, raises difficult regulatory problems. See generally *Records, Computers and the Rights of Citizens* (Report of DHEW Secretary's Advisory Committee on Automated Personal Data Systems, July 1973), and the *Juvenile Records and Information Systems* volume.

PART IV: EMERGENCY TEMPORARY CUSTODY
OF AN ENDANGERED CHILD

4.1 Authorized emergency custody of endangered child.

A. Any physician, police or law enforcement official, or agent or employee of an agency designated pursuant to Standard 4.1 C.

should be authorized to take physical custody of a child, notwithstanding the wishes of the child's parents or other such caretakers, if the physician, official, or agent or employee has probable cause to believe such custody is necessary to prevent the child's imminent death or serious bodily injury and that the child's parents or other such caretakers are unable or unwilling to protect the child from such imminent death or injury; provided that where risk to the child appears created solely because the child has been left unattended at home, such physician, official, or agent or employee should be authorized only to provide an emergency caretaker to attend the child at home until the child's parents return or sufficient time elapses to indicate that the parents do not intend to return home; and provided further that no such physician, official, or agent or employee is authorized to take physical custody of a child unless risk to the child is so imminent that there is no time to secure such court approval. Any physician or police or law enforcement official who takes custody of a child pursuant to this standard should immediately contact an agency designated pursuant to Standard 4.1 C., which should thereupon take custody of the child for such disposition as indicated in Standard 4.2.

Commentary

This provision, directed toward the protection of children whose lives or physical well-being are in serious and immediate danger is atypical of American child abuse and neglect statutes. In six states reporting laws include clauses permitting the emergency removal of children from their homes. See Ky. Rev. Stat. § 119.335(4), (Cum. Supp. 1972); Md. Ann. Code, art. 27 35A(f-1) (Cum. Supp. 1973); N.Y. Fam. Ct. Act § 1024–1025, and N.Y. Soc. Serv. Law § 414(2); S.C. Code Ann. § 20-310.2 (Supp. 1972); Tenn. Code Ann. § 37-1206 (Cum. Supp. 1973); Tex. Fam. Code, ch. 34, 34.05(d). In New York authority is granted to physicians, law enforcement officials, and social service workers to take immediate custody in cases of "imminent danger" to a child. When such action is taken, the Family Court must be notified forthwith, and child protective proceedings must be commenced by the appropriate social service agency at the next weekday session of the court. Authority of a similar nature is given to law enforcement officials in Maryland, Kentucky, and Tennessee. In Maryland, such removal is authorized subsequent to the law enforcement official being summoned by social agency personnel. In Kentucky, law enforcement officials may remove a child pursuant to a warrant, and must begin efforts to obtain a court order within twenty-four hours. Tennessee laws authorize "appropriate protective action" on the part of law enforcement officers. Both Texas and South Carolina require the filing of a petition with the court before emergency removal may be authorized. Statutes in eight states allow medical personnel to retain custody of an injured child against parental wishes for a specified period of time or until a court hearing can be held. See Conn. Gen. Stat. Rev. § 17-38a(d) (Supp. 1973); Ky. Rev. Stat. § 199.355(4) (Supp. 1973); Mass. Gen. Laws Ann., ch. 199-51c (Cum. Supp. 1974); Mich. Comp. Laws Ann. § 722.571(2) (Supp. 1973); N.J. Rev. Stat. § 9:6-8.16 (Supp. 1974); N.Y. Fam. Ct. Act § 1025(a); N.C. Gen. Stat. § 110-118(d) (Cum. Supp. 1974); Tenn. Code Ann. § 37-1204 (Cum. Supp. 1974). Two states require consultation with the welfare department before law enforcement officials may remove a child from his/her legal custodians. See Ohio Rev. Code Ann. § 2151.421C (Supp. 1972); Nev. Rev. Stat. § 200.502 (1971, as amended 1973). This consultation may be dispensed with in certain emergency situations.

All of these statutes are, we believe, inadequate to deal with the problem of crisis situations of abuse and neglect. Existing statutes are either too limited—restricting emergency action to only a segment of those most likely to come in contact with endangered children, or making procedural requirements precluding intervention that may be needed in an emergency—or too broad—incompletely defining authority and providing insufficient guidelines for implementation of emergency custody in the manner least detrimental to the child.

The reservations of commentators and legislators, as reflected in the literature and in the rarity of emergency custody provisions in the law, are not difficult to comprehend. DeFrancis and Lucht express the fear that such laws "substitute good motives for effective skilled services" and invite over-zealous officials and less skilled agency personnel to avoid difficult case by case decisions by summary and routine removal of children from their homes. V. DeFrancis and C. Lucht, *Child Abuse Legislation in the 1970's* 15, 185 (rev. ed. 1974); see McCoid, "The Battered Child and Other Assaults Upon the Family," 50 *Minn. Law Rev.* 1, 49-50 (1956); Paulsen, "Child Abuse Reporting Laws: The Shape of the Legislation," 67 *Colum. L. Rev.* 1, 46 (1967). Moreover, the costs and risks of emergency custody, in terms of the child's psychological trauma, disruption of the family, and possible violation of due process with regard to parental rights, are formidable.

These objections, however, are less arguments for the exclusion of emergency custody provisions from the law than they are factors that must be considered in drafting legislation. See, for example, the Model Child Abuse and Neglect Reporting Law, Section 6, and its accompanying commentary in A. Sussman, "Reporting Child Abuse and Neglect: Guidelines for Legislation," 4, 29–33 (1975). The child who is in true immediate danger needs protection. Yet misuse and overuse of emergency measures are dangers to be reckoned with. The provisions of this section are intended to facilitate intervention in cases where the child's situation is so hazardous that immediate protection is mandatory, while concurrently minimizing the dangers of overuse and unnecessary detrimental effects on the child and family.

Standard 4.1 A. sets four important limitations on the taking of emergency temporary custody of an endangered child:

1. Removal or retentive action is authorized only by specific types of personnel.

2. Emergency removal is limited to situations of imminent danger of death or serious injury where there is no time to take steps seeking a court order.

3. An individual taking emergency custody is required to immediately contact and turn custody over to an agency authorized to handle such cases.

4. Where a child's danger is the result solely of his/her being unattended, removal is not to be effected until the alternative course of sending an agency caretaker into the home has been tried, and the parent has not returned and the time lapse indicates that he/she does not intend to return.

This standard gives emergency custodial authority to physicians since they typically encounter severely endangered children in, for example, emergency clinics of hospitals. But the subsection further requires that physicians taking custody must immediately contact a specially designated agency which in turn would evaluate the imminent need for emergency custody and take custody itself where appropriate. Such agency personnel are also authorized to take direct emergency custody of children by this subsection. A specialized child protection agency is thus given a central role in initially evaluating the need for emergency custody and in providing that custody where necessary. The processes and standards by which such agency is designated are indicated in 4.1 C. Standard 4.1 A. envisions further that police or law enforcement officials would also be authorized to take emergency custody of endangered children. It might be preferable, because of the likelihood that police intervention might appear punitive (however unintended) and that police officers will lack requisite training and skills in protecting the emotional wellbeing of children and families, that the specialized agency personnel assume this exclusive role (beyond physicians likely first to identify endangered children).

When an agency takes physical custody of a child, it must act immediately to safeguard the child, as prescribed by Standard 4.2 A., and to report such action to the court, as provided in Standard 4.2 B.

This stipulation that an agency must send a caretaker into the home of a child endangered because of being unattended before that child may be actually removed reflects one of the basic premises of this statute. That is, removal of a child from the home is a drastic measure and should be avoided whenever there are any other available means for protecting the child.

B. Any physician, police or law enforcement official, or agent or employee of an agency who takes custody or care of a child pursuant to Standard 4.1 A. should be immune from any civil or criminal liability as a consequence of such action, provided that such person was acting in good faith in such action. In any proceeding regarding such liability, good faith should be presumed.

Commentary

The goal of protecting endangered children would be defeated if those contemplating protective measures in an emergency hesitated in fear of future legal sanctions. A requirement of good faith is an adequate restriction here on wrongful use of emergency custody. Only if there is probable cause to believe that a child's death or serious harm is so imminent that there is insufficient time to seek court intervention may an individual in good faith take such action. It is vital to the interests of the child, however, that legal standards are not so restrictive as to discourage emergency action where that action is appropriate. Compare the similar immunity provision in Standard 3.1 C. *supra.*

C. The state department of social services (or equivalent state agency) should be required to designate at least one agency within each geographic locality within the state, of those agencies listed as qualified report recipient agencies pursuant to Standard 3.2, whose agents or employees would be authorized to take custody of children pursuant to Standard 4.1. To qualify for such designation, an agency must demonstrate to the satisfaction of the state department that it has adequate capacity to safeguard the physical and emotional well-being of children requiring emergency temporary custody pursuant

to this Part. The state department should be required to promulgate regulations specifying standards for personnel qualification, custodial facilities, and other aspects of temporary custodial care which an agency must provide, or have access to, regarding children subject to this Part. Each agency designated should thereafter be required to demonstrate, in conjunction with review proceedings pursuant to Standard 3.2 C., that it continues to meet the requirements for designation pursuant to this standard, in view of its efficacy in safeguarding the well-being of children subject to this Part.

Commentary

Removal of a child from a dangerous home situation is obviously useful only where the child is removed to an environment less detrimental to his/her wellbeing. High standards of custodial care, strictly enforced and periodically reviewed, are necessary to insure that children temporarily removed from their homes are protected as much and damaged as little as possible. To this end, only specially qualified and carefully investigated agencies and facilities should be involved in the very delicate and difficult situation of temporary emergency custodial care. Under current child protective systems, one of the greatest problems is that the inadequacy of resources for caring for children removed from their families frequently renders removal essentially useless as a protective device. Wald, "State Intervention on Behalf of Neglected Children: A Search for Realistic Standards," 27 *Stan. L. Rev.* 985, 987 (1975). This subsection provides for designation of a specialized agency with demonstrated capacity to provide adequate emergency custody. We anticipate that such designated agency would also qualify as a report recipient agency pursuant to Standard 3.2, and—as envisioned in that standard—that some jurisdictions might have more than one such designated agency, thus enlisting a wider range of trained personnel and funding sources, both public and private, than now appears in current official child-protective practices.

4.2 Agency disposition of children in emergency temporary custody.

A. An agency taking custody of a child pursuant to Standard 4.1 should place the child in a nonsecure setting which will adequately safeguard his/her physical and emotional well-being. Such agency should be authorized to provide immediately, or secure the provision of, emergency medical care if necessary to prevent the child's imminent death or serious bodily injury, notwithstanding the wishes of the child's parents or other such persons. The agency should ensure that the child's parents or other such caretakers have opportunity to visit with the child, at least every day for the duration of custody pursuant to this Part (including without limitation the provision of transportation for the parents or other such persons) unless such visits, even if supervised, would be seriously harmful to the child (due account being given, among other considerations, to the child's wishes regarding visits).

Commentary

Authorization of the custodial agency to safeguard a child's well-being through appropriate temporary placement or the providing of medical care is a necessary corollary to the concept of emergency protective action. Assumption of custody by the agency would offer little benefit if the child's emotional and physical needs were not cared for. It is envisioned that these custodial facilities would not also primarily house children charged with or found guilty of delinquent acts and that these facilities would be open, nonsecure buildings.

Interference with parental or similar emotional ties is extremely painful for a child, irrespective of how well or poorly the custodial function has been served. J. Goldstein, A. Freud, and A. Solnit, *Beyond the Best Interests of the Child*, 20, 31-34 (1973). A major danger in any case of a child's removal from home and particularly in instances of independent emergency removal by a stranger, is that the psychological difficulties of separation and removal may be as damaging to the child as the harm removal was intended to prevent. J. Bowlby, *Child Care and the Growth of Love*, 13-20 (2nd ed. 1965); Goldstein, Freud and Solnit, *supra*, note 9 at 19-20; N. Littner, *Some Traumatic Effects of Separation and Placement* (1956). That such psychological harm should be risked without the careful consideration afforded by court review is a major source of reservations on the desirability of emergency custody provisions. By providing the opportunity and means of parental visitation, however, the dangers of interrupting the continuity of relationships may be minimized.

Often a parent will lack means of transportation to visit his/her child. Because the child's need to maintain contact with that parent is typically so critical, no matter how apparently harmful the parent's past conduct, this subsection further envisions provision of state resources for transportation as preferable policy notwithstanding its expense.

In some cases, parental visits, even if directly supervised, might be seriously harmful to the child. The child's wishes regarding parental visits might be one important consideration in determining whether such visits would be harmful. In any event, if parental visits are denied, this action should be taken only after a person trained in child psychiatry or psychology (a psychiatrist, psychologist, or psychiatric social worker) has clearly found that the child would be harmed by such visits. If visits were curtailed, the agency should be required to justify its view regarding the inadvisability of parental visits in its submission to the court pursuant to Standard 4.2 B.

Some might support, on the other hand, parental visits in all cases, arguing as follows: 1. that the abrupt severance of contact between parent and child—even if the parent had been seriously abusive toward the child—would only add psychological injury to the child; 2. that the child could be protected both from this added injury and from possible additional abusive conduct by the parent if these visits were supervised; 3. that the agency that is willing to take the extraordinary step of emergency removal of a child is unlikely to view any parental claims for visits with adequately unbiased judgment and will therefore inappropriately discount the child's psychological needs for continued contact with his/her parents notwithstanding their possible abusive conduct; and 4. that the child's explicit wishes regarding visits in the traumatic setting necessarily accompanying any sudden removal from parental custody is likely to be an unreliable indication of the child's underlying feelings and, at least for the short time that emergency custody will continue before court disposition of a petition, it is better in general to shield the child from being forced to choose between loyalty to his/her parents, however abusive they might appear to an outside observer, and need for protection from his/her temporary emergency custodians.

B. No later than the first business day after taking custody of a child pursuant to Standard 4.1, the agency should be required to report such action to the court authorized to conduct proceedings by Part V and to explain the specific circumstances justifying the taking of custody and the specific measures implemented to safeguard the physical and emotional well-being of the child. The agency should, at the same time, submit a petition without prior screening by the intake processing agency, under Standard 5.1 B., except that if the agency decides against such submission, it should immediately return the child to the custody of his/her parents or other such caretakers.

Commentary

This provision for speedy reporting of emergency action to the court and commencement of regular legal proceedings reflects at least three different intentions of the standard. First, custody assumed pursuant to this Part is intended to be strictly temporary. The by-passing of normal court review channels is justifiable only insofar as the shortness of time and the immediacy of the child's peril prohibit such review. Such custody should not be allowed to continue beyond the time when court review is obtainable. Second, the inherent danger of careless or erroneous use of emergency custody demands that such action be examined by a court as quickly as possible. The requirement of an immediate report, within the bounds of the business week, creates an additional safeguard against misuse of the statute by insuring that unwarranted assumption of emergency custody will be noticed and terminated with all possible speed. Third, the child's needs mandate strict agency accountability and quick judicial attention. In the interests of minimizing harm to the child—both physical harm and psychological damage risked by disruption of family and emotional ties—it is vital that the adequacy of measures implemented for protection and care of the child be insured. Hence, judicial scrutiny of the specific action taken should commence as soon as circumstances permit. Moreover, this standard is intended to encourage more careful and timely agency scrutiny of the handling of cases in anticipation of imminent court proceedings. Pre-court screening of the petition by an intake processing agency provided by Standard 5.1 B. would only delay court review and is not necessary because of the intensive agency screening that should precede the agency's continuing emergency custody of the child. If pursuit of court jurisdiction pursuant to Part V is not appropriate, the presumption of parental autonomy in childrearing mandates that the child be immediately returned home.

4.3 Court review regarding children in emergency temporary custody.

A. Immediately upon receipt of a petition submitted pursuant to Standard 4.2, the court should direct notification pursuant to Standard 5.1 C., appointment of counsel for the child pursuant to Standard 5.1 D., and referral of the petition for prosecution pursuant to Standard 5.1 B. On the same business day if at all practicable, and no later than the next business day, the court should convene a hearing to determine whether emergency temporary custody of the child should be continued.

Commentary

This section mandates specific court action under Part V of these standards. The guiding principle here is the recognition of the importance of certainty and permanence to the child's psychological well-being. If there is no compelling reason to displace the presumption of parental autonomy, return to the custody of parents or other such caretakers should take place immediately. If custody is to be denied to the child's parents or caretakers, it is in the child's best interests to make a judicial determination swiftly in order to speed and facilitate permanent placement of the child. The child's capacity to cope with loss and uncertainty is limited by what, in adult terms, seems a distorted sense of time. Delay in achieving a permanent status and resultant uncertainty and distress, therefore, may be of a longer duration in the child's world than in adult perception. See J. Goldstein, A. Freud, and A. Solnit, *Beyond the Best Interests of the Child*, 40–45 (1973). The prolonging of temporary custody performs a disservice to the child in that it disrupts and precludes the formation of meaningful, permanent, and stable emotional bonds.

B. The court should be authorized to continue emergency temporary custody of the child, pursuant to Standard 4.1, if it determines:

1. custody of the child with his/her parents or other such caretakers named in the petition would create an imminent substantial risk of death or serious bodily injury to the child, and no provision of services or other arrangement is available which would adequately safeguard the child in such custody against such risk;

2. the conditions of custody away from the child's parents or other such caretakers are adequate to safeguard his/her physical and emotional well-being (including without limitation direction by the court to provide emergency medical care to the child if necessary to prevent the risk found pursuant to subsection 1.); and

3. the child's parents or other such persons named in the petition would be provided opportunity to visit with the child at least every day for the duration of custody pursuant to this Part (including without limitation the provision of transportation for the parents or other such caretakers unless such visits, even if supervised, would be seriously harmful to the child (due account

being given, among other considerations, to the child's wishes regarding visits).

Commentary

Efforts to proceed with all due speed notwithstanding, emergency temporary custody will, under certain circumstances, have to be continued while legal proceedings commence and judicial determinations are made. Such continuation, however, is only justified provided that certain guidelines, already reflected in these standards, continue to apply (see generally the commentary to Standard 4.2 A.):

1. appropriate steps toward final resolution of the child's status are being taken with all possible speed;

2. the necessity for emergency custody, because of the immediacy and seriousness of threatened harm to the child and the impossibility of other protective measures or procedures, is sufficient to outweigh strong presumptions of parental autonomy and the integrity of the family unit, and to outweigh as well risks to the psychological well-being of the child;

3. emergency custodial care and facilities are such that physical and emotional harms to the child are minimized by presence in such custody;

4. the child's need for continuity and the dangers of disrupted emotional ties are recognized and appropriately cared for with measures encouraging and fostering continued contact between the child and parent.

4.4 Custody during pendency of proceeding.

Upon motion of any party to a proceeding pursuant to Part V, at any time during the pendency of the proceeding, the court may, following a hearing, authorize emergency temporary custody of a child with an agency designated pursuant to Standard 4.1 C., if the court determines such custody is justified pursuant to the criteria specified in Standard 4.3 B.

Commentary

Court-authorized emergency temporary custody is perhaps a less problematic measure than independent action by a physician or agency worker. At least theoretically, the dangers of irresponsible and unnecessary use of emergency custody are lessened by judicial consideration given to the matter in a hearing. Nevertheless, most of the difficulties and dangers discussed in the foregoing commentary are still present and the standards and guidelines as noted in Standard 4.3 above must continue to be applied.

PART V: COURT PROCEEDINGS*

5.1 Complaint and petition.
   A. Submission of complaint.
      1. Any person may submit a complaint to the juvenile court alleging and specifying reasons why the juvenile court should find a child within the jurisdiction of the court, pursuant to the standards set out in Part II. Any complaint that serves as the basis for a filed petition of endangerment should be sworn to and signed by a person who has personal knowledge of the facts or is informed of them and believes that they are true.

Commentary

State statutes typically place no restriction on the persons authorized to submit wardship petitions. In practice, however, greater credence is undoubtedly given to petitions submitted by child protective agencies familiar to the courts. It is anticipated that the demonstrated expertise of the abuse report recipient agencies, listed by the State Department of Social Services pursuant to Standard 3.2, will lead the intake processing agency and court to give special credence to petitions submitted by these agencies. Nonetheless, it is considered unwise to restrict access only through these agencies. It is likely that most complaints and petitions will be filed by the agencies, but these standards preserve access to the intake processing agency and courts for any person who believes a child is endangered.

Under existing state laws, certain persons who see children in professional capacities—physicians, including psychiatrists, and in some jurisdictions psychologists and social workers—are (or appear to be) barred from communicating information about the child to any third party without express permission from the child's parents. This result appears to follow from the general rule that patients control access to their personal medical information and that parents exercise this control as proxies for their children. Some courts might construe an exception to this rule when it appears that parents are acting against their children's best interest, and thus authorize professionals to

---

*Robert Burt and Michael Wald were not the reporters for this revised edition. Martin Guggenheim was the special editor.

divulge information notwithstanding parental objections. Uncertainty on this score was, however, one important element which led states in the mid-1960s to adopt mandatory child abuse reporting laws. See Daley, "Willful Child Abuse and State Reporting Statutes," 23 *U. of Miami L. Rev.* 283, 330 (1969). States which have extensively broadened the scope of these mandatory reporting laws have, of course, eliminated the legal issue discussed here. But for the reasons set out in Part III, these standards restrict mandatory reporting to physical abuse. Thus certain professionals would be uncertain about their authority to report parental conduct which is seriously harmful to children but does not constitute abuse (that is, intentional infliction of physical injury).

It might be argued that any professional who believes that parental conduct warrants reporting should have absolute discretion for such action. We believe, however, that the general principle that all persons must give basic respect to parents' control over their children is most consistent with our social traditions and with the psychological tenet that an intense bonding between parent and child should be fostered in all ways possible. This principle does not warrant absolute respect, no matter what circumstances occur. But the principle should be strongly favored in the practical operations of state child protective legislation. A legal rule which authorized—and, in effect, invited—any professional to disregard the traditional norms of confidentiality in dealing with children would unduly denigrate the principle of parental control. A contrary principle, however, which forbade professionals in all circumstances from reporting their concerns about children would unduly derogate from the needs of some children to be protected from their parents.

A middle ground, which would encourage professionals to think twice before breaching confidentiality but which would permit that breach for "good cause shown," is struck by this standard. The professional person who is bound by general norms of confidentiality under state law could be freed from those norms upon application to the intake processing agency, see Standard 5.1 B. *infra*, indicating in anonymous format the information he/she possesses about a child and the harmfulness of the child's custodial environment. The agency would authorize reporting of the identity of this child if it determined that the professional's allegations, if proven, would justify court jurisdiction—if, that is, the child's condition and parental conduct described allegedly violated the society's minimum norms for childrearing conduct.

2. Any person submitting a complaint or any person providing information upon which a complaint or petition might be based should be immune from any civil or criminal liability as a result of such action, or as a result of participating in any subsequent proceedings regarding such action, provided that such person was acting in good faith in such action. In any proceeding regarding such liability good faith should be presumed.

Commentary

This provision bestowing civil and criminal immunity for persons who in good faith submit complaints or petitions or generally provide information to court or noncourt agencies (such as police or school authorities), is typical of the majority of existing state laws. Some eight states provide absolute immunity for such action, but we are persuaded that a "good faith" requirement is not onerous and provides needed protection against malicious or vexatious petitions, a problem which has particular relevance to bitter and prolonged divorce custody disputes. See Katz et al., "Child Neglect Laws in America," 9 *Fam. L. Q.* 1, 43–45 (Table IX) (1975).

B. Intake review of complaints.
    1. Upon receipt of a complaint, an intake officer of the juvenile probation agency should promptly determine whether the allegations, on their face, are sufficiently specific and, if proven, would constitute grounds for court jurisdiction pursuant to the standards set out in Part II. If the intake officer determines that the allegations, on their face, are not sufficiently specific, or, if proven, would not constitute grounds for court intervention, the intake officer should dismiss the complaint. If the legal sufficiency of the complaint is unclear, the intake officer should ask the appropriate prosecuting official for a determination of its sufficiency. If the intake officer determines that the complaint is sufficient, the officer should determine a disposition of the complaint. The following are permissible dispositions at intake:
    a. Unconditional dismissal of a complaint.
    Unconditional dismissal of a complaint is the termination of all proceedings arising out of the complaint.
    b. Judicial disposition of a complaint.
    Judicial disposition of a complaint is the initiation of formal judicial proceedings through the filing of a petition.
    c. Referral to a community agency.
    Referral to a community agency is the referral of the child and his/her parents to an agency, including a child protective services agency, for further consideration.

2. In determining a disposition of a complaint at intake, the intake officer should:

    a. determine whether coercive intervention appears authorized as provided in Standard 2.1 A.-F.;

    b. determine whether judicial intervention appears necessary to protect the child from being endangered in the future, as provided in Standard 2.2; and

    c. consider the resources available both within and without the juvenile justice system.

3. The standards for intake procedures set out in Section IV of *The Juvenile Probation Function: Intake and Predisposition Investigative Services* should apply to intake review of complaints of endangerment, except that the privilege against self-incrimination at intake should apply to the parent or other custodian who is the subject of the complaint pursuant to the standards in Part II of this volume, and a right to assistance of counsel should be available to that parent or other adult custodian as a waivable right. The standards incorporated by reference are *Juvenile Probation Function* Standards 2.9 Necessity for and desirability of written guidelines and rules; 2.10 Initiation of intake proceedings and receipt of complaint by intake officer; 2.11 Intake investigation; 2.12 Juvenile's privilege against self-incrimination at intake; 2.13 Juvenile's right to assistance of counsel at intake; 2.14 Intake interviews and dispositional conferences; and 2.15 Length of intake process. In addition, *Juvenile Probation Function* Standard 2.16, Role of intake officer and prosecutor in filing of petition: right of complainant to file a petition, also should apply to the intake review of complaints of endangerment, except that the references to a petition in those cases in which the conduct charged "would constitute a crime if committed by an adult" should be deemed to refer to a petition of endangerment in this volume.

Commentary

This provision follows the model of the intake processing agency provided in *The Juvenile Probation Function: Intake and Predisposition Investigative Services* volume for the juvenile court. It provides for an initial screening, on an *ex parte* basis without hearing, of all complaints submitted except those filed under Standard 4.2 B. The essential function of this screening is promptly to dispose of clearly meritless complaints, to ensure that all petitions accepted for filing contain sufficient specificity, to ensure that parents are clearly apprised of the charges against them, and to divert complaints to noncourt disposition where appropriate. The agency's disposition is appealable in court. Courts have ultimate responsibility under these standards for the application and elucidation of the basic norms of state child-protective activities. Delegating this role exclusively to a subordinate bureaucracy would limit the public visibility and articulation of those norms.

C. Parties.

The following should be parties to all proceedings regarding a child alleged to be or adjudicated endangered:

1. the child;

2. the child's parents, guardians, and, if relevant, any other adults having substantial ties to the child who have been performing the caretaking role; and

3. the petitioner.

Commentary

This standard specifies the necessary parties in all endangered child proceedings, from initial hearings on emergency temporary removal to proceedings regarding termination of parental rights. Party status is conferred not only on parents who have current custody of the child, but also on noncustodial parents, such as divorced spouses. Although the noncustodial parents' conduct toward the child will not necessarily be at issue in the proceedings, their interests in the child are strong enough to warrant their participation.

In addition, party status is provided for guardians and, where relevant, any other adults having substantial ties to the child who have been performing the caretaking role. This would include foster parents or members of the "extended family" who have actually been caring for the child. It is important to involve these persons in the proceedings in order to avoid discontinuities in the child's relationships to parental figures and to properly examine the child's needs in light of his/her cultural background and values. Finally, the standard makes clear that the child is an independent party, entitled to all the rights of other parties.

5.2 Preadjudication proceedings.

A. Written petition.

Each jurisdiction should provide by law that the filing of a written petition, sworn to and signed by a person who has personal knowledge of the facts or is informed of them and believes they are true, giving the parents adequate notice of the charges is a requisite for endangerment proceedings to begin. If appropriate challenge is made to the legal sufficiency of the petition, the judge of the juvenile court should rule on that challenge before calling upon the parents to plead.

B. Filing and signing of the petition.

Petitions alleging endangerment should be prepared, filed, and signed by the juvenile prosecutor to certify that he or she has read the petition and that to the best of his or her knowledge, information, and belief there is good ground to support it.

Commentary

The standards for preadjudication proceedings derive directly from the *Pretrial Court Procedures* and *Adjudication* volumes, prescribing the requirements for initiating formal judicial proceedings after a delinquency complaint has been screened by the juvenile probation intake agency and the juvenile prosecutor, with modifications necessitated by the fact that the parent, and not the juvenile, is the respondent in endangerment proceedings. See *Adjudication* Standard 1.1 and *Pretrial Court Proceedings* Standards 1.1 to 1.4.

C. Notification of filing, service, and initial appearance.

Upon filing of the petition, the court should issue a summons directing the parties to appear at a specified time and place and serve the summons, with a copy of the petition attached, at least twenty-four hours in advance of the first appearance, upon the parents of the child alleged to be endangered. If, after reasonable effort, personal service is not made, the court should order substituted service. The initial appearance before the court should occur within [one] week of the filing of the petition, except if a child is in emergency temporary custody pursuant to the standards in Part IV, the first appearance should occur on the same business day, if possible, and no later than the next business day. At the first appearance, the court should:

1. notify the parents that such petition has been filed;

2. provide the parents with a copy of such petition, including identification by name of the person submitting such petition;

3. inform the parents of the nature and possible consequences of the proceedings and that they have a right to representation by counsel at all stages of the proceedings regarding such petition;

4. inform the parents that if they are unable to afford counsel, the court will appoint counsel at public expense, provided that, if a conflict of interest appears likely between parents named in the petition, the court may in its discretion appoint separate counsel for each parent; and

5. inform the parents of their right to confront and cross-examine witnesses and to request a probable cause hearing.

Commentary

This subsection, and the immediately succeeding subsections D. and E., provide the initial procedural steps following the filing of the petition. In this subsection, the parental right to counsel is guaranteed, and appointment of counsel for indigent parents is provided. The court should directly inform the parents of their rights to impress on them the seriousness of the proceedings and to guard against casual or ill-considered waiver of their rights.

Legal support is strong for the proposition that notice must be given to all interested parties in proceedings involving custody or termination of parental rights. Case law in general has upheld the right of parents to notification in child protective proceedings. See A. Sussman, *Reporting Child Abuse and Neglect: Guidelines for Legislation* 107 and citations (1975). Parental right to counsel, however, is far less clear in current law. Recent decisions in some jurisdictions have held that parents are entitled to representation by counsel, see *State v. Jamison*, 444 P.2d 15 (Ore. 1968), or appointed counsel, *Shapp v. Knight*, 475 S.W.2d 704 (Ark. 1972); *In re B.*, 30 N.Y.2d 352, 285 N.E.2d 288 (1972). Nevertheless, parents' rights to counsel in such proceedings is still very much a subject of controversy, see Sussman, *supra* 108–110. At present thirty-six jurisdictions give both parents and children a right to counsel in neglect hearings, and twenty-five jurisdictions provide a similarly broad right to appointed counsel. Parents are only granted a right to counsel in four jurisdictions, and to appointed counsel in six. Katz et al., "Child Neglect Laws in America," 9 *Fam. L. Q.* 1, 32–33 (1975).

We believe, both as a matter of policy and as a matter of constitutional law, that parents should be guaranteed the assistance of counsel in these proceedings. The potential deprivation and stigmatization imposed on parents in these proceedings, which may result from the loss of custody of their child, mirror the kinds of impositions which have led the Supreme Court in other apparently noncriminal proceedings to require constitutionally-derived criminal law guarantees such as the right to counsel. See *Kennedy v. Mendoza-Martinez*, 372 U.S. 144 (1963). Further, numerous decisions of the Supreme Court indicate that parental authority to rear children without state intervention while not an absolute right, nonetheless ranks among the fundamental values of our society. See, *e.g.*, *Meyer v. Nebraska* 262 U.S. 390 (1923); *Stanley v. Illinois*, 405 U.S. 645 (1972). From these two propositions—the "closeness of the criminal analogue to the operations of [neglect and abuse] laws and the hallowed status of the parent-child relation in our society"—the parental right to counsel in these proceedings follows as a matter of constitutional law. See Burt, "Forcing Protection on Children and their Parents: The Impact of *Wyman v. James*," 69 *Mich. L. Rev.* 1259, 1277-78, 1281-82 (1971). See also Burt, "Developing Constitutional Rights in, of and for Children," 39 *Law & Contemp. Probs.* (1976).

Subsection C. 2. of this standard provides that the parent named in the petition must be notified of the name of the person submitting the petition. This provision is consistent with the general posture of extensive discovery rights to parents and child mandated by Standard 5.2 I. This requirement would not, however, eliminate the possibility that petitions might be submitted with sources of information kept confidential from parents and child at this initial portion of the proceeding, since child protective agencies in many cases will themselves submit petitions. Accordingly, persons who wish to keep their identities secret from those named in the petition can contact child protective agencies with their information. These agencies may be expected, however, to screen out inappropriate petitions before submitting them. At later stages of the proceedings, in the agency investigation report under Standard 6.1 B. and in the court proceedings on contested petitions under Standard 5.3, the possibility of secrecy is sharply and necessarily curtailed for informants who provide critical data allegedly to substantiate a petition.

In some circumstances a conflict of interests may appear between the child's parents—if, for example, the parents have been divorced, the custodial parent's conduct toward the child is the subject of the petition and the noncustodial parent wishes to establish the other's unfitness for continued custody. Subsection 4. gives discretion to the court, where a conflict appears likely, to appoint separate counsel for each parent.

D. Appointment of counsel for child.

Upon filing, the court should be required to appoint counsel at public expense to represent the child identified in the petition, as a party to the proceedings. No reimbursement should be sought from the parents or the child for the cost of such counsel, regardless of the parents' or child's financial resources.

Commentary

This subsection mandates the appointment of counsel for the child named in the petition. There are good reasons to believe this guarantee is constitutionally mandated in light of the significant consequences to the child if court wardship were ultimately imposed. Though the court would obviously consider such imposition necessary to protect the child, nonetheless wardship might involve state-imposed custodial arrangements for the child and might even carry some stigma invoked in the "abused" or "neglected" label. The reasoning underlying the Supreme Court's mandate of counsel for minors in *In re Gault*, 387 U.S. 1 (1967) thus applies readily to minors involved in wardship proceedings (though *Gault* itself applied only to proceedings in which the child was charged with conduct that would be criminal if performed by an adult). At present, the statutes of thirty-five states guarantee appointed counsel to children in neglect proceedings. See Katz et al., "Child Neglect Laws in America," 9 *Fam. L. Q.* 1, Table I (1975). Further, the federal Child Abuse Prevention and Treatment Act, 42 U.S.C. § § 5101–5106 (1974), requires that states appoint a guardian ad litem for children in these proceedings, as a condition of eligibility for federal program support. This subsection also specifies that counsel for the child should be compensated by public funds irrespective of the parents' or child's financial condition. Assuring that counsel is not compensated from the parents' funds is to guard against potential conflicts of interest, or even the appearance of conflict. Keeping the child's resources separate serves similar purposes because of the likelihood that the child's funds might be perceived as intermingled with general family resources; in any event, if a child subject to wardship proceedings did have separate resources, it would seem wise to preserve those resources for the child's future welfare rather than requiring their expenditure for services of counsel. See generally A. Sussman, *Reporting Child Abuse and Neglect: Guidelines for Legislation* 107–108 (1974).

E. Attendance at all proceedings.

In all proceedings regarding the petition, the parents of the child should be entitled to attend, except that the proceeding may go forward without such presence if the parents fail to appear after reasonable notification (including without limitation efforts by court-designated persons to contact the parents by telephone and by visitation to the parents' last known address of residence within the jurisdiction of the court). The child identified in such petition should attend such proceedings unless the court finds, on motion of any party, that such attendance would be detrimental to the child. If the parents or custodians named in the petition fail to attend, the court may proceed to the hearing only if the child is represented by counsel. If the parents or custodians named in the petition were not present at the hearing and appear thereafter and move the court for a rehearing, the court should grant the motion unless it finds that they willfully refused to appear at the hearing or that the rehearing would be unjust because of the lapse of time since the hearing was held.

Commentary

Elemental notions of due process require that all affected parties be given adequate opportunity to be present in judicial proceedings affecting important interests such as those at stake here. See *Stanley v. Illinois*, 405 U.S. 645 (1972). It is equally clear, as a matter of general law, that parties' failure to attend proceedings after adequate attempts at notification cannot itself stymie the public purposes to be served by the proceedings. In these proceedings, the need to protect children provides a clear interest mandating that proceedings should go forward if parents fail to attend, after reasonable attempts at notification. The question of proceeding without the presence of the child raises different issues. Even in criminal matters, where the accused's presence at trial is explicitly guaranteed by the Constitution, it is now clear that countervailing interests in the conduct of an orderly trial can justify proceeding without the presence of the accused. *Illinois v. Allen*, 397 U.S. 337 (1970). The child has important personal interests at stake in these proceedings, and those interests might ordinarily justify his/her presence at trial. Nonetheless, some children might be seriously psychologically harmed if they witnessed the testimony regarding their parents' conduct toward them or other stressful aspects of the proceeding. Thus there can be justification for excluding a child from presence at some part, or all, of the proceedings. The laws of twenty-two states currently provide that the child's attendance may be waived at such proceedings. Katz et al., "Child Neglect Laws in America," 9 *Fam. L.Q.* 1, 32–33 (1975). This subsection ensures, however, that such exclusion will not be automatic, and that before any such exclusion is ordered specific proof must be adduced and the court must specifically find that the particular child would be harmed by attending the proceedings. Such proof could consist, for example, of psychological or psychiatric evaluations of the child, *in camera*, on-the-record interviews with the child by the court or other sources calculated to provide specific data regarding the impact of attendance on the child. Further, the subsection provides that exclusion of the child from the proceedings must be initiated on motion of one of the parties, rather than *sua sponte* by the court, so that the moving party will bear the responsibility of placing evidence before the court regarding the need for the child's exclusion.

F. Evidence at all proceedings.

In all proceedings regarding the petition, sworn testimony and other competent and relevant evidence may be admitted pursuant to the principles governing evidence in civil matters in the courts of general jurisdiction in the state. The court may admit testimony by the child who is the subject of the petition or by any other children whose testimony might be relevant regarding the petition if, upon motion of the party wishing to proffer the testimony of such child, the court determines that the child is sufficiently mature to provide competent evidence and that testifying will not be detrimental to the child. In making such determination regarding the child's proffered testimony, the court may direct psychological or other examinations and impose appropriate conditions for taking any testimony to safeguard the child from detriment. However, the court should not have access to any investigational or social history report prior to adjudication unless it has been admitted into evidence. The privileged character of communications between husband and wife and between professional person and his or her patient or client, except the privilege between attorney and client, should not be a ground for excluding evidence that would otherwise be admissible.

Commentary

This subsection provides that admissibility of testimentary and documentary evidence in these proceedings should be governed by the ordinary rules for civil proceedings in the jurisdiction. The subsection further provides that the court may admit testimony by the child subject of the petition, or other children with knowledge likely to be relevant to the petition (such as siblings of the subject child) upon two specific determinations: that the child is sufficiently mature to provide competent evidence and that such testimony will not be detrimental to the child. As in most state child abuse statutes, privileged communications, except the attorney-client privilege, are abrogated for the purpose of endangerment proceedings.

G. Temporary custody.

If the child remains in emergency temporary custody pursuant to Standard 4.3, no later than [two] working days following the filing of the petition, the court should convene a hearing to determine whether emergency temporary custody should be continued.

Once the parents have been informed of the proceeding and counsel has been assigned or retained, the court should hold a second detention hearing upon the request of the parents. At this hearing, the burden should be on the petitioner to show by relevant, material, and competent evidence, subject to cross-examination, that continued emergency temporary custody is necessary, pursuant to the standards set out in Standard 4.3 B.

Commentary

Subsection G. specifies a circumstance in which an immediate court hearing is mandatory: when the child has been placed, and remains, in emergency temporary custody pursuant to Part IV. The potential consequences to the child of separation from parents are significant. At such hearing, the court should take care that the interests of the child are adequately protected under the standards specified in this Part and the standards governing voluntary placement (Part X) or emergency temporary custody (Part IV). Subsection G. provides stringent time limits within which hearings must be convened for children in emergency temporary custody to assure that home removal which began as a "temporary emergency" does not extend, by default, into a longer term arrangement without intensive examination of the consequences of such separation to the child and the possible alternative arrangements in the home that might better protect the child and family.

H. Appointment of independent experts.

Any party to the proceeding may petition the court for appointment of experts, at public expense, for independent evaluation of the matter before the court. The court should grant such petition, unless it finds the expert unnecessary.

Commentary

In order to preserve the adversarial character of the proceedings, and to assure effective and vigorous representation of all interests in that proceeding, it is essential that all parties have fullest possible access to expert assistance. Accordingly, parties must be given fullest possible access to independent experts. The potential expense of that access must, in some degree, serve as a constraint. If the contesting party can independently afford access to experts, no such constraint appears. But in the typical case, the parents and/or child in particular will lack financial resources for such purpose and independent evaluation, if it takes place at all, must occur at public expense. This subsection authorizes public funding for such independent expert evaluation, unless the court find no need for the appointment of the particular expert requested. These experts may be drawn from medical, psychological, social welfare, or other disciplines. The overarching principle is the imperative necessity to provide full adversarial scrutiny of matters affecting the interests of children and their families when state intervention into family life is at stake.

I. Discovery.

The standards governing disclosure of matters in connection with proceedings to determine whether the petition should be granted, disposition of granted petitions (Part VI), or review proceedings (Part VII) should be the same for the child and the parents as for the respondent in delinquency cases set out in the *Pretrial Court Proceedings* volume.

Commentary

The issues presented regarding scope of discovery in endangerment proceedings are the same, and mandate the same resolutions, as in delinquency proceedings. These issues have received extensive consideration in the *Pretrial Court Proceedings* volume for delinquency petitions, and the resolution of the issues struck there should equally apply in this context. The single difference is that both the parents and child, in the endangerment proceeding, have the same access to pretrial discovery as is provided for the subject of the delinquency petition.

J. Subpoenas.

Upon request of any party, a subpoena should be issued by the court (or its clerk) commanding the attendance and testimony of any person at any proceeding conducted pursuant to this Part or commanding the production of documents for use in any such proceeding, except that the attendance and testimony of any children (including the child subject of the petition) should be governed by Standard 5.2 E. and F. Failure by any person without adequate excuse to obey a subpoena served upon him/her may be deemed a contempt of the court subject to civil contempt penalties.

Commentary

This provision is another aspect of the principle generally enunciated in these standards—to guarantee the fully adversarial character of the proceedings. The right of each party to compel attendance of witnesses is essential for adequate presentation of all interests at stake in the proceedings. The qualifications on compelled testimony from juveniles are the same as those set out in Standard 5.2 E. and F., *supra.*

K. Interpreters at all proceedings.

The court should appoint an interpreter or otherwise ensure that language barriers do not deprive the parents, child, witnesses, or other participants of the ability to understand and participate effectively in all stages of the proceedings.

Commentary

The standard providing for the appointment at public expense of interpreters for parties, witnesses, or other essential persons who may be handicapped by a language barrier so that they would be unable to participate effectively in the proceedings is similar to *Pretrial Court Proceedings* Standard 2.3 and *Adjudication* Standard 2.7. It is intended to cover the use of an interpreter for a person who is deaf or mute, as well as one who cannot speak or understand English competently. The standard applies to intake, preadjudication, and dispositional proceedings in addition to adjudication proceedings.

5.3 Adjudication proceedings.

A. Proceedings to determine contested petition.

In any proceeding to determine whether the petition should be granted, the following should apply:

1. Upon request of the child or the parents, the sole trier of fact should be a jury whose verdict must be unanimous, and which may consist of as few as six persons. In the absence of such request from either such party, the trier of fact should be the court. Under no circumstances should the trier of fact, or the judge prior to adjudication, have access to any investigational or social history report, unless it has been duly admitted into evidence at the hearing, as provided in Standard 5.2 F.

2. The burden should rest on the prosecutor of the petition to prove by clear and convincing evidence allegations sufficient to support the petition.

3. Proof that access has been refused to sources of or means for obtaining information, or that the parents have refused to attend or testify without adequate excuse, or regarding conduct of the parents toward another child should be admissible, if the court determines such proof relevant to the allegations in the petition; except that proof of either such matter, standing alone, should not be sufficient to sustain the granting of the petition.

4. Time for hearing. A hearing regarding a child who has remained in emergency temporary custody should take place no later than [twenty-five] days after the filing of the petition. If, within [twenty-five] days, the petitioner is not ready to go forward with the hearing, the court must order the child returned to his or her parents and dismiss the petition with prejudice unless there is good cause shown for the delay. In the event such cause is shown, the court must continue to find that conditions exist, pursuant to Standard 4.3, justifying the continuation of the child in emergency temporary custody. In no event should a delay beyond [twenty-five] days be authorized for longer than [seven] additional days.

For all other cases under this part, a hearing should be held within [sixty] days of the filing of the petition. If at the end of this time the petition is not ready to proceed, the court should dismiss the petition with prejudice.

Commentary

Subsection 1. of this section provides a right to jury trial at the option of the child or parent named in the petition. *McKeiver v. Pennsylvania*, 403 U.S. 528 (1971), indicates that this right is not constitutionally mandated in wardship proceedings since the constitutionally based arguments for such mandate are, if anything, stronger in the delinquency proceeding context of that case. A right to trial by jury is currently provided in eight jurisdictions and granted specifically to parents in another four. Statutes in twenty-four jurisdictions, however, contain language precluding trial by jury. Katz et al., "Child Neglect Laws in America," 9 *Fam. L. Q.* 1, 32–33 (1975). As a matter of policy, we believe that the right to a jury trial is important to ensure that state intervention into family childrearing practices reflects widely shared community norms that any randomly selected jury would adhere to. Under subsection 1. this right is withheld from the prosecution to ensure that the jury will be invoked only by a party—the parent or child—with the most direct personal interests at stake, and typically as a tactic to increase the burden on the proponent of the petition. This burden of persuasion appropriately reflects the general principle enunciated in these standards presuming against state interventions. Specifying that the jury may consist of as few as six persons reflects the greater flexibility regarding jury size now permitted even in criminal cases in light of *Williams v. Florida*, 399 U.S. 78 (1970), and *Colgrove v. Battin*, 413 U.S. 149 (1973).

Subsection 2. makes explicit that the burden of proof is on the prosecutor of the petition. The standard of proof specified is, however, not the criminal standard of "beyond reasonable doubt" but rather the civil law standard of "clear and convincing evidence." Criminal law norms are not fully applicable to these proceedings. Rather these proceedings are more hybrid versions of criminal and civil proceedings, reflecting the competing policies of guaranteeing families and children against inappropriate state intervention but giving adequate assurance that children will be protected against parentally inflicted harms. Because direct proof of parental conduct is frequently difficult to adduce, particularly regarding preschool children, the criminal law standard of "beyond reasonable doubt" would be unduly restrictive of the possibility that state intervention might adequately protect children in need. See Dembitz, "Child Abuse and the Law—Fact and Fiction," 24 *Record of N.Y.C.B.A.* 613 (1969).

Subsection 3. mandates the evidentiary weight that may be given to two items: proof that parents have refused to provide information in the investigation report or testify at the postinvestigation proceeding, and proof regarding parents' conduct toward another child. The subsection provides that either such matter may be relevant to ultimate adjudication of the merits of the petition and proof of such matters is thus admissible. But both such matters can produce an unjustifiably heavy pejorative impact on the factfinder and lead the factfinder wrongly to wish to "penalize" a parent who refused to "cooperate with investigators" or to conclusively (and wrongly) presume that a parent who behaves harmfully toward one child necessarily is unfit in dealing with all other children. To guard against the inevitably prejudicial impact of such proof, this subsection specifies that proof of either such matter, standing alone, would not be sufficient to sustain the granting of the petition, and that either such matter may only be cumulatively supportive of the petition. This subsection thus rejects the rule that the parents' uncooperativeness alone is sufficient to sustain a petition, compare *In re Vulon Children*, 56 Misc. 2d 19, 288 N.Y.S. 2d 203 (Fam. Ct. 1968) similarly rejecting such rule, or that parental abuse or neglect of one child is alone sufficient to sustain a finding of endangerment for other children in the absence of any evidence whatsoever regarding those other children, compare *In re Milton Edwards*, 76 Misc. 2d 781, 351 N.Y.S.2d 601 (Fam. Ct. 1972) adopting such rule.

Subsection 4. specifies fixed maximum time periods in which a hearing must be held after a petition of endangerment has been filed. It distinguishes between a situation in which the child has been removed from home and placed in temporary custody, requiring the hearing within twenty-five days, and one in which the child is not in custody, setting a sixty-day limit for such hearings. An extension of no more than seven days is authorized for children in custody.

B. Uncontested petitions.

If the parents wish to admit to all or any part of the allegations in the petition, sufficient to give the court authority to order a disposition of the proceeding other than dismissal as set out in Part VI, the court should convene a hearing at which testimony should be taken regarding the voluntariness and validity of the parents' decision. The judge should not accept a plea admitting an allegation of the petition without first addressing the parents personally, in language calculated to communicate effectively with them, to:

1. Determine that the parents understand the nature of the allegations;

2. Inform the parents of the right to a hearing at which the petitioner must confront respondent with witnesses and prove the allegations by clear and convincing competent evidence and at which the parents' attorney will be permitted to cross-examine the witnesses called by the petitioner and to call witnesses on the parents' behalf;

3. Inform the parents of the right to remain silent with respect to the allegations of the petition as well as of the right to testify if desired;

4. Inform the parents of the right to appeal from the decision reached in the trial;

5. Inform the parents of the right to a trial by jury;

6. Inform the parents that one gives up those rights by a plea admitting an allegation of the petition;

7. Inform the parents that if the court accepts the plea, the court can enter any final order of disposition set forth in Part VI;

8. Determine that the plea is voluntary; and

9. Determine that the parents were given the effective assistance of an attorney, if the parents were represented by counsel.

The court should allow the parents to withdraw a plea admitting an allegation of the petition whenever the parents prove that withdrawal is necessary to correct a manifest injustice. If the court accepts an admission, it should enter an order finding that the child is endangered.

Commentary

The standards for uncontested endangerment petitions are designed to ensure that the parents or other custodians have acted with full awareness of the consequences of their decision not to contest the charges and that their waiver of the right to an adversary proceeding is voluntary and uncoerced. The provisions are based on *Adjudication* Standards 3.1 to 3.6 governing acceptance of a plea admitting an allegation in a delinquency petition, as modified by the fact that the respondent in an endangerment proceeding usually is an adult.

C. Recording proceedings.

1. A verbatim record should be made and preserved of all proceedings, whether or not the allegations in the petition are contested.

2. The record should be preserved and, with any exhibits, kept confidential.

3. The requirement of preservation should be subordinated to any order for expungement of the record and the requirement of confidentiality should be subordinated to court orders on behalf of the parents, child, or petitioner for a verbatim transcript of the record for use in subsequent legal proceedings.

Commentary

The requirement of a verbatim record of all proceedings to facilitate subsequent legal action, such as appeal of a final order, initiation of a proceeding for termination of parental rights, or court review of a placement, is consistent with the procedural safeguards provided in other volumes in this series. See *Pretrial Court Proceedings* Standard 6.4 and *Adjudication* Standard 2.1. Provisions for confidentiality of records and for the priority of an order of expungement over the need for preservation of records are based on the *Adjudication* standards.

5.4 Findings.

A. The trier of fact should record its findings specifically. Findings of fact and law should be articulated separately on the record. If the trier of fact determines that facts sufficient to sustain the petition have been established, the court should enter an order finding that the child is endangered. If the trier of fact determines that facts sufficient to sustain the petition have not been established, the court should dismiss the petition.

B. Each jurisdiction should provide by law that a finding by juvenile court that a child is endangered should only be used for the purpose of providing the court with the authority to order an appropriate disposition for the child pursuant to Standard 6.3.

Commentary

This standard provides that an adjudication proceeding should culminate in recorded findings of fact and law. The only permissible legal consequence of a finding that a child is endangered is the authority for the court to convene a dispositional hearing in order to devise an appropriate order of disposition. See *Adjudication* Standard 5.3.

5.5 Appeals.

Appeals from a finding that a child is endangered should not be allowed as of right. Interlocutory appeals from such orders may be allowed only in the discretion of the appellate court. Appeals as of right exist only from a final order of disposition. The standards governing appeals from proceedings under this Part should be the same as those set out in the *Appeals and Collateral Review* standards, except that the parties entitled to take an appeal under *Appeals and Collateral Review* Standard 2.2 also should include the petitioner pursuant to Standard 5.1 C. above.

Commentary

Under Standard 5.5, an appeal from a finding of endangerment is not a matter of right prior to a final order of disposition. The purpose of relying on the court's discretion to limit such appeals prior to the dispositional hearing is to expedite an appropriate outcome for an endangered child.

PART VI: DISPOSITIONS

6.1 Predisposition investigation and reports.

A. Predisposition investigation.

After the court has entered a finding pursuant to Standard 5.4 F. that a child is endangered, it should authorize an investigation to be conducted by the probation department to supply the necessary information for an order of disposition.

B. Predisposition report.

The predisposition report should include the following information:

1. a description of the specific programs and/or placements, for both the parents and the child, which will be needed in order to prevent further harm to the child, the reasons why such programs and/or placements are likely to be useful, the availability of any

proposed services, and the agency's plans for ensuring that the services will be delivered;

2. a statement of the indications (*e.g.*, specific changes in parental behavior) that will be used to determine that the family no longer needs supervision or that placement is no longer necessary;

3. an estimate of the time in which the goals of intervention should be achieved or in which it will be known they cannot be achieved.

4. In any case where removal from parental custody is recommended, the report should contain:

a. a full description of the reasons why the child cannot be adequately protected in the home, including a description of any previous efforts to work with the parents with the child in the home, the "in-home treatment programs," *e.g.*, homemakers, which have been considered and rejected, and the parents' attitude toward placement of the child;

b. a statement of the likely harms the child will suffer as a result of removal (this section should include an exploration of the nature of the parent-child attachment and the anticipated effect of separation and loss to both the parents and the child);

c. a description of the steps that will be taken to minimize harm to the child that may result if separation occurs.

5. If no removal from parental custody is recommended, the report should indicate what services or custodial arrangements, if any, have been offered to and/or accepted by the parents of the child.

C. The investigating agency should be required to provide its report to the court and the court should provide copies of such report to all parties to the proceedings.

Commentary

The predisposition investigative report typically will provide the most extensive critical behavioral data on which any state intervention to protect the child will be based. It is therefore essential that these data are as complete and helpful as possible. This standard accordingly requires detailed specificity in its data and findings well beyond the typical highly generalized "boilerplate" language about "less than optimal child-rearing environment" that currently afflicts too many agency-to-court reports in these matters. The subsections of this provision spell out precisely what data and what predictions are required for any rational judgment that state intervention might be required. The standard further provides that, if no wardship is recommended, the report should nonetheless specify what services have been offered and accepted by the parents, in order to give some protection against unduly coerced acceptance of services by parents as a price of avoiding a court wardship recommendation. If, that is, the investigative report indicates that no wardship is recommended but that the parents have accepted extensive and onerous intrusions into their family life, counsel and the court should be alerted to the possibility that these services were not free from coercion.

6.2 Proceeding to determine disposition.

Following a finding pursuant to Standard 5.4 that a child is endangered, the court should, as soon as practicable, but no later than [forty-five] days thereafter, convene a hearing to determine the disposition of the petition. If the child is in emergency temporary custody, the court should be required to convene the hearing no later than [twenty] working days following the finding that the child is endangered. All parties to the proceeding should participate in the hearing, and all matters relevant to the court's determination should be presented in evidence at the hearing. In deciding the appropriate disposition, the court should have available and should consider the dispositional report prepared by the investigating agency pursuant to Standard 6.1 B.

Commentary

After a child has been found endangered, this standard provides for a hearing separate from the adjudicatory hearing to determine whether continued state involvement with the family is necessary, and if so, what form this involvement should take. In accordance with general practice in most jurisdictions, this second hearing is called the dispositional hearing.

It is of central importance that the dispositional hearing be held separately from the adjudicatory hearing, even if they are held on the same day. At the dispositional hearing the court will be provided with substantial information about the family and the child. Some of this information might be very prejudicial if considered at the adjudicatory stage. For example, a trier of fact might be influenced by knowing that a family was the recipient of welfare services or that a parent was a drug addict; yet such information might be irrelevant on the factual issue of whether a child had been sexually abused, needed medical care, etc.

The standard specifies that all parties, including the child, should be able to present any evidence relevant to the question of the appropriate disposition. Each party should also have the right to examine evidence presented by other parties, to call his or her own witnesses, and to cross-examine witnesses of other parties, including the person who prepared the social report required by Standard 6.1.

The standard does establish set time periods for holding this hearing. These time periods are designed to enable the parties to work out a treatment plan that meets the needs of the child and family. Depending upon the services needed, this plan may be developed immediately after the adjudicatory hearing or it may take several weeks or longer following that hearing.

However, in order to provide children with stable, continuous living environments as quickly as possible, more stringent time limits are established if the child is in temporary custody. Most temporary child care facilities are not able to provide a child with an adequate adult-child relationship, nor can they provide for the child's long-term needs. Therefore, it is essential to either have the child returned to his/her parents as rapidly as possible, or placed in an alternative setting designed to fully meet the child's needs.

At the dispositional hearing the court will generally hear evidence presented by the parents and by the child. However, as specified by Standard 6.4 *infra*, the burden shall be upon the petitioner to show the need for continued coercive intervention. A report recommending intervention should contain a specific plan designed to protect the child from further harm and to insure him/her a permanent living environment, preferably with his/her own parents or guardians.

The purpose of the dispositional report is to inform the court, and all of the parties, of the dispositional recommendation of the investigating agency prior to the court hearing. This will allow all parties to prepare their responses. The report is not meant to replace the testimony of the investigator who wrote the report, although the parties may waive cross-examination of the report writer.

At present most courts, at least in larger jurisdictions, receive and consider such reports. Unfortunately, the reports are frequently conclusory in form and contain substantial amounts of hearsay. Moreover, they often fail to discuss critical questions, such as what treatment programs will be utilized to make intervention effective and whether suggested programs are in fact available. In order to overcome these deficiencies, Standard 6.1 B. delineates a number of specific questions that must be addressed in the report relating to the major issues before the court. It must also be recognized that unless the social workers are adequately trained and educated, the opinions expressed in such reports may not qualify as expert opinions, and the courts should weigh the recommendations accordingly.

6.3 Available dispositions.

A. A court should have at least the following dispositional alternatives and resources:

1. dismissal of the case;

2. wardship with informal supervision;

3. ordering the parent to accept social work supervision;

4. ordering the parent and/or the child to accept individual or family therapy or medical treatment;

5. ordering the state or parents to employ a homemaker in the home;

6. placement of the child in a day care program;

7. placement of the child with a relative, in a foster family or group home, or in a residential treatment center.

B. A court should have authority to order that the parent accept, and that the state provide, any of the above services.

C. It should be the state's responsibility to provide an adequate level of services.

Commentary

One of the central defects of all current systems of intervention is that intervention takes place without adequate services being available to meet the needs of the child and parent. Because of inadequate or nonexistent resources, courts often must utilize intervention strategies that are inappropriate. See B. Bernstein, *A Preliminary Report: Foster Care Needs and Alternatives to Placement* (N.Y. Bd. of Social Welfare, 1975). As a result, intervention is often ineffective and even harmful to the child.

It is a basic judgment in these standards that intervention is not justified unless there are adequate resources available of sufficient quality to make the intervention beneficial to the child, and to the maximum degree possible, to his/her family. It is pure hypocrisy for legislatures to authorize intervention, not provide resources, and still believe that children are being protected by neglect laws.

This standard specifies the resources that should, at the very minimum, be available to the court. It does not provide guidelines for determining when a court should make any particular disposition. Guidelines for this decision are contained in Standard 6.4 *infra*. The purpose of this standard is to delineate the *minimum types* of services needed to make the entire set of proposals contained in this volume useful. It must also be recognized that the quantity and quality of such services is critical. This volume does not address issues of quantity and quality. Minimal standards for some services have been offered by other standard setting groups. See, *e.g.*, Child Welfare League of America, *Standards for Homemaker Services for Children;* C.W.L.A., *Standards for Day Care Services;* American Public Welfare Association, *Standards for Foster Family Services Systems.*

Dismissal of the case. Even when a child comes within one of the statutory grounds, coercive intervention may be inappropriate. See Standard 2.2 *supra.* At the dispositional hearing the court should consider carefully whether the child will be endangered unless brought under court supervision. If not, the court should be required to dismiss the petition.

Wardship with informal supervision. In some situations the court might believe there is a need for continued review of the family situation, but concludes that no regular casework or other form of supervision is necessary. For example, in a case of inadequate protection the court might want to review the situation in six months, but not require any specific casework plan. Such instances may be infrequent, but a court should have this option available.

Casework supervision. Because the option of removal is greatly restricted by these standards, see 6.4 C. *infra*, the most frequent disposition will involve provision of some type of services to the parents and/or child while the child remains in his/her home. Usually this should consist of "hard" services, such as homemakers, day care, housing. In addition, the court should be able to require the parents to accept social work services from a social work agency. These services can take a variety of forms. At a minimum, it might consist only of periodic checks on the child's wellbeing. In most cases the worker also should be responsible for seeing that any services ordered by the court are, in fact, provided to the parents and/or the child. The worker may also provide direct counseling, where appropriate. To make such services meaningful, there must be available to the court a sufficient number of trained workers, with manageable caseloads.

Provision of treatment. At present there is a paucity of medical and counseling services available to help parents and children under court supervision. Yet a number of studies have demonstrated that, particularly in cases of child abuse, a coordinated program of psychiatric counseling and social work help can prevent the need to remove the child and help the family function adequately without endangering the child. See, *e.g.*, B. Steele, *Working With Abusive Parents* (1975). Programs developed in a number of cities can serve as models for the provision of such treatment services. See, *e.g.*, R. Helfer, *The Diagnostic Process and Treatment Programs for Child Abuse and Neglect* (1975).

Homemakers. Homemakers are persons who come into a home to help the parents care for their children and to teach parenting skills. See *CWLA Standards for Homemaker Services, supra.* It is well documented that provision of such services can prevent the removal of children; moreover the cost of a homemaker is less than foster care. See D. Fanshel and E. Shinn, *Dollars and Sense in Foster Care* (1972); M. Burt and L. Balyeat, *Options for Improving the Care of Neglected and Dependent Children* (1971).

The provision of homemakers can be the most effective means of intervention in most cases arising under Standard 2.1 B. It is essential that adequate funds be provided for homemakers to achieve the goals established in this volume.

Day care. Some children cannot be protected solely by casework and/or various treatment services, at least until these services have been offered for a period of time. At present most of these children are placed in foster care, from which they frequently never return. See commentary to Standard 7.1 *infra*.

There is now evidence that many of these children do not have to be totally removed from their homes. Instead, they can be protected, and their parents helped, by placing them in a day care facility with the parent retaining basic custody and control. See Pavenstedt, "An Intervention Program for Infants from High Risk Homes," 63 *Am. J. Pub. Health* 393 (1973).

Such services should not be exclusively limited to endangered children, however. Unfortunately, services limited to endangered children often tend to be of lower quality. Moreover, there is substantial reason to believe that if adequate day care services, as well as other social programs, were more generally available, many children would not be neglected or abused. See, *e.g.*, Bronfenbrenner, "Is Early Intervention Effective," in *2 A Report on Longitudinal Evaluations of Preschool Programs* (HEW Monograph No. (OHD) 74-25, 1974). Therefore, day care services should be offered as part of an overall community program for all children.

Removal. Removal of a child from his or her parent to a relative's home, foster family, or residential treatment center should occur only when less drastic means are unavailable to protect the child. See Standard 6.4 C. However, foster care will continue to be necessary. Even with better services, foster care facilities must be upgraded to make removal beneficial to the child.

Evidence from several states indicates that children are often placed in inadequate institutions or foster homes. See Gil, "Institutions for Children" in A. Schorr, *Children and Decent People* (1974). Too often we merely substitute inadequate state care for inadequate parental care. Therefore, each state should examine what out of home services are needed to develop a program to insure that the quality of alternative living situations for endangered children is sufficiently high.

In order for intervention to be successful, a court must have authority to order the parents to participate in a treatment program. In some states the court action is on behalf of the child, and it is unclear whether the court has continuing jurisdiction over the parents. This standard specifies that a court should have such authority.

Under this standard, the court also is given authority to order state agencies, and private agencies performing any services paid for by the state, to provide services to families under court supervision. At present most courts cannot order such agencies to provide services, and as a result, dispositional orders may be rendered ineffective. If intervention is to help children, prevent their removal from their families, or facilitate return of children to their families as quickly as possible, it is essential that courts have authority to order any agency to provide needed services to the child and parents.

Again, it must be recognized that courts cannot order provision of services that do not exist. The success of these standards depends on the availability of quality services, services that not only have trained personnel, but workers who understand the culture and language of the clients they serve.

Standard 6.3 C. requires the state to provide an adequate level of services. In that connection, it is permissible for the state to purchase services from outside sources. Contracting for services from private agencies is used extensively in many states. For a discussion of the advantages and disadvantages of purchasing services, see the commentary to *Dispositions* Standard 4.1 B.

It should be noted further that although *Dispositions* Standard 4.1 provides for a juvenile's right to services, *Dispositions* Standard 4.2 provides that juveniles adjudicated delinquent have the right to refuse *all* services. An endangered child should have no fewer rights. Therefore, the inclusion under Standard 6.3 A. 7. of placement in a residential treatment center among the other custodial dispositions following removal, such as placement in a foster or group home, calls for even greater safeguards than the principle of least restrictive alternatives referred to above would compel. Not only must the child's need for such treatment and the reasons why it cannot be provided without removing the child from home be established, but the presence of informed uncoerced consent by the juvenile to such treatment also should be found by the court before ordering the disposition of placement in a treatment facility.

6.4 Standards for choosing a disposition.
    A. General goal.
    The goal of all dispositions should be to protect the child from the harm justifying intervention in the least restrictive manner available to the court.
    B. Dispositions other than removal of the child.
    In ordering a disposition other than removal of the child from his/her home, the court should choose a program designed to alleviate the immediate danger to the child, to mitigate or cure any damage the child has already suffered, and to aid the parents so that the child will not be endangered in the future. In selecting a program, the court should choose those services which least interfere with family autonomy, provided that the services are adequate to protect the child.
    C. Removal.
        1. A child should not be removed from his/her home unless the court finds that:
            a. the child has been physically abused as defined in Standard 2.1 A. and there is a preponderance of evidence that the child cannot be protected from further physical abuse without being removed from his/her home; or
            b. the child has been endangered in one of the other ways specified by statute and there is clear and convincing evidence that the child cannot be protected from further harm of the type justifying intervention unless removed from his/her home.
        2. Even if a court finds subsections 1. a. or b. applicable, before any child is removed from his/her home, the court must find that there is a placement in fact available in which the child will not be endangered.
        3. The court should not be authorized to remove a child when the child is endangered solely due to environmental conditions

beyond the control of the parents, which the parents would be willing to remedy if they were able to do so.

4. Those advocating removal should bear the burden of proof on all these issues.

Commentary

General goal. At present, virtually all state statutes direct courts to select that disposition which is "in the best interest" of the child. The standard proposed herein specifically rejects the "best interest" test. In its place, the standard provides that the goal of the disposition is to protect the child *from the specific harm justifying intervention.* In addition, removal of the child from the home is specifically forbidden unless the child cannot be protected by any other means. Children should not be removed from home except when less restrictive dispositions are unavailable.

The "best interest" test is rejected for a number of reasons. First, no legislature has provided statutory guidelines which spell out the factors a court should consider in determining the child's best interests. Obviously, this term may mean different things. Should a court be concerned with the child's physical wellbeing, intellectual development, material comforts, emotional stability? What weight should be placed on each of these? Should a court determine whether the child is more likely to become delinquent, go to college, have close, warm relationships with an adult, grow up "happy" in his/her own home or in some other placement? Should courts consider the likely impact of each possible disposition on each of these variables, or on any other variables; and compare the home to each one to see which one has the most pluses? Are they to determine the child's best interest in the short run or the long run?

In the absence of legislative definition, there is considerable variation among judges in applying the test. Decisions may reflect individual judges' views of a proper upbringing. As a result, there has been unequal treatment of parents and children, discrimination on the basis of race and social class, and judicial decisions based on value judgments not commonly held by society or approved by the legislature. See *In re Raya*, 255 Cal. App. 2d 260, 63 *Cal. Rptr.* 252 (1967); A. Shyne, E. Sherman and B. Haring, *Factors Associated with Placement Decisions in Child Welfare* 69–84 (1971).

Moreover, the "best interest" test increases the chances of inappropriate intervention, and especially of unwarranted removal of the child. Under the best interest standard, a social worker or judge may try to protect children from "evils" in the home environment even though there is no sound basis for believing that these factors will have any short- or long-term negative impact on the child. The "best interest" test allows courts to order dispositions in an effort to protect a child from harms other than those specified in Standard 2.1 A.-F. *supra*. See, *e.g.*, *In re Cager*, 251 Md. 473, 248 A.2d 384 (1968). The grounds for intervention specified in that section preclude intervention for alleged harms where there is reason to believe that in general, intervention will not benefit most children. If the initial exclusion of these "harms" is correct, they should not be relevant in the dispositional phase of neglect proceedings.

Even if a legislature were to define best interest more specifically, the test would still be unsatisfactory, especially for decisions regarding removal of a child. Any test that calls for weighing the likely impact of home versus foster care with regard to a number of different factors, however carefully defined, requires complex calculations which are impossible for judges to make. As Professor Mnookin has recently stated, under the best interest test a judge must:

> . . . compare the probable consequences for the child of remaining in the home with the probable consequences of removal. How might a judge make this comparison? He or she would need considerable information and predictive ability. The information would include knowledge of how the parents had behaved in the past, the effect of this parental behavior on the child, and the child's present condition. Then the judge would need to predict the probable future behavior of the parents if the child were to remain in the home and to gauge the probable effects of his behavior on the child. Obviously, more than one outcome is possible, so the judge would have to assess the probability of various outcomes and evaluate the seriousness of the possible benefits and harms associated with each. Next, the judge would have to compare this set of possible consequences with those if the child were placed in a foster home. This would require predicting the effect of removing the child from home, school, friends, and familiar surroundings, as well as predicting the child's experience while in the foster care system. Such predictions involve estimates of the child's future relationship with the foster parents, the child's future contact with natural parents and siblings, the number of foster homes in which the child ultimately will have to be placed, the length of time spent in foster care, the potential for acquiring a stable home, and myriad other factors. Mnookin, "Foster Care: In Whose Best Interest," 43 *Harv. Ed. Rev.* 599 (1973).

We simply do not have sufficient data on the impact of removal, or sound clinical criteria for determining how a child will do in placement, to decide the questions Mnookin identifies, regardless of whether the factors which must be predicted are identified in advance or left to the court to choose. In the absence of adequate predictive ability, it is essential to adopt a test which is within the competence of courts and social workers to administer.

Dispositions other than removal. Dispositions involving removal entail the most serious consequences for both the child and parents. For this reason, and because of the absence of data which provide any sound evidence as to when any particular disposition short of removal is appropriate, the standards provide specific guidelines only as to the removal decision. Thus, the standards do not specify when a court should order counseling, homemaker services, day care, or any other program short of removal.

However, it must be recognized that any intervention can be harmful, rather than helpful, to the child and entails a substantial invasion of family privacy and parental autonomy. Therefore, all forms of coercive intervention should be limited to only those actions that are necessary to protect the endangered child from future harm. If the family desires other services, they can request that these services be provided on a voluntary basis.

For example, if a child is endangered because of dangerous home conditions, coercive intervention might only require helping the parent correct the conditions and provision of a homemaker for a period of time to insure that the parent is able to keep the home safe. If the parent also suffers from an alcohol problem, alcohol rehabilitation services should be offered to the parent but should not be required unless the alcoholism prevents the parent from protecting the child or maintaining the home in a safe condition.

It is certainly true that many parents who endanger their children exhibit a multitude of problems, all of which may in some way deprive the child of an ideal or even "good" environment. But given the limited resources available, our lack of knowledge about helping such families, see, *e.g.*, Fischer, "Is Casework Effective: A Review," *Social Work* 5 (Jan. 1973); G. Brown, *The Multi-Problem Dilemma: A Social Research Demonstration With Multi-Problem Families* (1968), and the resultant potential for keeping such families under court supervision for years, it is preferable to require that parents accept only those services essential to insure that the child is protected and to continue coercive supervision only while the child remains in danger.

Removal. The proposed standard permits removal only when the child cannot be protected from the specific danger justifying removal without resorting to removal. The burden of proof is on the intervening agency to demonstrate the need for removal—by a "preponderance of the evidence" in cases arising under Standard 2.1 A. and by "clear and convincing" evidence in all other cases.

The standard places two additional limitations on the authority of a court to order removal. First, Standard 6.4 C. 2. requires the court to find that there is a placement *actually available* for the child in which the child will not be endangered. Second, Standard 6.4 C. 3. states that removal should not be authorized in any case where the child is endangered solely because of environmental conditions beyond control of his/her parents and that the parents would be willing to rectify if given the opportunity or means.

To help the court in making these decisions, Standard 6.1, *supra* requires that the investigating agency present information on these issues whenever removal is recommended.

Many of the general reasons for adopting this test are discussed in the commentary to 6.4 A. In addition to the reasons stated there, the proposed standard on removal is consistent with the purposes of the initial intervention. We should not allow courts to find a child endangered merely because he/she might be better off living elsewhere or under state supervision. If this were the law, it might be used for a massive reallocation of children to new parents. Therefore, the standards permit intervention only where it is needed to protect a child from serious harm. Thus, the relevant question at disposition is how can we protect the child from this harm. If the child can be protected without removal, there is no reason to allow more intrusive state intervention.

Second, the proposed test avoids many of the problems caused by the best interest test. While a court still faces a difficult factual determination with regard to whether the specific harm can be avoided without removal, there is at least a precise issue to decide. The court is not required to make value judgments or to decide issues beyond its competence. The standard can generally be applied evenhandedly. Of course, different courts may be more or less prone to interpret facts in a manner favoring removal or nonremoval, but this is a problem inherent in the judicial system.

Finally, the test helps minimize the possibility of unwarranted removal. The test should sharply reduce the number of children now being removed. See Mnookin, "Foster Care: In Whose Best Interest," 43 *Harv. Ed. Rev.* 699, 693 (1973). This decision reflects the generally prevailing view that removal has often done more harm than good for many children. See Mnookin, *supra;* H. Stone, *Foster Care in Question* (1969). Children often have strong psychological attachments even to unfit parents. See J. Bowlby, *Child Care and the Growth of Love* 80 (1965); J. Goldstein, A. Freud and A. Solnit, *Beyond the Best Interests of the Child* (1973). When those ties are broken, the child suffers short-term trauma and possibly long-term emotional damage.

Once in foster care, the child may suffer from a number of problems, including difficulty in establishing an identity, guilt feelings over having "abandoned" his/her parents, and significant difficulties in adjusting to new "parents," "siblings," peers, and school environment. See E. Weinstein, *The Self-Image of the Foster Child* (1960).

In addition to the many problems caused by separation and the status of being a foster child, existing alternatives to the child's own home may be quite undesirable. Because of a shortage of foster parent homes, group homes, and good residential treatment facilities, children often must spend weeks or months in impersonal "holding" institutions. Many such institutions do not provide adequately for the child's emotional wellbeing. Gil, "Institutions for Children" in A. Schorr, *Children and Decent People* (1974). Some cannot even protect the child's physical wellbeing. See Oelsner, "Juvenile Justice: Failures in a System of Detention," *New York Times*, April 4, 1973, at p. 1, col. 4. In order to keep children out of institutions, placement may be made in a less than adequate foster home.

Finally, children in foster care frequently are subjected to multiple placements; each such move is thought to destroy the continuity and stability needed to help a child achieve stable emotional development. See Bowlby, *supra*; Goldstein, Freud and Solnit, *supra*. Although the standards proposed in Part VII *infra* are designed to minimize the possibility of multiple placement, it is unlikely they can be eliminated.

When a child is seriously endangered, removal may well be in his/her interests. This may be the only way to protect the child. However, if a child can be protected from the specific harms justifying intervention without removal, he/she should not be forced to suffer the harms associated with removal in the hope that his/her overall wellbeing will be furthered thereby. This is accepting a known cost without any assurance of long run benefit for the child.

Burden of proof. The standards place the burden of proof on the agency requesting removal to demonstrate the need for removal. At present no state laws address the issue of burden of proof.

Those favoring removal should bear the burden for several reasons. First, placing the burden on those seeking removal is consistent with the value placed on family autonomy. At least in the absence of evidence showing the benefits of removal, we should continue to support notions of family autonomy and place the burden on those seeking separation.

Second, placing the burden on the intervening agency is fairer in terms of the parties' ability to present evidence. The agencies, not the parents, know about the resources which might help the parent keep the child. Even a parent with counsel may not be able to put together a plan for safeguarding the child at home, especially if state agencies are not cooperative.

Third, placing the burden on the agencies will facilitate implementation of the proposed substantive standard. In order to show that removal is necessary, the agency staff will have to examine the alternatives within their knowledge and to explain why these are not satisfactory. Faced with this burden, agency personnel might be encouraged to find ways to keep children at home rather than taking the easier road of removal. They have no incentive to do so with the burden on the parent.

Finally, removal often has a negative impact on other children in the family. If one child is removed, other children in the family may worry that they will be the next to go. This uncertainty and anxiety can be quite harmful. In addition, when services are used to keep an endangered child in his or her home, these services also may benefit other children in the home who are not legally neglected. Therefore, the overall wellbeing of all the children in the home may be promoted.

It should be recognized, moreover, that keeping children at home can achieve substantial cost savings. See D. Fanshel and E. Shinn, *Dollars and Sense in Foster Care* (1972). Many states are paying five to ten times more to support children living out of their homes than to maintain them in their homes. These cost savings could be used to provide programs to protect children at home.

Level of proof. While the burden is always on those advocating removal, the level of proof differs depending on the basis for intervention. The need for removal must be shown by clear and convincing evidence if intervention is premised on Standard 2.1 B.-F.; by a preponderance of the evidence when the child comes within 2.1 A.—physical abuse.

Physical abuse, as compared to unsafe home conditions, emotional damage, sexual abuse, or contributing to delinquency usually involves the most substantial threat of permanent injury and even death. Such abuse can take place rapidly. Without placing someone in the home on a twenty-four-hour basis, there is no way to prevent its occurrence with certainty. While removal is by no means always necessary to protect the child, especially in cases of less serious injuries, the best available evidence indicates that some parents are likely to reinjure their children, even if they participate in a good treatment program. Unfortunately, we cannot predict exactly which parents will abuse their children even if supervised. Given the magnitude of the harm, the relative certainty that removal will prevent further physical harm, and the substantial evidence that many parents repeatedly abuse their children, it is too risky for the child to require the higher standard of proof in abuse cases.

In all the nonphysical abuse situations justifying intervention, the possibility of protecting the child at home is higher. Therefore, Standard 6.4 C. 1. b. requires clear and convincing evidence before removal may be ordered to protect children in these cases.

In cases involving unsafe home conditions, prediction about the likelihood of future harm is more speculative; there are successful intervention programs such as homemaker services, and in-home services that provide the opportunity to learn whether the parents can or will change the conditions. In cases involving emotional damage, the emotional problems often are so closely tied to the parent-child relationship that treatment can be given only if the child remains in the family. Also, removal may simply be substituting a different trauma for the damage in the home. Virtually all children suffer emotional trauma from separation. A court should be quite certain that removal is essential before adding this trauma to the child's problems.

In sexual abuse cases removal is often ordered because of moral outrage at the parent's act. Yet the child may not be suffering any clear harm or may be further harmed by removal. Also, as with emotional harm, family therapy may be the best, and perhaps the only really effective way to remedy whatever harm has occurred, and with such therapy protection of the child in the home is possible.

Even though all these factors make removal inappropriate in many cases, there are still situations where the child should be removed from the home. The kind of evidence used to meet the clear and convincing standard might include a failure of previous in-home services to alleviate the situation, the child's desire to leave the home, a parental condition such as drug addiction or alcoholism, which causes the inadequate care, and which cannot be treated rapidly enough to assure the child's safety, or the absence of parental desire to keep the child. Also if the extent of harm in the particular case is very severe, removal is more likely to be appropriate. On the other hand, courts should be more hesitant to order removal where the parent-child ties are strong.

Requiring any particular standard of proof or varying the test by the type of harm involved does not guarantee that courts will treat the classes of cases differently, let alone that they will utilize removal only when appropriate. We have no proof that different burdens of proof actually affect judicial decisions. However, the terms "preponderance" and "clear and convincing" do have legal meaning. See *Alsager v. District Court of Polk County*, 406 F. Supp. 11 (N.D. Iowa 1975); *In re Gibson*, 24 Ill. App. 3d 981, 322 N.E.2d 223 (1975); *In re Simmons Children*, 154 W. Va. 491, 177 S.E.2d 19 (1970). The different levels of proof required convey to a judge a difference in legislative preference with regard to removal. They provide a basis for appellate review which may result in better trial advocacy by attorneys.

Limitations on the general standard.   Subsections C. 2. and 3. place two additional limitations on the court's authority to remove a child: 6.4 C. 2. is applicable in all cases, while 6.4 C. 3. applies a special rule for cases where the child is endangered by environmental conditions beyond his/her parents' control.

Subsection C. 2. does not require a comparison of the relative merits of the parental home versus some type of foster home. It only requires that a court, after finding that a child cannot be protected in his/her own home, also must find that there is a placement, *that is in fact available*, in which the child can be protected from further harm.

At present children often are removed on the assumption that they will receive a foster home or a residential treatment placement, but these placements fail to materialize. As a result, many children spend weeks, months, or even their entire placement period in institutions which can't provide for any of their needs. In some cases the child may even be physically injured in the institution. Even when gross harm is avoided, inadequate institutions or foster homes may cause severe emotional damage to the child, damage at least as great as would have occurred if the child had been left at home.

In some instances the threat of substantial harm at home, for example, severe physical abuse, may be so great that the court will have to assume that any placement is better than leaving the child at home. However, when the nature of the harm is not as severe, a court should not order placement unless an adequate foster home or other treatment facility is actually available for that child. This requirement is especially critical for cases involving emotionally damaged or sexually abused children who are placed in order to provide them with treatment for emotional problems. The court should consider carefully whether an environment is available that will be conducive to the child's mental health.

Subsection C. 3. reflects that value judgment previously discussed, see commentary to Standard 2.1 *infra*, that the state should not use endangerment laws to protect children who are endangered only because the state has failed to provide their families with adequate food, housing, or a safe neighborhood in which to live. Although, as discussed in the commentary to Standard 2.1, coercive intervention may sometimes be needed in such situations (since it may be the only way to provide the family with services or income), subsection C. 3. specifies that regardless of the danger to the children, removal may not be utilized in such cases. This reflects the judgment that it is wrong for the law to permit thousands of dollars a year to be spent on placement of a child when that same amount, provided to his/her family, would enable the family to provide adequate care and protection for the child.

The type of problem to which this subsection applies has arisen, in recent years, in New York City and other large urban areas. For example, because of housing shortages some families live in condemned buildings, buildings sufficiently unsafe that the child comes within Standard 2.1 B. In many instances, however, the parent would like to move and provide safe housing but there is no public housing, or other affordable housing, available. The standards would allow coercive intervention—as a last resort means of providing services—but would forbid removal.

Finally, it must be stressed again that in ordering any disposition, including removal, the court should be cognizant of the child's cultural background and heritage and should choose a disposition which will allow the child to continue these identifications. Every effort should be made to place a child with relatives or other adults who have been significant in the child's life. If this is not possible, placement should be with foster parents of the same ethnic or cultural background as the child, or if this is not possible, with foster parents trained to understand, respect, and encourage the child's identification with that cultural heritage.

To accomplish such placements, each state should review its foster home licensing standards and practices to be certain that they do not discriminate against minority group applicants. In addition, relatives should be compensated at the same rate as nonrelated foster parents. At present relatives receive a much smaller amount which prevents many poorer families from taking custody even though placement with the relative would be beneficial to the child. This practice may be unconstitutional, as well as poor policy.

6.5 Initial plans.

A. Children left in their own home.

Whenever a child is left in his/her own home, the agency should develop with the parents a specific plan, detailing any changes in parental behavior or home conditions that must be made in order for the child not to be endangered. The plan should also specify the services that will be provided to the parent and/or the child to insure that the child will not be endangered. If there is a dispute regarding any aspect of the plan, final resolution should be by the court.

B. Children removed from their homes.

Before a child is ordered removed from his/her home, the agency charged with his/her care should provide the court with a specific plan as to where the child will be placed, what steps will be taken to return the child home, and what actions the agency will take to maintain parent-child ties. Whenever possible, this plan should be developed in consultation with the parents, who should be encouraged to help in the placement. If there is a dispute regarding any aspect of the plan, final resolution should be by the court.

1. The plan should specify what services the parents will receive in order to enable them to resume custody and what actions the parents must take in order to resume custody.

2. The plan should provide for the maximum parent-child contact possible, unless the court finds that visitation should be limited because it will be seriously detrimental to the child.

3. A child generally should be placed as close to home as possible, preferably in his/her own neighborhood, unless the court finds that placement at a greater distance is necessary to promote the child's well-being. In the absence of good cause to the contrary, preference should be given to a placement with the child's relatives.

Commentary

Perhaps the most consistent criticism of the present system focuses on the lack of planning about a child's future after a court assumes jurisdiction. In both cases of removal and of home supervision those plans that do exist are vague and the goals ill defined. The problem is especially acute when a child is removed from his/her home. As a recent study of one state's agencies concluded:

> The conclusion must be reached that for a substantial proportion of caseworkers foster care practice is not goal-oriented but oriented to maintenance of existing arrangements as a status quo. It is a practice of drift characterized by inertia, inactivity except in crisis, indecisiveness about goals or probable direction, discrepancy between goals and activity, and an unwillingness to make decisions and judgments about evidence that would rule out unacceptable alternatives and move toward justifiable ones. Regional Research Institute for Human Services, *Barriers to Planning for Children in Foster Care: A Summary* 15 (School of Social Work, Portland State University, Feb. 1976).

Many of the problems in planning stem from large caseloads, high worker turnover, and inadequate resources. However, inadequate funding and insufficient resources do not account for the entire problem. It is essential that agencies follow sound planning principles regardless of caseload size or available resources. See Gambrill and Wiltse, "Foster Care: Prescriptions for Change," 32 *Public Welfare* 39 (Summer 1974); Stein, Gambrill and Wiltse, "Foster Care: The Use of Contracts," 32 *Public Welfare* 20 (Fall 1974); *Barriers to Planning for Children in Foster Care, supra.* The absence of adequate planning has resulted in a number of problems. When the child is left at home, failure to develop plans often delays or thwarts the effective provision of services. It can also preclude sound evaluation of the intervention effort. As a result, home situations may not improve, the child may be reinjured, and removal becomes necessary. On the other hand, in some instances casework continues for years and years, at great public cost, with little benefit to the children and a substantial invasion of family privacy.

The absence of planning is even more detrimental when a child is removed from the home, since insufficient planning often means prolonged separations. Adequate planning is critical in a system designed to provide children with stable placements. For these reasons, Standard 6.5 requires that specific plans be developed in all cases where the court assumes jurisdiction. In general, these plans should be presented to the court at the time of the dispositional hearing, although in some cases, *if a child is not removed from his/her home*, they can be presented to the court within two weeks of the dispositional hearing. Such delay may be necessary to allow the parent to fully participate in the development of the plan.

Children left in their own home. When a child is left at home, the plan should focus on the services that will be provided to the parents and child and the measures that will be used to determine when supervision is no longer necessary. If protection of the child involves, for example, sending a homemaker or public health nurse into the home, or requires that the child be brought to a day care center each day, the plan should specify why these services are necessary, whether they are available, and who will be responsible for insuring that they are in fact provided.

The parent should be fully involved in the development of the plan. This should indicate to them that the proceedings are meant to be helpful, not punitive. It should also make them aware of what changes are needed before supervision will be terminated. The parent should also have the opportunity to object to any aspect of the proposed plan, such as a requirement that they engage in any specific type of therapy. The court is empowered to make the final determination in such instances.

Children removed from their homes. If the agency is recommending that a child be removed from the home, the initial plan should be required at the time of the dispositional hearing. This is essential since part of the plan will focus on the availability of a suitable placement for the child. No child should be removed unless an adequate placement, as defined in Standard 6.4 C., is available.

The central focus of the plan should be on the steps that will be taken to facilitate the return of the child as quickly as possible and on the means that will be utilized to maintain parent-child contact.

Too often under current practice, there is no direction or incentive for parents or agency to work towards return of the child. The court rarely, if ever, requires a plan and does not review the case to see what is being done. The pressures of agency workload, aggravated by inadequate staffing and financing, are such that as long as a child in placement raises no problems, he/she will not get any attention. Dealing with the parents may be time-consuming and, according to the agency's priorities, unproductive. If a child is not having difficulty in placement, the agency may consider it to be in the child's "best interest" to remain in placement, even if the child would now be safe in his/her own home. Therefore, no effort is made to work towards return. The financial considerations of agencies involved in placements should not be allowed to encourage continued placement. To be consistent with the underlying goals of these standards— that children's interests are generally best served by assuring them a continuous safe home with their parents—it is imperative that any plan for removal include clear commitments by parents and agency to take the necessary action to return the child to a safe home. See *Barriers to Planning for Children in Foster Care, supra.*

To accomplish the goal of returning children whenever possible, the standard requires that the plan contain at least three features. First, the plan itself should identify those changes in parental behavior, home conditions, or the child's condition which must occur in order for the child to be returned. In this way the parents will know what they are expected to do and the social worker in charge of the case will know the goals of casework in the specific case.

Equally important, the plan should identify the specific services that will be provided to the parents to help them regain custody. In this way the parents are informed of what services they may expect, so that they can complain to the court if these services are not in fact being provided. Moreover, the court should know what services are in fact available and will be provided before it decides whether to place a child. The court should not abdicate its responsibility to see that the purposes of placement are served. Judges must be forced to realistically assess the likelihood that removal will accomplish its goals.

Whenever possible, the parents should be encouraged to participate in the placement plans. Of course, many parents will be contesting placement and may not be cooperative. However, if the parents do participate, they may be able to identify special needs of the child and may even be able to suggest nearby relatives or friends with whom the child can be placed. Again, requesting their participation will demonstrate that this procedure is designed to be supportive and therapeutic, not punitive. In addition, the parents are more likely to wholeheartedly participate in a program that incorporates some of their wishes.

Second, the standard requires agencies to encourage and facilitate maximum parent-child contact following removal, unless the court finds that contact should be limited because it will be seriously detrimental to the child. At present parental visitation of children in foster care is often minimal, averaging less than one contact per month. In some cases this reflects parental disinterest. More often, however, parents are either forbidden to visit or they are discouraged from doing so by agency policies limiting time and place of visits, or by social workers. See A. Gruber, *Foster Home Care in Massachusetts* 50 (1973). Rarely are parents encouraged to visit and aided in doing so.

Policies forbidding or restricting visitation are extremely detrimental. Visitation serves a number of important functions. It minimizes the child's feelings of abandonment, maintains parent-child attachments, maximizes continuity, and provides an opportunity for the foster parents to obtain information that will help them deal with the inevitable hardships of foster care on the child. See J. Goldstein, A. Freud and A. Solnit, *Beyond the Best Interests of the Child* 40–41 (1973); American Public Welfare Association, *Standards for Foster Family Service Systems* 64, 67–75 (1975).

Most importantly, an extensive program of visitation forces parents to decide whether they really want to retain contact with and resume custody of the child. A recent study of 624 children placed in New York City found that the amount of parental visiting was the best predictor of whether the child eventually returned home. Fanshel, "Parental Visiting of Children in Foster Care: Key to Discharge?" 49 *Soc. Serv. Rev.* 493 (1975). Some parents do not want to resume custody, although they may be unable to face this reality. Agency staff workers may be reluctant to force the parents to face this decision. In some instances, the staff may sympathize with the parents and keep believing unrealistically that they eventually will resume custody. If the agency were to encourage and facilitate visitation, this would enable both the parents and the staff to assess realistically, and as quickly as possible, the likelihood of return.

Parental participation should not be limited to visiting. After placement, they should be encouraged to participate in the child's care by, for example, buying him/her clothing, taking him/her to doctor's appointments, and participating in school affairs. This would help maintain parent-child ties, keep up parental interest, and allow the supervising agency to assess the parents' competence to resume custody. Adoption of such procedures would be a drastic change for most agencies. But only through such changes can agency policy be reoriented toward reuniting families.

Finally, the standard provides that the child should generally be placed as close to home as possible. This proposal also is contrary to established practice in many agencies. Children are often placed out of county and even out of state. This is sometimes necessary because of the shortage of foster homes or the special needs of the child. However, absent such considerations, the child should be placed in his/her own neighborhood, since this will help limit the trauma of removal by assuring continuity and stability of some aspects of the child's life. Moreover, proximity to the parents will increase their opportunity to visit and to participate meaningfully in the child's care and development.

In order to make such placements, it may be necessary to change foster home licensing laws, which often discriminate against applicants because their housing is considered "inadequate," to provide higher compensation and status to foster parents so that more people will apply, and to provide the same compensation to relatives who become foster parents as to nonrelatives. Standard 6.5 B. 3. states a preference for placement with relatives, if it is feasible.

In some cases, the plan also might provide for the training of the foster parents in parenting and other necessary skills.

6.6 Rights of parents, custodians, and children following removal.

A. All placements are for a temporary period. Every effort should be made to facilitate the return of the child as quickly as possible.

B. When a child is removed from his/her home, his/her parents should retain the right to consent to major medical decisions, to the child's marriage, or to the child's joining the armed services, unless parental consent is not generally required for any of these decisions or the court finds that the parents' refusal to consent would be seriously detrimental to the child.

C. Depending on the child's age and maturity, the agency should also solicit and consider the child's participation in decisions regarding his/her care while in placement.

D. Unless a child is being returned to his/her parents, the child should not be removed from a foster home in which he/she has resided for at least one year without providing the foster parents with notice and an opportunity to be heard before a court. If the foster parents object to the removal and wish to continue to care for the child, the child should not be removed when the removal would be detrimental to the child's emotional well-being.

Commentary

This standard makes explicit the premise of the previous standards, *i.e.*, that foster care is designed to be temporary and that every effort should be made to return the child as quickly as possible. When this cannot be done, termination of parental rights may be appropriate. Standards for termination are provided in Part VIII. The reasons for making care temporary have been developed in the Commentary to Standards 1.6, 6.4 C., and 6.5.

The standard also specifies certain decisions about which the parent must be consulted when a child is in foster care. As stated in Standard 6.5, the goal should be to encourage parental participation in as many of the decisions regarding the child's care as possible. The specific areas singled out in this standard are those generally considered the minimum "residual rights" parents retain when a child is removed from their custody. See United States Children's Bureau Standards, *Legislative Guides for the Termination of Parental Rights and Responsibilities and the Adoption of Children* 3–4 (1961). However, these rights should not be absolute. First, a state may decide that a child of a given age can marry, join the Army, or consent to some or all aspects of medical care without parental permission. Standards for when children should be given these rights are contained in the *Rights of Minors* volume.

In addition, Standard 6.6 B. provides that a court can dispense with parental permission if it finds that the parents' refusal to consent will be seriously detrimental to the child. This situation will probably arise mostly in medical care cases. In such cases the court should be guided by Standard 2.1 E. and commentary.

Standard 6.6 C. provides that the child, as well as the parents, should be consulted about these and other major decisions regarding his/her care while in placement. Obviously, the amount of consultation will vary with the child's age and maturity. Teenagers should be given a substantial say about such things as whether they want to live in a particular placement, while five-year-olds would have considerably less say, although they should be told about all major decisions and provided with an opportunity to express their feelings and anxieties. Regardless of the child's age, however, it must be recognized that children are not pawns who can be moved about for bureaucratic reasons. Their needs and desires should be the central focus of foster care policy and activities.

Standard 6.6 D. provides for foster parents to acquire procedural and substantive rights to the custody of their foster child after one year of custody unless the child is being returned. This significant provision constitutes an attempt to overcome the greatest defect— instability—in long-term foster care and at the same time to consider the rights of natural parents.

Courts and commentators have long noted the excessive movement of children within the foster care system. *Smith v. Organization of Foster Families for Equality and Reform*, 431 U.S. 816 (1977); Wald, "State Intervention on Behalf of 'Neglected' Children," 28 *Stan. L. Rev.* 623, 645–646 (1976); Mnookin, "Foster-Care—In Whose Best Interest?" 43 *Harv. Educ. Rev.* 599, 625–626; Fanshel, "Status Changes of Children in Foster Care," 55 *Child Welfare* 143 (1976); D. Fanshel and E. B. Shinn, *Children in Foster Care: A Longitudinal Investigation* (1978). Multiple placements are particularly harmful. Having already been separated from their parents, foster children are more vulnerable to the destructiveness of the parent-child relationship. Each move further destroys the continuity and stability necessary for a child to develop in a healthy and happy manner. See, *e.g.*, J. Goldstein, A. Freud, and A. Solnit, *Beyond the Best Interests of the Child* (1973); J. Bowlby, *Attachment and Loss*, Vol. II, *Separation* (1973).

Many of the removals of children from foster homes are caused by the agencies despite the objection of the foster parents. Wald, "State Intervention on Behalf of 'Neglected' Children: A Search for Realistic Standards," 27 *Stan. L. Rev.* 985, 944 (1975); Mnookin, *supra*, 43 *Harv. Educ. Rev.* at 612; Katz, "Foster Parents Versus Agencies: A Case Study in the Judicial Application of 'The Best Interests of the Child' Doctrine," 65 *Mich. L. Rev.* 145 (1969). Because of the instability of foster care, a number of commentators have recommended shortening the time within which parental rights may be terminated elsewhere. This is too drastic a remedy. More importantly, it is an unnecessary remedy. Relative stability can be obtained without any cost to the natural parents by providing to foster parents substantive rights to the care of their foster children. These rights are not as broad as those of natural parents. But they would make significant inroads into the unfettered discretion presently exercised by foster care agencies. See, *e.g.*, *Drummond v. Fulton County Department of Family and Children's Services*, 563 F.2d 1200 (5th Cir. 1977), *cert. denied*, 436 U.S. 908 (1978). The court would be able to monitor the placement through the procedures set forth in Part VII. If the agency sought to move the child out of a suitable foster home, the foster parent would have standing and substantive grounds upon which to object.

PART VII: MONITORING OF CHILDREN UNDER COURT SUPERVISION AND TERMINATION OF SUPERVISION

7.1 Periodic court reviews.

The status of all children under court supervision should be reviewed by the court in a formal hearing held at least once every six months following the initial dispositional hearing. The court may also review a case, upon request of the grievance officer or any party, at any time prior to the six-month review. At least [fourteen] days prior to a review hearing, the agency workers in charge of providing services to the child and parents should submit to the court a supplemental report indicating the services offered to the parents and child, the impact of such services, and should make a dispositional recommendation. Copies of this report should go to all parties and their counsel. The parents, unless they are physically unable to do so, and a representative of the supervising agency, should be required to attend each six-month review hearing. The court may also require or permit the attendance of any other necessary persons.

Commentary

Virtually all experts agree that the present system of intervention is marked by a lack of planning and by a failure to provide services to parents and children following intervention. See commentary to Standard 6.3 *supra*. It is essential that this problem, especially critical when children are in foster care, be remedied. The intervention process must be designed to provide children with stable living situations within a reasonable time, from the child's perspective.

Currently, in most states the evaluation of the effects of intervention is left pretty much to the social welfare agency. Though parents or agency can request a court hearing, they rarely do. Only eighteen states require regular review but do not specify the purpose of the review. When hearings do occur, they are often ex parte, pro forma proceedings that rarely result in any changes. They may last only a few minutes or even seconds, with neither a caseworker nor parents present.

Standard 7.1 reflects the judgment that systematic planning and the achievement of the goals of intervention are best insured by requiring periodic court review of the status of all children under court supervision. The court retains ultimate responsibility for insuring the wellbeing of all children for whom it has ordered intervention.

It is clear that in order to ensure the effective implementation of the plans established at the time of intervention, some means of checking both agency and parental performance is needed. Review must be ongoing and begin as soon as intervention occurs. The longer the agency delays in working with the parents, the less likely the parents will be to respond to agency efforts. Moreover, it is necessary to discover inadequate casework as quickly as possible in order to minimize the length of the child's stay in foster care when he/she is placed.

Review could be done either administratively or by court. Proposals for periodic court reviews have been strongly opposed by some social workers, who believe that administrative review within the supervising agency is preferable. They claim that court reviews are unnecessary, time consuming, and threatening to the parents. They would eliminate such hearings or hold them only yearly or biennially.

However, internal agency review does not provide an adequate check on agency procedures. See Festinger, "The New York Court Review of Children in Foster Care," 54 *Child Welfare* 211, 243–44 (1975); Chappell, "Organizing Periodic Review in Foster Care: The South Carolina Story," 54 *Child Welfare* 477 (1975). When the parents are not receiving adequate services, court hearings provide a forum in which they and the child through his/her attorney can challenge the agency's inaction. A court review is superior to lodging a complaint with the agency, since parents likely will assume that the authorities within the agency will support the caseworker. Moreover, the presence of counsel at a court hearing may make it easier for parents to raise complaints about the agency.

Court review is particularly important if the child is in foster care. The hearing provides a mechanism for reviewing parental performance so that it can be determined whether they have shown an interest in resuming custody. At such hearings both the supervising agency and the child's attorney can document the parents' failure to work toward resuming custody. It is essential that parental noncooperation be documented as quickly as possible. Otherwise it will be difficult to obtain termination if and when this is necessary. In a number of cases, courts have refused to order termination because the judge sympathized with the claim that the agency had not provided parents with services, had discouraged visitation, or had made return difficult. See *Juvenile Department of Marion County v. Mack*, 12 Ore. App. 570, 507 P.2d 161 (1973).

The parents' perception in these cases may have been totally accurate. Even when the parents' claims are false, however, most agencies lack adequate records to prove that services were offered and refused. Rapid staff turnover often makes it impossible to find the social workers who can testify about their activities to help the parent.

A policy that denies termination because the parents were not offered services penalizes the child in order to protect the parent. The child has already been in care for some time before the termination hearing and may have become strongly attached to his/her foster parents. If, in fact, the parents have refused services, return is unlikely. Unfortunately, under the current system the case will be continued while the child remains in an uncertain placement. Regular court reviews would prevent such occurrences.

Third, court review may serve as an incentive to both the agency and the parents. Socialworkers will attempt to conform their behavior to the court's expectations in order to avoid criticism at review hearings. The realization that the court will review their conduct, and possibly terminate their parental rights, may induce parents to show greater interest in their children.

While annual reviews would be less costly and time consuming, a year is too long to leave a child in foster care without review. From the child's perspective, six months is a very long period away from home. Yet, agencies become accustomed to leaving children in care until the next court review. Therefore, quicker review is needed.

For all these reasons the standards strongly recommend requiring court hearings. The six month time frame established by Standard 7.1 sets the maximum allowable interval between judicial reviews. Any party may petition the court for earlier review. If the child in foster care can be safely returned home within a shorter period of time, for example, three months, such action is to be strongly encouraged. Review hearings should not be *pro forma* reviews. The standard directs that the status of each child in placement be carefully and thoroughly examined in a judicial hearing. All interested parties should be accorded the right to counsel and the admission of evidence should be governed by the rules applicable to civil cases. Standards 7.4 and 7.5 detail specific findings the court must make at the hearing.

The supervising agency should prepare a report detailing the actions it has taken and the current situation. If the child is in placement, and continued placement or termination of parental rights is being recommended, the report should specify the reasons for the recommendation. To insure that all parties have adequate time to consider the recommendation and to prepare a response when desired, these reports should be sent to all parties at least two weeks prior to the hearing.

In reviewing the progress made in each case, the court should be guided by the goals established in the initial plan. See Standard 6.5 *supra.*

7.2 Interim reports.

The agency charged with supervising a child in placement should be responsible for ensuring that all ordered services are provided. It should report to the court if it is unable to provide such services, for whatever reason. The agency may perform services other than those ordered, as necessitated by the case situation.

Commentary

This standard is designed to assure that the program developed to insure that a child will not be endangered again, or to facilitate returning a child from foster care, will be carried out as nearly as possible the way the court ordered, by placing specific responsibility on the agency to either do what it proposed or inform the court if it cannot. It requires the agency to report any major problems it is having in implementing the court-ordered plan.

If the agency is unsuccessful in implementing the plan, either because of inadequate resources or noncooperation by the parents or other agencies, reporting this to the court may generate court action to find additional resources, to order other agencies to provide services, or to resolve any problems with the parents. Moreover, outside review may push each worker into maximum effort on each case. In this way, progress towards the goal of terminating supervision or reuniting families will be disrupted as little as possible.

The agency should be required to assign a specific person to supervise the case. This will make it easier for the court to monitor the family's progress and will tell parents exactly who is responsible for helping them. Evidence from several states indicates that in many instances there is no worker assigned to a case, especially when the child is in foster care. The child may have a worker assigned to him/her, but no one may be providing services to the parent. In such situations the chances of reunion are minimal. See A. Gruber, *Foster Home Care in Massachusetts* 28–29, 50–52 (1973).

7.3 Grievance officers.

There should be available in every community, either within the agency supervising a child found endangered or in a separate agency, a position of grievance officer. This person should be available to receive complaints from any parent or child who feels he/she is not receiving the services ordered by the court. The court should inform the parents and the child and/or the child's counsel of the name of such officer, how to contact him/her, and the services the grievance officer can provide.

Commentary

While the adequacy of agency and parental actions will be reviewed at each review hearing, six months is too long to wait to remedy problems. Particularly if a child is in foster care, six months delay in remedying inadequate efforts to reunite the family will prolong the length of foster care and its attendant harms.

Therefore, some type of administrative review should be developed so that parents and children can receive help if they believe that they are not receiving the services ordered by the court or if there are any major problems regarding the foster care arrangement which cannot be satisfactorily resolved by the supervising agency. Standard 7.3 provides that each community establish some type of review body to perform this function.

The standard does not provide any details regarding the exact structure or functions of this review agency. A number of jurisdictions have been experimenting with different types of review boards—ombudsmen, grievance officers, community boards, child advocacy centers. See Rodham, "Children Under Law," 43 *Harv. Ed. Rev.* 487 (1973); Chappell, "Organizing Periodic Review in Foster Care: The South Carolina Story," 54 *Child Welfare* 477; Report of the Joint Commission on Mental Health of Children, "Crisis in Mental Health: Challenge for the 1970s," ch. 1 (1970). There are not enough data about the operation of any given system to justify mandating or recommending any one structure. Communities should experiment with different types of review bodies and evaluate their efficacy in promoting the overall goals of the intervention system.

7.4 Standard for termination of services when child not removed from home.

A. At each six-month review hearing of a case where the child has not been removed from his/her home, the court should establish on record whether the conditions still exist that required initial intervention. If not, the court should terminate jurisdiction.

B. If the conditions that require continued supervision still exist, the court should establish:

    1. what services have been provided to or offered to the parents;

    2. whether the parents are satisfied with the delivery of services;

    3. whether the agency is satisfied with the cooperation given to it by the parents;

    4. whether additional services should be ordered and when termination of supervision can be expected.

C. Court jurisdiction should terminate automatically eighteen months after the initial finding of jurisdiction, unless, pursuant to motion by any party, the court finds, following a formal hearing, that there is clear and convincing evidence that the child is still endangered or would be endangered if services are withdrawn.

Commentary

Standard 7.4 A. provides the substantive test for determining when court supervision should cease. Basically it requires that coercive intervention terminate when the reason for the initial intervention is no longer present, *i.e.*, the child is no longer endangered.

Under this standard, the court should not just routinely continue cases, but should require specific evidence that intervention is still required. While formal testimony is not mandated in every case, the court should ask the parents whether they believe services are still needed. If they do not, the agency should have to justify the need for continued intervention.

In showing the need for continued services, the agency or counsel for any of the parties should have to demonstrate that the conditions or factors that justified initial intervention still exist or that there is a substantial likelihood that the conditions or factors would reappear if the supervision or services being provided by the agency were withdrawn. While it is certainly true that in some cases a family will need continued support and/or therapy if it is to remain a viable unit, the court should make certain that services are not being extended solely because they would be useful, when they are not necessary to protect the child. In such cases if the parents want services to continue, they can be provided on a voluntary basis.

Standard 7.4 B. is designed to insure that if supervision is continued, the court is fully aware of whether its order regarding provision of services has been carried out. In addition, requiring specific findings on the parents' attitude toward the services affords the parents the opportunity to raise any complaints or problems they might be having. At present court hearings are often very perfunctory and the parties may be afraid to discuss issues not brought up by the judge.

The specific questions will also give the agency the opportunity to confront the parents with any deficiencies in cooperation with the agency. Finally, the court should make certain that all parties are agreed to the future steps that will be taken so that supervision can terminate.

Requiring these specific findings will undoubtedly increase the length of these hearings and add to the court's burdens. Sufficient judicial personnel is essential if these standards are to become operational. The added expense should be offset by a decrease in the length of time families remain under supervision. Hopefully, the hearings will result in more effective provision of services, thereby strengthening the families and limiting the need for future state involvement.

Under present law in the great majority of states, there is no maximum period of supervision once a court assumes jurisdiction. Generally, the case will remain "open" until the supervising agency requests that supervision be terminated.

Standard 7.4 C. provides that court jurisdiction terminate automatically after eighteen months unless one of the parties requests continued supervision and shows, at a formal hearing, that the child is still endangered or will be endangered if services stop. There is little reason to believe that services for a longer period are necessary in the vast majority of cases. Yet, in some places, agencies keep open cases for years. This may divert resources from more exigent cases, or may result in "inflated" caseload statistics where no services are in fact provided. Since supervision can constitute a substantial burden on the family, as well as a substantial public cost, there should be a maximum time limit after which it should automatically terminate.

However, there may be a small percent of cases where withdrawal of services would substantially endanger the child. Rather than requiring filing of a new petition, and invoking all the procedures connected with an initial adjudication, 7.4 C. provides that supervision can be continued beyond eighteen months if the agency files a formal request for continued supervision and demonstrates at the eighteen month review hearing that there is a clear and convincing need for continued services. However, the burden here is a higher one than at the six or twelve month review. At those hearings the agency only need show that there are substantial reasons for continued supervision. Standard 7.4 C. envisions a court finding essentially equivalent to an initial finding of endangerment for supervision to be continued.

7.5 Standard for return of children in placement.

A. Whenever a child is in foster care, the court should determine at each six-month review hearing whether the child can be returned home, and if not, whether parental rights should be terminated under the standards in Part VIII.

B. A child should be returned home unless the court finds by a preponderance of the evidence that the child will not be endangered, in the manner specified in Part II, if returned home. When a child is returned, casework supervision should continue for a period of six months, at which point there should be a hearing on the need for continued intervention as specified in Standard 7.4 A.

C. At each review hearing where the child is not returned home and parental rights are not terminated, the court should establish on the record:

1. what services have been provided to or offered to the parents to facilitate reunion;

2. whether the parents are satisfied with the services offered;

3. the extent to which the parents have visited the child and any reasons why visitation has not occurred or been infrequent;

4. whether the agency is satisfied with the cooperation given to it by the parents;

5. whether additional services are needed to facilitate the return of the child to his/her parents or guardians; if so, the court should order such services;

6. when return of the child can be expected.

D. If a child is not returned to his/her parents at such review hearing, and parental rights are not terminated, the court should advise the parents that termination of parental rights may occur at a proceeding initiated under the standards in Part VIII.

Commentary

Standard for return. As specified in Standard 7.1, the central goal of periodic court review is to return children home or to assure them another permanent placement, within a reasonable time period, from the child's perspective. Therefore, the possibility of return, and of termination, should be considered at each hearing. Standard 7.5 focuses on the substantive test for when to return a child. Standards for termination are proposed in Part VIII.

Most jurisdictions apply the "best interest" test to determine whether or not to return a child in placement. These standards provide a new test, making the test for return the same as that for removal, *i.e.*, whether the child can be protected adequately from the specific harm(s) justifying removal.

The issue is a close one, since a balancing test has more merit at this point than at initial disposition hearings, especially when a child is doing well in foster care. Despite the attractiveness of the "best interest" approach, the proposed test is preferable. First, if children are not returned because they are doing "well" in foster care, this may encourage foster parents and child care agencies to resist helping the natural parents resume custody. A foster parent who wanted to adopt would have great incentive to discourage efforts by the parents to retain contact with the child. They might also encourage the child to reject the parents, which can create conflict for the child resulting in emotional harm. In addition, social workers may have less incentive to work with the natural parents, especially if they believe that return home would be detrimental to the child, even if the home were "safe."

Second, choosing this standard enables parents who have demonstrated the willingness and capability to improve themselves and the home conditions to regain custody of their children. Even though foster care may be "better" than a poor but safe home, the standard set in 7.5 B. is more appropriate considering the goals of ensuring continuity, stability, and autonomy of families whenever possible and the limited purposes for which coercive intervention is justified.

Finally, no legislature has defined the specific factors a court should consider in measuring the child's wellbeing. The vagueness of current law may reflect legislative unwillingness to resolve the value judgments involved in defining "best interest." Even if a number of factors were specified, it might still be extremely difficult to determine whether improvement had occurred or whether the improvement was attributable to being in foster care. For some possible factors, like emotional wellbeing, there are no agreed upon measures. Other factors, like school performance, may be inapplicable in a given case if a child is too young to be in school. Moreover, the fact that a child's school performance or physical health improves while in placement does not necessarily mean that remaining in placement is in the child's best interest. Even if it is assumed that the improvement is attributable to the foster home, it would be impossible to tell how the child would perform with regard to any of these measures if returned home. While there is more information available after six months than at the time of initial placement, we still do not have the ability to assess the likely impact of one environment versus the other.

Application of the proposed standard also requires predictions. However, the determinations required are within the skills of courts and social welfare agencies. Persons who have treated the parents can provide their evaluation of the parents' readiness to resume custody. Safety of the home environment can be tested by returning the child gradually, with observation during the visits. On the basis of this and other information, the judge can decide if the child will be safe in the home, and if so, order his or her return.

Comparing this determination with the problems of deciding whether return is in an individual child's best interest demonstrates the improvement these standards would be over the current system.

Some courts have been attracted to the best interest test by cases in which the issue of return arose after the child had been in care many years, usually in the same foster home. See *Stapleton v. Dauphin County Child Care Service*, 228 Pa. Super. 371, 324 A.2d 562 (1974). Not surprisingly, judges are reluctant to return a child to natural parents who have not had custody for many years just because the child will not be physically beaten or sexually abused if returned. They recognize that in most such situations the foster parents are the child's "psychological parents." See J. Goldstein, A. Freud and A. Solnit, *Beyond the Best Interests of the Child* (1973).

Adopting the same standard for return as for initial removal will result in returning some children who are doing well in foster care. Even though their wellbeing may deteriorate at home, that cost is outweighed by the benefit of making foster care truly temporary. As a result, the best decision, from each child's perspective, cannot be made in every case. The best we can hope for is a system that promotes the best interest of most children.

Burden of proof. The burden of proof question is critical in the return decision process. Because the substantive standard—whether the child can be protected from harm upon return—requires a prediction about the likelihood of future endangerment, conclusive evidence cannot be produced by either the parents seeking return or the agency opposing it. Given the difficulty of making such predictions with a high degree of certainty, placement of the burden will be determinative in many cases.

The standards place the burden on the agency. To the extent that implications about future harm can be raised, the agency clearly has greater access to pertinent information and the greater ability to persuade the court. For example, the agency can show that the parents have not cooperated with a treatment program, have not shown an interest in the child, or have failed to care for other children in the home. It can also produce expert testimony indicating that because of a mental condition, alcoholism, or some other problem, the parents probably will endanger the child again. Given such evidence, a judge is unlikely to return the child.

While the parents cannot prove that the home environment will be safe until they have resumed custody, the agency can test the safety of the home environment by returning the child home on a gradual basis, starting with one-day visits and progressing to visits of several days before a final decision is made. The caseworker can observe the parent-child interaction during these visits to determine whether the child can be protected. Of course, parents will act differently under such conditions, but such procedures should uncover homes that remain clearly dangerous.

When a child is returned home, supervision of the family should be mandatory for at least six months, in order to insure that the child is not endangered again. At that point the case should be reviewed on the need for continued supervision, applying Standard 7.4 regarding cases where children are at home.

Children not returned. Standard 7.5 C. lists the specific issues on which the court must make findings if a child is not returned home at a review hearing. The reasons for requiring specific findings are basically the same as those discussed in the commentary to 7.4 B. The court needs the information specified in 7.5 C. in order to make a realistic assessment of the likelihood of return and to make a meaningful decision about the care of the child for the next six months. If services have been offered and accepted, and everyone is satisfied with them, it may be simply that the changes necessary before the child can be safely returned just take time, and a continuation of the current program would be appropriate. If the parents have visited often and participated conscientiously in the care of the child, but have not participated in the services or counseling offered, perhaps changes in that aspect of the program can be ordered.

Court reviews should not be limited to these issues. However, the specific questions posed in the standard provide the basic information any court would need to make sound planning decisions for the child's future.

Warnings as to termination. The final part of this standard is the requirement that the court explain to the parents that the child must have a permanent home.

Perhaps the warning may supply some incentive to participate more fully in the programs available to facilitate reunion if that has been the reason for slow progress. It also makes it clear to the parents that the child's needs will be met first, and if they continue to be unable to protect their child, even through no fault of their own, they must bear the brunt of their problems, and the court will still protect the child if termination of parental rights becomes necessary under the standards proposed in Part VIII.

PART VIII: TERMINATION OF PARENTAL RIGHTS*

8.1 Court proceedings.

Each jurisdiction should provide by law that the filing of a written petition giving the parents and the child adequate notice of the basis upon which termination of parental rights is sought is a requisite to a proceeding to terminate parental rights.

Commentary

All terminations of parental rights, voluntary and involuntary, should occur in accordance with court proceedings, initiated for that express purpose and not as an incidental outcome of other judicial or nonjudicial inquiries. The seriousness of the event compels adherence to formal procedural requirements.

8.2 Voluntary termination (relinquishment).

A. The court may terminate parental rights based on the consent of the parents upon a petition duly presented. The petitioner may be either the parents or an agency that has custody of the child. Such a petition may not be filed until at least seventy-two hours after the child's birth.

B. The court should accept a relinquishment or voluntary consent to termination of parental rights only if:

1. The parents appear personally before the court in a hearing that should be recorded pursuant to Standard 5.3 C. The court should address the parents and determine that the parents' consent to the termination of parental rights is the product of a voluntary decision. The court should address the parents in language calculated to communicate effectively with the parents and determine:

---

*Robert Burt and Michael Wald were not the reporters for this revised edition. Martin Guggenheim was the special editor.

a. that the parents understand that they have the right to the custody of the child;

b. that the parents may lose the right to the custody of the child only in accordance with procedures set forth in Standard 8.3;

c. that relinquishment will result in the permanent termination of all legal relationship and control over the child; or

2. If the court finds that the parents are unable to appear in person at the hearing, the court may accept the written consent or relinquishment given before a judge of any court of record, accompanied by the judge's signed findings. These findings should recite that the judge questioned the parents and found that the consent was informed and voluntary.

C. If the court is satisfied that the parents voluntarily wish to terminate parental rights, the court should enter an interlocutory order of termination. Such order should not become final for at least thirty days, during which time the parents may, for any reason, revoke the consent. After thirty days, the provisions for an interlocutory order for termination of parental rights set forth in Standard 8.5 should apply.

D. Once an order has been made final, it should be reconsidered only upon a motion by or on behalf of the parents alleging that the parents' consent was obtained through fraud or duress. Such a motion should be filed no later than two years after a final order terminating parental rights has been issued by the court.

E. Regardless of the provisions of Standard 8.2 B. 1.–2., a court should not be authorized to order termination if any of the exceptions in Standard 8.4 are applicable.

Commentary

This standard requires that all voluntary terminations be approved by the court to ensure the knowing and uncoerced relinquishment by the parents of their parental rights. Because termination of the parent-child relationship is so drastic, all terminations, voluntary or involuntary, should be heard in a court. Parents should appear personally to be informed of the significance of the decision, to guard against overbearing pressures in favor of a voluntary surrender, and to make a record protecting the integrity of the decision to surrender if it should be attacked in the future. See Areen, "Intervention Between Parent and Child; A Reappraisal of the State's Role in Child Neglect and Abuses Cases," 63 *Geo. L.J.* 887, 992 (1975). Thus, a surrender in person can serve to protect the child and adoptive parents from challenge after the thirty-day revocation period has expired. Congress, in enacting the Indian Child Welfare Act of 1978, 25 U.S.C. §§ 1901–1963, has seen fit to require the personal court appearance of Indian parents who wish to surrender their parental rights. *Id*. at § 1913(a). The personal appearance of parents generally, however, is not required by state laws, even in model laws. See, *e.g.*, Katz, *Model Act to Free Children for Permanent Placement*, § 3.

Some would argue that requiring a personal appearance is unduly burdensome on the courts, the parents, and other personnel. Others claim it is unduly restrictive by failing to allow for exceptions.

An important exception to the requirement of personal appearance before the court accepting the surrender does exist. Where the personal appearance would be difficult or impossible, the court may accept the written consent of the parent, provided a personal appearance was made before *some* court. In order for this alternative to be available, the record must reflect that the court before which the surrender was made questioned the parent and found that the consent was an informed and voluntary act. It may be that there will be circumstances in which requiring the personal appearance will prevent surrender from occurring because of the difficulty in having the parent appear. Such cases might include parents who are hospitalized, institutionalized, or otherwise unavailable. Requirement of the mere ritual of an appearance may be unwise. On balance, however, a law requiring the personal appearance seems the wisest course. It properly accords the importance to the decision that the surrender represents. Permanent surrender of parental rights should require personal appearance as well.

Nevertheless, when this standard was revised by the executive committee, several members expressed concern over the inhibiting effect of formal court proceedings as a prerequisite to relinquishment of parental rights and suggested adding an informal alternative, such as the use of a court officer or referee to investigate and confirm the parents' informed consent. However, *Court Organization and Administration* Standard 3.2 requires that all judicial proceedings be heard by a judge and rejects the use of referees and nonjudicial personnel in general if the procedure entails a judicial process.

Surrender should not be allowed until the child is at least seventy-two hours old in order to ensure that the decision is not reached in haste and is not too close to the emotionally charged period of birth.

Subsection C. provides that parents may revoke within thirty days for any reason. If they do so, they should be given custody of the child upon the application to revoke. Subsection C. also makes voluntary termination subject to the one-year interlocutory order required in Standard 8.5 for all terminations, voluntary or involuntary. This provides an opportunity to review the child's circumstances and determine whether a suitable placement has been secured.

Finally, subsection D. allows a surrender to be attacked once the thirty-day period has expired only upon the ground that it was obtained through fraud or duress. See, 25 U.S.C. § 1913(d). Such a claim may be made only within two years of the final order terminating parental rights. There was some disagreement among the members of the executive committee with respect to the two-year time limit in Standard 8.2 D. Several members argued that this standard permitted excessive disturbance of an adoption or other permanent placement and should be reduced to six months. It was decided that the two-year period was necessary to allow for instances in which fraud is not discovered immediately because of the parents' absence, physical or mental condition, extreme youth, or other special circumstance.

8.3 Involuntary termination.

A. Court proceedings to terminate parental rights involuntarily.

No court should terminate parental rights without the consent of the parents except upon instituting a separate proceeding in juvenile court in accordance with the provisions set forth in this Part.

B. Procedure.

1. Written petition. The grounds for termination should be stated with specificity in the petition in accordance with the standards set forth in subsection C.

2. Petitioner. The following persons are eligible to file a petition under this Part:

a. an agency that has custody of a child;

b. either parent seeking termination with respect to the other parent;

c. a foster parent or guardian who has had continuous custody for at least eighteen months who alleges abandonment pursuant to Standard 8.3 C. 1. c. or a foster parent or guardian who has had continuous custody for at least three years who alleges any other basis for termination;

d. a guardian of the child's person, legal custodian, or the child's guardian ad litem appointed in a prior proceeding.

3. Prosecutor. Upon receipt of the petition, the appropriate prosecution official should examine it to determine its legal sufficiency. If the prosecutor determines that the petition is legally sufficient, it should be filed and signed by a person who has

personal knowledge of the facts or is informed of them and believes that they are true. All petitions should be countersigned and filed by the prosecutor. The prosecutor may refuse to file a petition only on the grounds of legal insufficiency.

4. Parties. The following should be parties to all proceedings to terminate parental rights:

a. the child;

b. the child's parents, guardians, custodian, and, if relevant, any other adults having substantial ties to the child who have been assuming the duties of the caretaking role;

c. the petitioner.

5. Service of summons and petition. Upon the filing of a petition, the clerk should issue a summons. The summons should direct the parties to appear before the court at a specified time and place for an initial appearance on the petition. A copy of the petition should be attached to the summons. Service of the summons with the petition should be made promptly upon the parents of the child. The summons should advise the parents of the purpose of the proceedings and of their right to counsel. Service of the summons and petition, if made personally, should be made at least twenty-four hours in advance of the first appearance. If, after reasonable effort, personal service is not made, the court may make an order providing for substituted service in the manner provided for substituted service in civil courts of record.

6. First appearance. At the first appearance, the court should provide the parents with a copy of the petition, including identification by name and association of the person submitting such petition, and inform the parents on the record of the following:

a. the nature and possible consequences of the proceedings;

b. the parents' and the child's right to representation by counsel at all stages of the proceeding regarding such petition, and their right to appointed counsel at public expense if they are unable to afford counsel;

c. their right to confront and cross-examine witnesses; and

d. their right to remain silent.

7. Appointment of counsel for child. Counsel should also be appointed at public expense to represent the child identified in the petition, as a part to the proceedings. No reimbursement should be sought from the parents or the child for the cost of such counsel, regardless of their financial resources.

8. Attendance at all proceedings. In all proceedings regarding the petition, the presence of the parents should be required, except that the proceedings may go forward without such presence

if the parents fail to appear after reasonable notification (including, without limitation, efforts by court-designated persons to contact the parents by telephone and visitation to the parents' last known address within the jurisdiction of the court). The child identified in such petition should attend such proceedings unless the court finds on motion of any party that the attendance of a child under the age of twelve years would be detrimental to the child.

If the parents or custodians named in the petition fail to attend, the court may proceed to the termination hearing. If counsel for the parent has already been assigned by the court or has entered a notice of appearance, he or she should participate in the hearing. If the parents or custodians named in the petition were not present at the hearing and appear thereafter and move the court for a rehearing, the court should grant the motion unless it finds that they willfully refused to appear at the hearing or that the rehearing would be unjust because of the lapse of time since the hearing was held.

9. Interpreters. The court should appoint an interpreter or otherwise ensure that language barriers do not deprive the parents, child, witnesses, or other participants of the ability to understand and participate effectively in all stages of the proceedings.

10. Discovery. General civil rules of procedure, including discovery and pretrial practice, should be applicable to termination proceedings, provided, however, that after the filing of a petition, the court may cause any person within its jurisdiction, including the child and the parents, to be examined by a physician, psychiatrist, or psychologist when it appears that such an examination will be relevant to a proper determination of the charges. A party's willful and unexcused failure to comply with a lawful discovery order may be dealt with pursuant to the general civil rules of discovery, including the power of contempt. Except as otherwise provided, the standards governing disclosure of matters in connection with proceedings under this Part should be the same for the child and the parents as for the respondent in delinquency cases, as set out in the *Pretrial Court Proceedings* volume.

11. Appointment of independent experts. Any party to the proceeding may petition the court for appointment of experts, at public expense, for independent evaluation of the matter before the court. The court should grant such petition unless it finds the expert is unnecessary.

12. Subpoenas. Upon request of any party, a subpoena should be issued by the court (or its clerk), commanding the attendance

and testimony of any person at any proceeding conducted pursuant to this Part, or commanding the production of documents for use in any such proceeding.

13. Public access to adjudication proceedings. The court should honor any request by the parents or child that specified members of the public be permitted to observe the hearing.

14. Burden of proof. The burden should rest on the petitioner to prove by clear and convincing evidence allegations sufficient to support the petition.

15. Evidence. Only legally relevant material and competent evidence, subject to cross-examination by all parties, may be admissible to the hearing, pursuant to the principles governing evidence in civil matters in the courts of general jurisdiction in the state.

16. Findings. If the trier of fact, after a hearing, determines that facts exist sufficient to terminate parental rights pursuant to the standards set out in Standard 8.3 C., the court should convene a dispositional hearing in accordance with Standard 8.5.

If the finder of fact determines that facts sufficient to terminate parental rights have not been established, the court should dismiss the petition.

C. Basis for involuntary termination.

Before entering an interlocutory order of termination of parental rights, a court, after a hearing, must find one or more of the following facts:

1. The child has been abandoned. For the purposes of this Part, a child has been abandoned when:

a. his/her parents have not cared for or contacted him/her, although the parents are physically able to do so, for a period of [sixty] days, and the parents have failed to secure a living arrangement for the child that assures the child protection from harm that would authorize a judicial declaration of endangerment pursuant to Standard 2.1;

b. he/she has been found to be endangered pursuant to Part V and has been in placement, and the parents for a period of more than one year have failed to maintain contact with the child although physically able to do so, notwithstanding the diligent efforts of the agency to encourage and strengthen the parental relationship; or

c. he/she has been in the custody of a third party without court order, or by court order pursuant to Standard 10.7, for a period of eighteen months, and the parents for a period of more than eighteen months have failed to maintain contact with the child although physically able and not prevented from doing so by the custodian.

2. The child has been removed from the parents previously under the test established in Standard 6.4 C., has been returned to his/her parents, has been found to be endangered a second time, requiring removal, has been out of the home for at least six months, and there is a substantial likelihood that sufficient legal justification to keep the child from being returned home, as specified in Standard 6.4 C., will continue to exist in the foreseeable future.

3. The child has been found to be endangered in the manner specified in Standard 2.1 A., more than six months earlier another child in the family had been found endangered under 2.1 A., the child has been out of the home for at least six months, and there is a substantial likelihood that sufficient legal justification to keep the child from being returned home, as specified in Standard 6.4 C., will continue to exist in the foreseeable future.

4. The child was found to be endangered pursuant to Standard 5.4, the child has been in placement for two or more years if under the age of three, or three or more years if over the age of three, the agency has fulfilled its obligations undertaken pursuant to Standard 6.5 B., and there is a substantial likelihood that sufficient legal justification to keep the child from being returned home, as specified in Standard 6.4 C., will continue to exist in the foreseeable future.

5. The child has been in the custody of a third party without court order, or by court order pursuant to Standard 10.7, for a period of three years, the third party wishes to adopt the child, and

    a. the parents do not want or are unable to accept custody at the present time;

    b. return of the child to the parents will cause the child to suffer serious and sustained emotional harm; or

    c. the child is twelve years or older and wants to be adopted.

6. The child has been in voluntary placement by court order pursuant to Standard 10.7 for a period of three years and

    a. the parents do not want or are unable to accept custody at the present time;

    b. return of the child to the parents will cause the child to suffer serious and sustained emotional harm; or

    c. the child is twelve years or older and wants to be adopted.

Commentary

The drastic remedy of terminating parental rights should only be accomplished in a separate judicial proceeding, upon a written petition providing the parent with adequate notice and an opportunity to be heard. Because of the special issues to be addressed in termination proceedings, these proceedings should be separate from other actions the court previously may have heard.

It is noted that, unlike every other proceeding, the termination procedures as prescribed in the standards do not provide for the screening of petitions prior to their being filed. Although the inclusion of an intake process would lend a symmetry to the termination process by bringing it into line with all other juvenile court proceedings, there does not appear to be sufficient justification for it. Termination proceedings may be initiated only in strictly defined circumstances in which intake's customary role of adjusting complaints or referring cases to community agencies would be superimposed on situations in which a child care agency already is involved. In all circumstances where termination may be sought, the child will have been living away from home for a substantial period of time. Therefore, the future of the child should be decided by the court without further delay. Except for the intake screening process, the procedure for termination of parental rights is the same as the standards for endangerment proceedings set forth in Part V.

Standard 8.3 B. 2. limits the capacity to commence a termination proceeding to the agency or persons who have actual custody of the child or to persons who have been legally designated as guardian to the child. This scheme is substantially identical to the Model Law recommended by Professor Sanford Katz. See Katz, *Freeing Children for Placement Through a Model Act,* § 8. Although restrictive in the type of person who may file in that the standard does not authorize a petition by "any interested person," it does empower any person in direct relationship with the child to file.

The first appearance procedure in Standard 8.3 B. 6. is substantially identical to Standard 5.2 C. in this volume. It is contemplated that waiver of counsel by parents would be extremely rare. Because termination is so drastic and because it involves a complicated legal issue, as a rule parents need counsel to represent them. Generally, if the parent opposes termination, it would be inconsistent to waive assignment of counsel. If the parent does not oppose termination, the provisions of Standard 8.2 apply. In such a case, counsel may not be necessary.

All parties, including children, are entitled to attend the proceedings under Standard 8.3 B. 8. Children over the age of twelve years have an absolute right to appear if they wish. Children under the age of twelve years may be excluded over their objection only when the court finds that attendance would be detrimental to them. Such a finding should not be presumed. By contrast, the Model Act for Freeing Children for Permanent Placement provides for the exclusion of a child of any age if the court finds that exclusion would be in the child's "best interest." Children of any age, and especially mature children, have a sufficiently great interest in the outcome of the proceedings to be entitled to attend in the vast majority of cases. In addition, this subsection provides that if the hearing is to proceed without the parents' presence, the attorney for the parents should nonetheless appear if he or she has already been assigned or has filed a notice of appearance. Counsel should assume that the parents oppose termination and at the hearing should oppose the termination on their behalf, compelling proof that the statutory bases for termination have been met. Counsel's appearance, however, is not designed to prejudice the parents' rights in any respect. If termination is ordered after a hearing at which the parents did not appear, a request for rehearing by the parents should not be denied lightly. It should be denied only if one or both of the grounds in the subsection are met. Absent unusual circumstances, at least one year should have passed before the lapse of time would render a rehearing unjust.

Standard 8.3 B. 14. adopts the clear and convincing standard as the quantum of proof instead of the beyond a reasonable doubt or the preponderance of the evidence standards. This follows the trends in both state and federal courts. See Katz, "Freeing Children for Permanent Placement Through a Model Act," 12 *Fam. L.Q.* 203, 240 (1978).

Standard 8.3 C. provides the substantive test for involuntary termination. Abandonment is prescribed as the first basis. All laws and model acts recognize abandonment as an appropriate basis to free children for adoption. Abandonment can occur in three different ways. First, if a parent leaves the child for sixty days without ensuring that he or she is adequately cared for, although able to do so, termination of parental rights is permissible. Note that abandonment under this basis does not require a court to judge the subjective intention of the parent. The standard focuses on the child and authorizes termination when the child was left without adequate provision for care for the requisite time period. The one aspect of parental conduct that must be examined is whether the parent was able to care or to arrange care for the child. Incarcerated or institutionalized parents could not be found to abandon their children under this test. They are unable to care or to arrange care for their children.

Second, where the child has been removed from the custody of the parent by court order and the parent has failed to maintain contact with the child for more than one year, termination is authorized if two conditions are met. The parent must be physically able to maintain contact *and* the agency must have diligently encouraged and attempted to strengthen the parent-child relationship. A number of states place on the agency the responsibility to make diligent efforts to encourage and strengthen the parental relationship.

Third, where the child has been in the custody of a third party without court order, or by court order pursuant to Standard 10.7, where the placement is with a child care agency, a parent must have maintained contact within an eighteen-month period if physically able and not prevented from doing so by the custodian. A longer period of time is utilized for this situation than for court-ordered placement since the separation was voluntary and not based on any harm to the child. In such a circumstance, the likelihood of the child being harmed by the separation is not as great. Moreover, the third-party custodian-child relationship is protected after one year against intervention by all parties other than the parent, pursuant to Standard 6.6 D.

Under Standard 8.3 C. 2., if a child has twice been found to be endangered and twice removed from the parent's custody, termination is permissible unless the child can be returned home after six months in care. This subsection is premised on the belief that the harm to the child involved in being twice separated involuntarily, combined with the probability of remaining in foster care for the foreseeable future, justifies authorization to terminate. This subsection is inexorably connected with Standards 7.5 and 6.4 C. Children must be returned home except when it is necessary to protect the child from the specific harms that justified removal in the first place. Thus, in this subsection and in subsections 3. and 4., termination is unauthorized unless the court finds that continued separation is the least restrictive alternative available to the court to protect the child from being endangered.

Subsection 3. also recognizes that multiple parental conduct resulting in harm to children justifies a shorter time period within which to free children for adoption. To invoke this subsection, however, the second abuse must have occurred at least six months after the first. This is to avoid a situation in which siblings were endangered at or near the same time. The period of six months has been used to give parents some time within which to have rehabilitated themselves.

Subsection 4. contains several important and related concepts. Termination is authorized for children who were involuntarily removed from the parents only if the following three conditions are met: 1. the child must have been separated from his or her parents for at least two years if under the age of three, or three years if over three; 2. the agency must have complied with Standard 6.5, which requires providing services to the parents with the goal of returning the child to the parents and allowing for maximum parent-child contact during the placement; and 3. the court must find that return to the parents in the near future is unlikely due to the continued presence of the causes of endangerment. The time periods in this subsection are critical. There is an explicit rejection of proposals that advocate termination after the child is out of the home for six months or one year. See, *e.g.*, Areen, "Intervention Between Parent and Child: A Reappraisal of the State's Role in Child Neglect and Abuse Cases," 63 *Geo. L.J.* 887, 937 (1975) (six months for children under two, twelve months for children over two); Wald, "State Intervention on Behalf of 'Neglected' Children: Standards for Removal of Children from Their Homes, Monitoring the Status of Children in Foster Care, and Termination of Parental Rights," 28 *Stan. L. Rev.* 623, 6590–91 (1976) (six months for children under three, twelve months for children over three); Ketchum and Babcock, "Statutory Standards for the Involuntary Termination of Parental Rights," 29 *Rutgers L. Rev.* 530, 555 (1976) (one year for all children); Katz, "Freeing Children for Permanent Placement Through a Model Act," 12 *Fam. L.Q.* 203, 217 (1978) (one year for all children).

This standard does adopt the recommendation of several commentators of having different time frames for children based on age. Being out of the home for six months and even one year, however, is simply too brief to warrant termination of parental rights. It is recognized that potential harm can result to children who are kept in limbo status too long. At the same time, keeping open the possibility of reuniting children and parents to the more realistic period of two or three years conforms to the thrust of the volume, which is to preserve the parent-child relationship, if possible. Commentators have argued that maintaining children in foster care for two years is "too long a period, since it increases the chances of multiple placements and decreases the possibility of adoption." Wald, *supra* at 690. Such an assessment, however, is based on current practice rather than on a system operating under the standards proposed in this volume. The standards include four critical features that render the model likely to bear different results from the present system.

First, the standards express a strong preference for keeping children with their families or reuniting them as quickly as possible. Second, the standards require agencies to work affirmatively toward maintaining the parent-child relationship and attempting to rehabilitate the parents in order to effectuate a reuniting. Third, the standards require periodic court review of children in foster care in order to monitor the agencies' responsibilities. (See Standard 7.1.) Fourth, the standards give a preference to foster parents who had custody of children for at least one year, except when children are being returned to their natural parents.

Among the harms to be avoided by excessively long foster care are: 1. interrupting a child's relationship with his/her primary attachment figure more than once by returning the child to the parents after there is no longer any psychological attachment to them; and 2. avoiding unnecessary, harmful separations caused by shifting children about from one foster home to another. Both of these problems would be mitigated in a scheme that adheres to the standards articulated in this volume. Regular and frequent visitation, monitored by courts, would do a great deal to keep alive the parent-child relationship so that reuniting the family could in no way be compared with placing the child with yet another stranger. See Maccoby and Masters, "Attachment and Dependency," 2 *Manual of Child Psychology* (P. Mussen, ed., 3rd ed., 1970). Additionally, giving to foster parents a preference over all third parties other than the parents to keep custody of children once they have been in their care for one year will sharply reduce the number of placements and disruptions in a child's life.

Current data indicate that once a child is in foster care longer than six months, the chances of returning home diminish considerably. D. Fanshel and E. B. Shinn, *Children in Foster Care: A Longitudinal Investigation* (1978); Maas, "Children in Long-Term Foster Care," 48 *Child Welfare* 321 (1969). But creating laws to compel that result by cutting off parental rights after six months would be a serious mistake. The probability of children in foster care returning home diminishes with time because of the notorious abuses of foster care as presently administered. Commentators and studies have long lamented the inadequate efforts by child care agencies to maintain contact between children and parents or to assist in reuniting the family. Visiting between parents and children is the most important method of ensuring that a relationship is maintained. Studies indicate that the likelihood of a child being returned is highly correlated to parental visiting. Fanshel, "Parental Visiting of Children in Foster Care: Key to Discharge?" 40 *Soc. Serv. Rev.* 493 (1975). Nevertheless, an important national study of foster care recently "found over and over again policies and practices that make it difficult, if not impossible, for parents to visit their children." Children's Defense Fund, *Children Without Homes* 22 (1978). At least one county actually has a policy of forbidding visitation. *Ibid.* With this reality, it is not surprising that children who remain in foster care for more than six months face a probability of not being returned. This must be corrected by creating a process that ensures that more children will be returned, not by ratifying the present problems and terminating parental rights.

In addition to maintaining contact, working directly with the parents to help them cope with the difficulties that led to their children being placed in foster care is a necessary condition to many children going home. In practice, this function generally is not pursued as part of foster care and rarely are parents provided with any services once their children are in placement. S. Vasaly, *Foster Care in Five States: A Synthesis and Analysis of Studies from Arizona, California, Iowa, Massachusetts and Vermont* (H.E.W., 1978); D. Shapiro, *Agencies and Foster Children* (1976). Yet there is no question that increased visitation and providing services to parents would result in significantly greater numbers of children being returned home. When proper efforts to reunite a family are made, many children who have been out of their homes for several years, even those traditionally regarded as unlikely to return and adoptable, can be returned to their parents safely. One recent study underscores this fact. A demonstration project in Oregon, titled "Freeing Children for Permanent Placement," provides dramatic evidence of the impact intensive services can provide. The project developed screening criteria to identify within the state foster care caseload children who were in unplanned long-term care. Over 2,200 cases were screened. Of the group screened, 509 children were selected for intensive casework on the basis that they represented children who had been in foster care longer than one year and were regarded by their caseworkers as likely candidates for adoption because of their small chance of being reunited with their own families. Within three years, 26 percent had been returned home after being assigned to project counselors charged with effectuating a permanent plan for each child. Children's Defense Fund, *Children Without Homes* 162–163. Other studies confirm this. D. Shapiro, *Agencies and Foster Children*

73-88 (1976); Jones, Neuman, and Shyne, *A Second Chance for Families: Evaluation of a Program to Reduce Foster Care* (Child Welfare League of America, 1976).

Current data support the conclusion that parents, even parents who have physically abused their children, can be provided with the skills and means to care adequately for their children. But such programs often take more than six months. Even under present law, empirical data indicate that many children removed from their parents because of abuse and neglect are being returned after more than six months, and after more than one year in foster care. See Wald, "State Intervention on Behalf of Neglected Children," 28 *Stan. L. Rev.* 623, 662 n.158 (1976). If foster parents were properly trained and if placement agencies were motivated to maximize contact between foster children and their natural parents while providing the latter with rehabilitative services, it is anticipated that children would not be seriously traumatized by remaining in foster care for periods longer than those allowed by the standards unless they are subjected to multiple foster placements. On the contrary, there is evidence that children can resume prior relationships without harm. Thus, even if the child has become attached to another "psychological parent," the child may be quite able to withstand the breaking of this attachment, especially if a new one is developed. Wald, *supra* at 670-671.

These standards recognize the importance to children of permanence in the planning of their lives. Accordingly, time limits should be set to allow them to be adopted. But limits cannot be so short as to be unrealistic and unfair. Limits should not be imposed to make it easier to terminate rights of parents who could adequately care for their children if assisted. Instead, there must be a standard that on the one hand protects children from too many disruptions and on the other protects both parents and children from avoidable terminations. To terminate parental rights under Standards 8.3 C. 1. b. and C. 4., the court must find that the agency complied with its statutory duties. This requirement properly focuses attention on the responsibilities of the agency to facilitate contacts and attempt to correct the conditions that led to the removal. Once the court is satisfied that the agency met its responsibilities, termination is authorized only if return to the parents in the near future appears unlikely.

The grounds for termination in Standard 8.3 C. 1. through 4. provoked the most discussion among the members of the executive committee in connection with the adoption of the revised standards. Several members criticized the language concerning the parent's failure to maintain contact with a child in placement because it seemed to permit a single telephone call or postcard within a year to block termination. The argument prevailed, however, that the courts would not construe so tenuous an act as complying with the clearly ongoing sense of "maintain." It also was contended that although the burden is on the agency to provide services to the family, the parents should be required to demonstrate their own diligent efforts to take actions to resume custody as described in Standard 6.5 B.

Another point of dispute was the requirement in Standard 8.3 C. 2. that even after a child has been found endangered a second time, parental rights cannot be terminated until the child has been out of the home for an additional six months. The minority argued that the child had suffered enough already to warrant termination. Nevertheless, the revised standard was deemed consistent with the principle that termination should be the last resort, after every reasonable effort at family reunification had failed. Finally, some members objected to the time periods in Standard 8.3 C. as too lengthy. Therefore, brackets were added to all time periods to make adoption of recommended periods discretionary with individual jurisdictions.

Standards 8.3 C. 5. and 6. address the most difficult issue regarding private or voluntary placements, *i.e.*, what should happen if the parents are not able to resume custody after a substantial period of time. The position adopted is that even where the child does not live in the parental home for reasons other than a court order after a finding of endangerment, permanent termination of parental rights may be appropriate when the child has been out of the house for a significant period of time. The length of time should not vary according to the financial ability of the parents, and thus an identical period exists for both private placements and voluntary placements with agencies. The critical distinction between these subsections and subsection 4. is that these subsections deal with presumptively fit parents. The necessary conditions to terminate parental rights of presumptively fit parents should be different from those authorizing termination of rights of parents who have been found to have endangered their children. Parents who have not lost custody of their children pursuant to a judicial order that the children are endangered should have an absolute right to the custody of their children within three years of a separation. Once the children have lived outside of the parental home for three years, however, termination of parental rights may be ordered over parental objection in certain circumstances. Three years has been chosen as the appropriate length of time after which termination is permissible. Parents must be given an adequate opportunity to become capable of resuming the care and custody of their children. Institutionalized or incarcerated parents should not be punished with the permanent loss of their children for at least three years. Balancing parental rights against the right of the custodian to adopt and the right of the child to a permanent relationship requires a recognition that at some point parental rights should be terminated. The parent can avoid termination by resuming custody at any time up to three years. After three years, termination is possible. The conditions under which it is possible differ for private placements with relatives or friends and a voluntary placement with a child care agency that has been ratified by the court in accordance with Standard 10.7. For private placements, termination may not be ordered unless the custodian wants to adopt and commences an action. Termination should never be ordered to punish the parent or out of a sense that parents have forfeited their rights to a child. Requiring custodial consent to adopt protects against this possibility. The desire of the custodian to adopt is a necessary but not sufficient condition to termination. In addition, one of the following conditions must be found. First, the parents do not want or are unable to accept custody at the time the action is brought. Consent for the adoption, *per se*, is not required. If the parents do not want custody, parental rights may be terminated over their objection. Second, even if the parents do want custody, return of the child will cause the child to suffer serious and sustained emotional harm. See, *e.g.*, *In re B.G.*, 11 Cal. 3d 679, 523 P.2d 244 (1974). If there is an insufficient parent-child emotional bond, termination may be ordered. Finally, even if return of the child to the parents will not be harmful, termination may be ordered if the child is over twelve years and wants to be adopted.

The difference in conditions between private and voluntary placements is that in voluntary placements the custodian need not want to adopt. This distinction is made because in the voluntary placement, unlike the private placement, the custodian may not have had custody of the child for long. Where the custodian has had custody for over one year and termination is sought after the child has been out of the parental home for three years, it is expected that a purpose of termination would be to permit adoption by the custodian. Pursuant to Standard 6.6 D., the custodian acquires substantive rights after one year and would ordinarily be permitted to adopt if desired. Even where the custodian does not want to adopt, the child is not permitted to drift indefinitely as a ward of the state. Pursuant to Standard 8.7, termination may not be ordered if it does not appear that an adoption will occur. In addition, if the child has not been adopted within one year after termination is ordered, the court may vacate its order and reinstate parental rights.

8.4 Situations in which termination should not be ordered.

Even if a child comes within the provisions of Standard 8.2 or 8.3, a court should not order termination if it finds by clear and convincing evidence that any of the following are applicable:

A. because of the closeness of the parent-child relationship, it would be detrimental to the child to terminate parental rights;

B. the child is placed with a relative who does not wish to adopt the child;

C. because of the nature of the child's problems, the child is placed in a residential treatment facility, and continuation of parental rights will not prevent finding the child a permanent family placement if the parents cannot resume custody when residential care is no longer needed;

D. the child cannot be placed permanently in a family environment and failure to terminate will not impair the child's opportunity for a permanent placement in a family setting;

E. a child over age ten objects to termination.

Commentary

It is necessary to recognize that in a number of situations termination is inappropriate. Standard 8.4 specifies five situations where termination would not serve the goals of providing stable placements and protecting the child's well-being. A court should not order termination whenever one of these exceptions is applicable.

Termination would be detrimental to the child due to the strength of the parent-child relationship. There is substantial clinical evidence that some children in foster care retain very strong ties to their natural parents. In fact, some children continually run away to their own homes or have to be removed from foster homes because they refuse to accept anyone in place of their own parents. Even where the child has accepted a foster home, he/she may still retain strong emotional ties to his/her natural parents. The number of children with substantial ties may increase if the standards designed to enhance parent-child contact are followed. Since termination in such situations is likely to be harmful to the child, courts should retain parental ties if desired by both the parents and child.

In every case where the parents have continued to visit the child but cannot resume custody, or where a child appears to retain strong family ties, a social agency should explore with the child the question of termination. Standard 8.4 E. provides that if a child age ten or over objects to termination, that should be conclusive. Younger children should not be given the power to block termination, although their wishes, as expressed in interviews with well-trained mental health professionals, should be given great weight in determining whether termination is detrimental. Psychologically, younger children may not be able to comprehend the implications of the termination issue. In addition, giving them the full responsibility for the decision may be harmful, since they may feel that they are deserting their parents. Therefore the court, with the aid of expert opinion, should determine whether a younger child's attachment to his/her parents is such that termination would be seriously detrimental to him/her.

The standard does not provide a formula for determining when a child's ties with his/her parents warrant continuing the relationship. The court should consider the child's age, the length of time the child lived with his/her parents, the strength of the child's attachment to the foster parents if they are willing to adopt, and the opinion of mental health experts who interviewed the child.

Children placed with relatives who are willing to provide permanent care but do not wish to adopt. It is common practice to place children with relatives. Relatives often are more committed to the child and more willing to accept a child who behaves badly or exhibits special problems. When a child is placed with a relative, termination is both unnecessary and unwise unless the relative wishes to adopt the child or is unwilling to provide long-term care. As long as the relative is willing to provide care until the parents can resume custody, the child's need for stability and attachment is satisfied. In fact, initiating termination might place the relative in the awkward position of having to act against the parents.

If the relative is willing to adopt, however, and supportive of termination, it is unlikely that the relative will work with the parents to resume custody or to facilitate parent-child contact. In such instances, the court should order termination and adoption by the relative.

Children who need special treatment. For the most part, children who must be removed as a result of endangerment proceedings can be, and should be, placed in foster family homes. However, in a minority of cases, placement of the child in a permanent family setting may not be possible, either initially or at all. For example, if a child is suffering severe physical or emotional damage or retardation, the best plan may be placement in a residential treatment center. It may be impossible to find a permanent home until the child's problems are treated, if ever. In addition, older children may prefer to live in a group home rather than in a family setting.

When a child is placed in a residential treatment facility, termination generally is not needed to ensure a stable placement or to prevent breaking any new attachments the child forms. Moreover, terminating parental rights might result in leaving a child without any parents if another permanent home cannot be found when he/she is ready to leave the residential treatment facility. Even if reunion with the parents is unlikely, and the parents visit only sporadically, it is preferable to encourage them to visit and maintain ties with the child, since the child may derive psychological benefit from knowing he/she does in fact have parents.

However, a child should not have to remain in institutional care indefinitely. If after a period of residential care, the child would benefit from a family setting, and his/her parents cannot or will not resume custody, it may be desirable to terminate parental rights at some point in order to facilitate permanent placement. At present, some children remain in institutions because their parents refuse to take them home or to agree to placement with another family. Therefore, the child's caseworker or the residential center should be able to request that the court order termination in order to facilitate permanent placement. If the court finds that the child should be removed from the treatment center, that return home is not possible, and that permanent placement is available, it should order termination.

Permanent family placement is unavailable. The need for residential treatment is not the only reason why children cannot or should not be placed permanently. Some children, especially those over ten, will not accept placement in a family setting or could not function well in one. It also may be very difficult to find permanent family homes for older children even if they could benefit from such a placement. Therefore, placement in a group home might be the preferable or only available placement.

If permanent placement is not feasible or desired by the child, there is no reason to terminate parental rights. The child might wish, at some later time, to live with his/her parents. Therefore the court should not order termination if the parents, or counsel for the child, demonstrate that permanent placement in a family setting is not desirable or feasible.

This exception must be applied very cautiously, however. Agencies often greatly underestimate the possibility of finding a permanent home for hard to place children. The exception is meant to apply only where foster family placement is opposed by the child or when there is substantial evidence that a permanent placement is unavailable. In the latter situation the court should be especially careful in each six-month review of the child's status to check that the agency is trying to find the child a permanent home.

In some instances permanent placement is unavailable because the foster parents cannot afford to adopt the child. The family may need the foster care income, or more likely, the free medical care provided to the child. This is especially true if the child is handicapped.

To prevent this situation, all states should adopt a "subsidized adoption" law. Several models are available. See, *e.g.*, Office of Child Development, Model Subsidized Adoption Act (HEW 1975). While no specific model is proposed in this volume, subsidized adoptions can provide financial savings as well as help assure children permanent homes.

Children ten and over. The final exception provides that termination should not be permissible when a child of ten objects to termination. The standard reflects the conviction that children should be given a substantial say in decisions affecting their lives, in accordance with their capacity to exercise judgment.

The choice of any particular age is somewhat arbitrary, since there is little psychological evidence available to guide one in making this choice. The specific choice of ten reflects the judgment that children of this age have sufficient maturity to understand the decision and probably desire control over such decisions. If a child this age opposes termination, he/she may defeat efforts to provide him/her a stable, permanent environment. In addition, it is considerably more difficult to find permanent homes for children over this age, so termination may deprive them of any "parents."

Other possible ages are twelve or fourteen, the two most common ages at which children now are given the right to consent to adoption, choose their own guardians, and choose a custodian in a divorce dispute.

8.5 Dispositional proceedings.

A. Predisposition report.

Upon a finding that facts exist sufficient to terminate parental rights, the court should order a complete predisposition report prepared by the probation department for the dispositional hearing. A copy of the report should be provided to each of the parties to the proceeding. The report should include:

1. the present physical, mental, and emotional conditions of the child and his/her parents, including the results of all medical, psychiatric, or psychological examinations of the child or of any parent whose relationship to the child is subject to termination;

2. the nature of all past and existing relationships among the child, his/her siblings, and his/her parents;

3. the proposed plan for the child;

4. the child's own preferences; and

5. any other facts pertinent to determining whether parental rights should be terminated.

B. Dispositional hearing.

A dispositional hearing should be held within [forty-five] days of the finding pursuant to Standard 8.3 B. 16. All parties to the proceedings should be able to participate in this hearing, and all matters relevant to the court's determination should be presented in evidence.

Commentary

As with all other volumes in the Juvenile Justice Standards series, proceedings to terminate parental rights are bifurcated into the fact-finding hearing and the dispositional hearing. If the court finds that, based on one of the grounds in Standard 8.3 C., it is authorized to terminate parental rights, a dispositional hearing should be held to determine the order the court should enter.

Standard 8.5 A. requires that the court obtain a detailed dispositional report before the dispositional hearing begins. The report should provide the court with the relevant information necessary to make an information decision.

Standard 8.5 B. requires that the hearing be held within forty-five days of the termination hearing.

Even if the court finds at the fact-finding hearing facts sufficient to order termination under the provisions of Standard 8.3 C., termination should not be granted if conditions prescribed in Standard 8.4 are present.

8.6 Interlocutory order for termination of parental rights; appeals.

A. If the court after a hearing finds that one or more of the bases exist pursuant to Standard 8.3 C. and that none of the bases in Standard 8.4 C. is applicable, it should enter an interlocutory order terminating parental rights. An interlocutory order terminating parental rights may be made final or vacated in accordance with the provisions in Standard 8.7 B.

B. Appeals. An appeal may be taken as of right from a court order entered pursuant to Standard 8.3 B. 16., 8.6, or 8.7. The standards governing appeals from proceedings under this Part should be the same as those set out in the *Appeals and Collateral Review* standards, except that the parties entitled to take an appeal under *Appeals and Collateral Review* Standard 2.2 should include the petitioner, pursuant to Standard 8.3 B. 2. and 4. above.

Commentary

Standard 8.6 A. provides that even when the grounds for termination exist and no basis exists not to order it, the court should enter only an interlocutory order terminating parental rights so that the court has the opportunity to review the current status of the child to determine whether the plan stated to the court in the dispositional hearing has been carried out.

In order to protect the rights and interests of the parents and children, subsection B. allows for an appeal to be taken from the interlocutory order entered pursuant to subsection A. Though nominally an interlocutory order, which normally would not be appealable as of right, an order terminating parental rights would be made final when the court is notified that the child has been adopted. Since the possibility of the child's adoption is beyond the control of the parents once an order terminating rights has been entered, the parents should be permitted to appeal as of right as soon as the court has ordered the termination.

8.7 Actions following termination.

A. When parental rights are terminated, a court should order the child placed for adoption, placed with legal guardians, or left in long-term foster care. Where possible, adoption is preferable. However, a child should not be removed from a foster home if the foster parents are unwilling or unable to adopt the child, but are willing to provide, and are capable of providing, the child with a permanent home, and the removal of the child from the physical custody of the foster parents would be detrimental to his/her emotional well-being because the child has substantial psychological ties to the foster parents.

B. When an adoption or guardianship has been perfected, the court should make its interlocutory order final and terminate its jurisdiction over the child. If some other long-term placement for the child has been made, the court should continue the hearing to a specific future date not more than one year after the date of the order of continued jurisdiction. After the hearing, the court should extend the interlocutory order to a specified date to permit further efforts to provide a permanent placement, or vacate the interlocutory order and restore parental rights to the child's parents.

Commentary

When parental rights are terminated, there are three ways of providing the child a permanent placement: adoption, guardianship, or permanent placement in a single foster home. In general, adoption is the preferred disposition, since it provides the child with the most stable family setting.

In some situations adoption may not be the best alternative, however. When a child is strongly attached to foster parents who are unable or unwilling for substantial reasons to adopt him/her, it may be preferable to leave the child with the foster parents, if they agree to become legal guardians or are willing to keep him/her until majority. Yet in most states, child care agencies routinely remove children from foster homes, regardless of the child's relationship to the foster parents, if an adoptive home is available.

Such policies are detrimental to children. Therefore, while there should be a statutory preference for adoption, bolstered by an adoption subsidy law so that foster parents are not economically precluded from adopting, the court should be authorized to order guardianship or permanent placement with foster parents. This disposition is appropriate, however, only if the foster parents are willing and able to provide the child with a stable and permanent environment, and removal of the child from the physical custody of his/her foster parents would be detrimental to the child.

The proposed standards do not require that an adoptive home be available prior to termination. This requirement, adhered to by many child care agencies, is an unwarranted barrier to termination in many instances. It means that some children are never freed for adoption because they are considered "hard to place." Yet this becomes a self-fulfilling prophecy, since many agencies will not place a child in an adoptive home unless he/she is "free" for adoption.

It is possible that following termination a permanent placement will fail, or perhaps not be found. To guard against this possibility, a guardian should be appointed for every child following termination until they are adopted or placed in a permanent family. In some cases it may even be appropriate to allow the natural parents to assume custody at some later point, if the child has not been placed permanently. In every case the court should review the child's status at least yearly until the child is either adopted or living with legal guardians.

Another innovative procedure which might be tried is to allow children to continue to maintain relationships and visit with siblings, and perhaps even parents, following permanent placement. These ties may be extremely important to the child, although the parents will never be able to resume custody and the siblings cannot be placed together.

PART IX: CRIMINAL LIABILITY FOR PARENTAL CONDUCT

9.1 Limiting criminal prosecutions.

Criminal prosecution for conduct that is the subject of a petition for court jurisdiction filed pursuant to these standards should be authorized only if the court in which such petition has been filed certifies that such prosecution will not unduly harm the interests of the child named in the petition.

Commentary

Under current law, two radically different kinds of sanctions can be invoked against a parent who harms his/her child: the parent can permanently lose custody of the child (or have some other response applied from the armamentarium of child protective laws); or the parent can be jailed (or have some other imposition from the penal laws). In these settings, the child protective and penal systems are both intended to serve two general goals—to protect children from harm by deterring or reforming misconduct, and to express community outrage at parental misconduct.

Child abuse is universally defined and punished as a crime under state laws. See Katz, "Child Neglect Laws in America," 9 *Fam. L. Q.* 1, 3, 4 (1975). Furthermore, the legislatures of four states (Arizona, Maryland, Mississippi, and Nevada) have created a new crime of "child abuse" or "cruelty to children," giving rise to criminal sanctions in addition to those already existing for assault, battery, and homicide. V. DeFrancis and C. Lucht, *Child Abuse Legislation in the 1970's*, 15, chart at 29 (1974). Sanctions for neglect, however, form a far less clear pattern among the several jurisdictions. Penalties for neglect are presently found in the criminal codes of thirteen jurisdictions, while civil penalties are included in the statutes of nineteen jurisdictions. Fines range from $50 to $1,000, and prison sentences from thirty days to five years for abandonment or resulting death. In most cases, both imposition of a fine and imprisonment are possible. See Katz, *supra* at 63.

Notwithstanding the almost universal existence of penal provisions supplementing the various dispositions possible under the child protective system, only the purpose of protecting children from harm is straightforwardly expressed in the statutes. Katz, *supra* at 17–19.

It is difficult to document the general or specific deterrent impact of penal laws against parental misconduct—though perhaps no more difficult to establish than for the deterrent impact of most criminal law sanctions. There are, however, special circumstances that should lead toward greater skepticism of the worth of penal sanctions for child protective purposes. First of all, invocation of imprisonment against a parent clearly works against the child's psychological interest in many ways—by removing the parent's physical presence which, no matter how abusive the parent's conduct, always has some deleterious consequence for the child; by imposing an added burden of guilt on the child beyond the irrationally magnified burden already carried by most (particularly younger) children harmed by their parents; and by fanning the parent's already smoldering anger at the child.

The question posed by an imposition of jail for parental misconduct, in short, is whether that parent should continue to have custody of the harmed child following his/her imprisonment. And if this question is posed in necessary tandem with the question of imprisonment, a further issue is thus raised: why shouldn't continued custody be the sole question raised by parental misconduct toward children? Where the child has died as a result of parental misconduct, the question of continued custody would obviously be moot (though the special problems of surviving siblings will be discussed later). But where the harmed child is alive, the question must be considered whether all of the purposes served by penal sanctions would be satisfied (and more attentively to the long-range interests of the child) by permitting invocation of sanctions drawn from child protective laws.

The failure of existing laws to ask that question harms the best interest of needy children. The current, overlapping regime of child protective and penal laws itself has a particularly exacerbating quality: each system is controlled by different personnel with different perspectives, and each system too readily may be invoked, without attention to the consequences for the other. Students of child abuse, for example, have noted that criminal laws against parents are only rarely invoked by prosecutors and such invocation appears triggered mostly by the extent of the newspaper coverage, and consequent public turmoil, about individual cases. See Terr and Watson, "The Battered Child Rebrutalized: Ten Cases of Medical-Legal Confusion," 124 *Am. J. Psychiatry* 1432 (1969). But though invocation of criminal sanctions is rare, the possibility of that invocation hangs heavy in every case in the minds of parents and of therapeutically oriented personnel attempting to work with, and build a trusting relationship with, parents in the future interests of their children. The problem of coordination could likely be solved by mandating case-by-case collaboration between prosecutors and child protective personnel. Mandating such collaboration obscures, however, the more fundamental question of the necessity and desirability for dual systems of sanctions for protecting children in any event.

While acknowledging that overlap between the criminal and child protective laws for the same parental conduct could have harmful consequences, the standard nonetheless looks to a case-by-case mediation of this conflict. It is considered important to maintain on the books, and in application to selected cases, criminal sanctions against outrageous abuses of parents against children. Harm to children, resulting from application of criminal sanctions to parents, could be adequately prevented if such sanctions were only possible when the court charged with the child protective function authorized such prosecution.

It can be argued to the contrary, however, that the pressures on the child protective court for invocation of criminal sanctions would be too strong—particularly in cases which fortuitously attract newspaper attention—and that all of the various legitimate purposes of the criminal sanction would be equally accomplished by sanctions available under child protective laws and the child would be better protected thereby. This position can be supported by the following arguments: that deterrence of future parental misconduct (generally or specifically) would be as much accomplished by invoking the possibility of permanent loss of child custody as by jail; that rehabilitative possibilities would be at least equally well served under the regime of child protective laws, and likely better served since persons with special therapeutic skills and sympathies would be more likely attracted to work in a child protective agency aegis; and that community outrage should, it seems, be equally satisfied, and the desires for the last measure of vengefulness through penal sanctions should be tempered by a realization that temporary separation of the child from his/her parent by jailing the parent will redound only to the greater harm of the child. It is true that, where a child dies as a result of parental misconduct and siblings remain living, those siblings will be injured by invocation of imprisonment against their parent (however much they also might need protection against that parent). But unfortunately, children are always harmed by separation from their parents when parents are jailed for harming the interests of other persons. Though principles of mercy might ask it, principles of equal treatment do not demand that surviving siblings have special claim on their murdering parent's company.

One further question must be addressed: that is, the definition of "parent." The social reality, of course, is that the "parenting function" is carried out by persons in widely divergent statuses; paramours may, for example, be more "psychological parents" than the absent biologic parent in a particular family unit. But for purposes of identifying parental misconduct which is properly subject only to child protective laws, it seems right to restrict this rubric only to "parents" who have a legally recognized right to custody of the child. The basic sanction under the child protective laws is the threat of loss of custody. Accordingly, other forms of adult-child relations must be subject to criminal law forums and sanctions, no matter how much out of step with the psychological reality of parent-child dynamic bonds in the individual case.

PART X: VOLUNTARY PLACEMENT

10.1 Definition.
For purposes of this Part, "voluntary placement" is any placement of a child under twelve years of age into foster care when the placement is made at the request of the child's parents and is made through a public or state supported private agency without any court involvement. This Part does not apply to placements in a state mental hospital or other residential facility for mentally ill or retarded children.

Commentary

The standards in this Part provide regulations for the "voluntary placement" process. Under existing law part of a parent's custodial rights includes the right to place the child in a living environment outside the natural parents' home. The range of such "placements" is enormous—from private schools to mental hospitals, from summer camps to foster family care with strangers. When these placements are made through a public agency, they are generally called "voluntary placements."

The standards are not meant to regulate all such placements. Obviously there are significant differences among them, although in many ways they all represent points on a continuum. The proposed standards are meant to apply only to placements into noninstitutional foster care, when the placement is made through a public or state supported private agency. Placements in private schools or placement of a child to live with relatives are excluded, unless there is state involvement. So are placements into state mental hospitals or residential institutions for mentally ill or severely retarded children.

Placements involving public support are singled out for three reasons. First, there is substantial evidence that some of these placements are made under coercion from welfare departments, which may threaten the parents with juvenile court proceedings if they do not place their child. See Levine, "Caveat Parens: A Demystification of the Child Protection System," 35 *U. Pitt. L. Rev.* 26–29 (1973); Campbell, "The Neglected Child: His and His Family's Treatment Under Massachusetts Law and Practice and Their Rights Under the Due Process Clause," 4 *Suff. U. L. Rev.* 649–51 (1970). Regulation is needed to prevent this. Second, there is also substantial evidence that as many as half of all voluntarily placed children are never reunited with their families, at least if they remain in care longer than six months. See Fanshel, "Status Changes of Children in Foster Care: Final Results of the Columbia University Longitudinal Study," 55 *Child Welfare* 143 (1976); A. Gruber, *Foster Home Care in Massachusetts* (1973); California Health & Welfare Agency, *Children in Foster Care* (Report Reg. No. 340-0395-501, 1974). Sometimes this is because the parents are not provided with services that would help them resume custody. Parents may even be discouraged from visiting or resuming custody. In other instances, the children are effectively abandoned by their parents. Many children are voluntarily placed by unmarried mothers who never assume any responsibility for them. These parents do not visit or maintain contact with their children. Regulation is needed to assure that such children are not left permanently in an unstable foster care situation. Finally, there is evidence that in some states welfare agencies make it difficult for parents to resume custody, even though the placement was voluntary. Regulations are needed to clarify parents' rights and to insure that they are fully aware of the consequences of a voluntary placement.

Placements in mental hospitals and similar facilities are not covered because there is now substantial doubt whether parents can place children in such institutions without court approval. Several courts have mandated full civil commitment procedures in such cases. See *Bartley v. Kremens*, 402 F. Supp. 1039 (1975), *cert. granted, Kremens v. Bartley*, 965 S. Ct. 558 (1976); *J. L. v. Parham*, 412 F. Supp. 112 (M.D. Ga. 1976). These standards adopt no position on the issues surrounding the placement of children into mental hospitals or similar facilities.

The standards are limited to placements of children under twelve. Placements of children twelve and over should require the child's consent.

These standards apply to placements made by both parents when they are living together or by the parent with legal custody if there is only one parent as a result of divorce, separation, death, or absence of the other parent. In such situations consent of the absent parent is not required.

10.2 Need for statutory regulation.

All states should adopt a statutory structure regulating voluntary placements.

Commentary

Although at least half the children in state-supported foster care are there through voluntary placements (as many as 150,000 children), only twenty-eight states currently have laws that in any way regulate such placements. Even in these states, most of the statutes contain virtually no guidelines regulating the placement process. The statutes generally consist only of one or two lines indicating that an agency may accept a child for placement upon the request of a parent.

Because voluntary placements substantially affect the legal rights and wellbeing of both parents and children, and because of the extensive evidence that the system is working improperly, see Wiltse and Gambrill, "Foster Care 1973: A Reappraisal," 32 *Public Welfare* 7 (Winter 1974); Gambrill and Wiltse, "Foster Care: Prescriptions for Change," 32 *Public Welfare* 39 (Summer 1974); commentary to Standard 10.1, *supra*, it is essential that the placement process be regulated by statute. If the system remains unregulated, it is clear that many thousands of children will be abandoned into the foster care system unnecessarily each year, at enormous financial expense to the public and emotional costs to the children and parents. The need for regulation has been recognized by many state agencies, standard setting groups, and expert commentators. See, *e.g.*, California Department of Health, "Regulations for Children in Out-of-Home Care" (Department of Health Manual 30-300 1975); American Public Welfare Association, "Standards for Foster Family Homes" XIX (1975); Gambrill and Wiltse, *supra*.

10.3 Preplacement inquiries.

Prior to accepting a child for voluntary placement, the agency worker should:

A. Explore fully with the parents the need for placement and the alternatives to placement of the child.

B. Prepare a social study on the need for placement; the study should explore alternatives to placement and elaborate the reasons why placement is necessary. However, a child may be placed prior to completion of the social study if the child would be endangered if left at home or the parents cannot care for the child at home even if provided with services.

C. Review with an agency supervisor the decision to place the child.

D. Determine that an adequate placement is in fact available for the child.

Commentary

The two most constant criticisms of the voluntary placement system are that many children are placed unnecessarily, since their parents would be able to retain custody if given adequate help in caring for the child, and that once children are placed they are left in care without sufficient effort to help their parents regain custody. Standard 10.3 provides a mechanism designed to insure that children are not placed unnecessarily. Standards 10.5–10.8 are designed to insure that when placement occurs, it will be for a temporary period.

All studies indicate that most placements are made at a time of parental crisis. See A. Gruber, *Foster Home Care in Massachusetts* (1973); S. Jenkins and M. Sauber, *Paths to Child Placement: Family Situations Prior to Foster Care* (1966). The reasons for placement can be divided into several categories. One group of parents places their children because they are unavailable to care for them. For example, a parent suffering from physical or mental illness who is about to enter a hospital, or a parent who is jailed may be unable to find anyone else to care for the children during the period they are out of the home. A second group consists of parents who feel unable to care for their children during a period of personal crisis. These include parents undergoing periods of severe marital conflict or severe financial difficulty, and parents who have recently lost a spouse due to divorce, separation, or death. A third group is composed of unmarried mothers, often teenaged, who place their children immediately upon or shortly after birth. Some of these mothers are uncertain whether they want the child; others expect that they will resume custody after they get a job, complete school, or establish a stable living situation. Finally, some parents place their children because the child is evidencing severe emotional, medical, or behavioral problems, and the parents feel unable to cope with the child at home. Often these parents request placement in a residential treatment center.

It is mostly the poor, especially poor single parents, who resort to voluntary placement. Parents living in poverty conditions often face the kinds of crises that lead to placement. They do not have the money to buy household help or relief from the burdens children can present. Faced with sudden illness or personal stress, they may have no relatives or friends able or willing to care for their children.

Because the parents seek placement at a time of crisis, they are generally unable to explore alternatives to placement. Yet a number of studies indicate that alternatives often exist. Provision of home-maker services, day care, crisis counseling, or short-term financial aid can help the parent through the crisis period without placement. See M. Jones, R. Neuman and A. Shyne, *A Second Chance for Families* (1976); Burt and Balyeat, "A New System for Improving the Care of Neglected and Abused Children," 53 *Child Welfare* 167 (1975); American Public Welfare Association, *Standards for Foster Family Systems* XVIII (1975). Avoiding placements spares both the child and parent the emotional trauma of separation. The child does not have to make the difficult adjustment to foster care. Moreover, provision of such services is considerably less expensive than providing services directly to the parent. Over 712 million dollars is now being spent annually to maintain children in foster care. See Subcomm. on Children & Youth of the Senate Comm. on Labor & Pub. Welfare, 94th Cong., 1st Sess., "Foster Care and Adoptions: Some Key Policy Issues" 2 (Comm. Print 1975) (prepared by P. Mott). It generally costs $400–$500 per month to maintain a child in foster care. Home services can be provided far less expensively. See D. Fanshel and E. Shinn, *Dollars and Sense in Foster Care* (1972); Burt and Balyeat, *supra.*

Therefore, Standard 10.3 requires that before accepting a child for placement, an agency should fully explore, itself and with the parents, the need for placement and alternatives to placement. To insure that this is done thoroughly, the standard provides that the agency worker should prepare a full social study on the need for placement, similar to the study provided for in Standard 6.1 B., *supra.* Such studies are now mandated in some states. See California Department of Health Manual, *supra.* To avoid the disparity in judgment common among workers, the decision to place the child should be approved by a supervisor. These reports will also be reviewed by the court if the child remains in care longer than six months. See Standard 10.7.

In most cases these reports should be prepared prior to placement. Emergency services can be provided to help the parents until the report is completed. If the child is in imminent danger, or the parent cannot continue custody or is in a hospital or jail, the report should be prepared within two weeks of accepting the child for placement.

Finally, the standard requires the agency to determine that there is an adequate placement available for the child. Frequently children are accepted for placement even though no foster family home is available. They may be forced to stay in an institution which may be worse for the child than the parents' home. See commentary to Standard 6.4 C. The parent should be fully apprised of the available placements and a child should not be accepted for placement if there is not a placement available adequate to protect his/her physical and emotional wellbeing.

In order to prevent unnecessary placements, it is essential that each community have adequate supportive services, such as homemakers, day care facilities, crisis intervention teams and even homes where the entire family can stay during a crisis. While development of these services entails a substantial initial investment, this is one case where these services should ultimately result in cost savings by reducing foster care costs. See D. Fanshel and E. Shinn, *supra*; M. Burt and L. Blair, *Options for Improving the Care of Neglected and Dependent Children* (1971).

10.4 Placement agreements.

When a child is accepted for placement, the agency should enter into a formal agreement with the parents specifying the rights and obligations of each party. The agreement should contain at least the following provisions:

A. a statement by the parents that the placement is completely voluntary on their part and not made under any threats or pressure from an agency;

B. a statement by the parents that they have discussed the need for placement, and alternatives to placement, with the agency worker and have concluded that they cannot care for their child at home;

C. notice that the parents may resume custody of their child within forty-eight hours of notifying the agency of their desire to do so;

D. a statement by the parents that they will maintain contact with the child while he/she is in placement;

E. a statement by the agency that it will provide the parents with services to enable them to resume custody of their child;

F. notification to the parents of the specific worker in charge of helping them resume custody and an agreement that the agency will inform the parents immediately if there is a change in workers assigned to them;

G. a statement that if the child remains in placement for longer than six months, the case will automatically be reviewed by the juvenile court, and that termination of parental rights might occur if the child remains in placement for eighteen months if the parents have failed to maintain contact or three years even if the parents have maintained contact.

Commentary

At present voluntary placement is often a very informal arrangement, with none of the rights and obligations of either the parents or agency specified at the time of placement. As a result, parents may be misled about the consequences of a placement. They may also be unaware of how they can resume custody of their child and what actions will be expected of them during placement. See Weiss and Chase, "The Case for Repeal of Section 383 of the New York Social Services Law," in "Legal Rights of Children," *Colum. J. of Human Rights and Social Welfare* (1973); Levine, "Caveat Parens: A Demystification of the Child Protection System," 35 *U. Pitt. L. Rev.* 26 (1973); Campbell, "The Neglected Child: His and His Family's Treatment Under Massachusetts Law and Practice and Their Rights Under the Due Process Clause," 4 *Suff. U. L. Rev.* 649 (1970).

Failure to adequately inform the parents of the consequences of placement may deprive them of substantial rights. Moreover, a formal placement is extremely important in insuring that the parents will remain actively involved with their child and work towards reunion. Although not currently required by law in most states, many agencies regularly enter into such agreements.

Use of formal placement agreements should not be left to agency discretion, however. These agreements should be mandated by statute. Standard 10.4 provides this mandate and also specifies the minimum contents of the agreement.

Subsection A. is intended to help prevent coercive "voluntary" placements. Before signing an agreement, the parents should be told that they have no obligation to do so and will not lose their children if they do not. If an agency believes the child is endangered, under the standards in Part II, it should file a petition with the court.

Subsection B. is designed to provide evidence that the agency has in fact explored alternatives with the parents.

Subsection C. makes clear that control of the child remains with the parent, not the agency. Some agencies discourage parents from visiting with or resuming custody of their children; in some states they may need a court order to resume custody even though the placement is voluntary. If we are going to allow parents the right to place their children, we should not discriminate against poor parents who need state help in making the placement. Obviously those parents who place a child without state help can reclaim the child any time. The same right should be afforded poorer parents. If the child is endangered, a juvenile court petition is the appropriate way to protect the child. If parents exercise their rights to resume custody pursuant to this subsection more than two times within a thirty-day period, the agency should refer the matter to the juvenile court.

Subsection D., in connection with the agreement specified in 10.6, is designed to insure that parents do not abandon their children through the voluntary placement process. The parents should commit themselves to retaining ties to the child. If they are unwilling to do so, the agency should file an endangerment petition. Having the commitment in writing is important, since if the parents later fail to retain ties and work towards reunion, the defense of lack of knowledge of their obligations will not be available in case of termination. See Standard 10.8.

As provided in 10.4 G., the possible consequences to the parent of not resuming custody, *i.e.*, court supervision and termination of parental rights, should be explicitly spelled out to the parents at the time of placement. While this may frighten some parents and discourage them from placing a child who needs placement, this cost must be borne if the child is to be guaranteed a permanent home after a reasonable period of time. It would be unfair to parents to institute court proceedings or to bring termination proceedings without having previously warned the parents of this possibility.

Subsections E. and F. should be included in order to inform the parents of the services they may expect and so that if court intervention becomes necessary after six months, the court can review the adequacy of the agency performance. See commentary to Standard 6.5 B.

10.5 Parental involvement in placement.

The agency should involve the parents and the child in the placement process to the maximum extent possible, including consulting with the parents and the child, if he/she is of sufficient maturity, in the choice of an appropriate placement, and should request the parents to participate in bringing the child to the new home or facility. Preference should be given to the placement of choice of the parents and the child, in the absence of good cause to the contrary.

Commentary

This standard specifies that the parents should be kept centrally involved with the child while he/she is in care. The reasons for this requirement are discussed in the Commentary to Standard 6.5 B. and 6.6 *supra*. See also Robertson and Robertson, "Young Children in Brief Separations: A Fresh Look," 26 *Psychoanalytic Study of the Child* 264 (1971); Goldstein, "Why Foster Care—For Whom, For How Long," 30 *Psychoanalytic Study of the Child* 647 (1975), which discuss the importance of parental participation in avoiding the trauma of separation. The right of parents to this participation is even clearer in the case of voluntary placements than after a finding of endangerment. If a parent needs to place a child voluntarily and has found a suitable prospective home for the child, that home should be used for the placement.

10.6 Written plans.

Within two weeks of accepting a child for placement, the agency and parents should develop a written plan describing the steps that will be taken by each to facilitate the quickest possible return of the child and to maximize parent-child contact during placement. The plan should contain at least the following elements:

A. provisions for maximum possible visitation;

B. a description of the specific services that will be provided by the agency to aid the parents;

C. a description of the specific changes in parental condition or home environment that are necessary in order for the parents to resume custody; and

D. provisions for helping the parents participate in the care of the child while he/she is in placement.

Commentary

This standard proposes that the agency conduct the same type of planning when a child enters care through voluntary placement as when a child is ordered into foster care by a juvenile court. All studies show that lack of planning results in long-term, impermanent care, regardless of the way children enter the foster care system. See Wiltse and Gambrill, "Foster Care 1973: A Reappraisal," 32 *Public Welfare* 7 (Winter 1974). For the reasons discussed in Standards 1.6 and 6.5 B., it is essential that adequate plans be developed to facilitate the return of children. The use of contracts, or formal agreements, between the parents and agency is particularly appropriate and useful when a child is placed voluntarily. See Stein, Gambrill and Wiltse, "Foster Care: The Use of Contracts," 32 *Public Welfare* 20 (Fall 1974); Maluccio and Marlow, "The Case for the Contract," 19 *Social Work* 28 (Jan. 1974).

10.7 Juvenile court supervision.

No child should remain in placement longer than six months unless the child is made a ward of the juvenile court, and the court, at a hearing in which both the parents and child are represented by counsel, finds that continued placement is necessary.

Commentary

Under this standard if a child remains in placement beyond six months, the placement agency would be required to file a petition with the juvenile court. The petition would state only that the child has been in care for six months and that the parents are unwilling or unable to resume custody. If after a hearing at which all parties are represented by counsel, the court finds that the parents are, in fact, unwilling or unable to resume custody, the court should assume jurisdiction over the family. The consequences of court jurisdiction are that the case would be regularly reviewed every six months as provided in Standard 7.1, and that the provisions of Standards 8.3 and 8.4 regarding termination of parental rights would become applicable. See Standard 10.8 and commentary.

The issue of whether there should be any court intervention following a voluntary placement is a controversial and complicated one. Expert commentators take positions ranging from eliminating all voluntary placements and requiring court approval of any placement to advocating total family autonomy, with no judicial review in any case. If it is decided that some judicial review is necessary, it must be decided when that review should occur and whether it should apply to all children in care or only certain groups.

Those who argue against any court involvement assert that in a system based on family autonomy, parental actions should be free from state control unless a child is endangered in a specific way. These commentators would argue that living in foster care is not endangerment *per se;* many groups of children, such as those in boarding schools, live away from their parents, yet there is no state intervention. Given this fact, mandatory court review constitutes unjustified discrimination against poor families, who must rely on state help when placing their children.

These standards reject this position. Some type of court review is essential to protect both the parents and the children. For the reasons discussed in the commentary to Standard 7.5 A., internal agency review does not provide adequate protection against either coercion of the parents or abandonment of children by parents after a child is in care. As Professor Festinger of the New York University School of Social Work has recently concluded, following her study of New York's court review procedures:

> [I]t seems unfortunate that the court review has been regarded by some in the child welfare field as an unnecessary watchdog looking over the shoulders of the agencies. . . . Clearly the [social work] field's verbal assurances and its long history of service to children do not meet the public's demand for accountability. . . . In view of the weaknesses of the existing accountability mechanism, and given a history of children remaining too long in foster care while unvisited, families who too

often do not receive needed services, and agencies that are often slow to move in the direction of adoption, the review process can . . . be regarded as a collaborative effort that endeavors to ensure the welfare of children. . . . Festinger, "The New York Court Review of Children in Foster Care," 54 *Child Welfare* 211, 243-44 (1975).

Given the extent of the deficiencies in the current system, it is reasonable to consider requiring court approval of all placements. Such a system would have a number of advantages. Court review might lead to better evaluation of the need for placement and a more extensive search for alternatives to placement. While courts presently act as perfunctorily as agencies in accepting placement, this should change under the proposed standards in this volume. Mandatory court review would also help screen out involuntary "voluntary" placements. Making all children in placement wards of the court also would facilitate monitoring the status of these children, thereby increasing the chances of an early decision on permanent placement.

However, there are substantial reasons for not mandating court approval in all cases. First, court review might discourage some parents from using placements who should be able to do so, for the child's benefit as well as the parents'. It is certainly likely that even with the development of additional social services some parents will need to place their children during a period of personal crisis. For example, if a single parent of an infant needs to be hospitalized for several weeks and has no one to care for the child, short-term placement in a foster home may be the best type of care for the child. In some cases placement is essential following a divorce or death of a spouse, since the custodial parent cannot provide adequately for the child.

It is possible that if parents had to go to court, they might either leave the child in an unsuitable home environment or place the child privately in an unsuitable home without state involvement.

Second, even if required court involvement did not discourage placements, it must also be considered that court hearings are costly and time consuming. It is questionable whether these costs are justified. Depending on the jurisdiction, anywhere between 20-50 percent of all children voluntarily placed are returned to their parents within a year, most within six months. See Festinger, *supra;* Jenkins, "Duration of Foster Care: Some Relevant Antecedent Variables," 46 *Child Welfare* 450 (1967). If administrative procedures are adequate to avoid unnecessary initial placements, then mandatory court approval would result in wasting the time of parents, judges, lawyers, and social workers.

A third reason for rejecting the elimination of placements without court approval is that requiring court intervention discriminates against the poor. Rich parents can place their children without state assistance and therefore are not generally subject to any type review. It is, arguably, unfair to require court review solely because the poorer parent must rely on state aid, both in finding a placement and in paying for the child's care while he/she is in placement.

For these reasons, mandatory review in all cases is rejected. Instead, the standards adopt a middle position, designed to allow parents the right to place their children for a limited amount of time without any outside review, but requiring review when the child has been left in care beyond six months. The best available data indicate that if a child is left in care longer than six months, the chances of return decline significantly. See Jenkins, *supra*; Festinger, *supra*; Gruber, *supra;* Fanshel, "The Exit of Children from Foster Care: An Interim Report," 50 *Child Welfare* 65 (1971). In order to protect these children from consignment to impermanent foster care, and to protect those parents who want to resume custody, court review is essential.

Therefore, as soon as a child has been in placement for six months, the supervising agency should file a petition in court. The court should assume jurisdiction unless the parents resume custody. The court should then make certain that a plan is developed for returning the child, following Standard 6.5. The parents should also be informed about the possibility of termination if they cannot resume custody, as provided in Standard 8.3 C. 6.

For the purposes of this standard, both parents, even if one is absent, should be notified of the court proceedings.

10.8 Termination of parental rights.

If a child is brought under court supervision, the standards for termination of parental rights contained in Part VIII should apply.

Commentary

Standard 10.8 addresses the most difficult issue regarding voluntary placements, *i.e.*, what should happen if the parent(s) are not able to resume custody for a substantial period of time. The position adopted is that despite the fact that the child is in care through parental action, not because the child is endangered, the child should not be allowed to remain in care indefinitely. Long-term foster care is as harmful to children placed voluntarily as it is to those in care because they were endangered. Therefore, the same standards are applied for termination as for endangered children. See Part VIII and commentary.

The proposed standards are aimed primarily at parents who abandon their children to the foster care system by failing to visit and plan for the return of their children. The standards may seem particularly harsh when applied to single parents who are imprisoned, in mental institutions, or who are suffering from drug or alcohol addiction. They may desire to keep their children, but are unable to do so. Loss of their children is certainly an added punishment. To some degree the impact of the standard may be mitigated if the parent is able to maintain a correspondence and visit regularly with his/her child in order to retain parental ties. In such instances the case might fall under exceptions 8.4 A. or E., since termination may be harmful to the child where the parent has retained contact. In many other cases the child can be placed with a relative who will continue to care for him/her, but who does not support termination of parental rights. Again termination would not be permissible. This may be especially true with regard to children who are older and who had been living with the parent at the time of imprisonment or commitment to a mental institution. See Standard 8.3 C. 6.

Dissenting Views*

Statement of Commissioner Wilfred W. Nuernberger

I dissent to the *Abuse and Neglect* volume for the following reasons:

No one would argue with protecting family autonomy but it should not abrogate the rights of children. I believe the volume is based on the premise that in every case of coercive intervention, termination of parental rights is a possibility and therefore the basis for intervention must be very restrictive. The result is that children are left unprotected except in the most severe cases of physical abuse. The neglect proceeding is an unusual proceeding because there are three parties involved, not two. Because of the age and immaturity of the child, the child is unable to take action to protect himself; although, if the child has reached adolescence and runs away from an intolerable home situation, the law will now protect him under the proposed standards for "Noncriminal Misbehavior." Unfortunately, those standards do not protect the very young unable to run away or the child who is unaware of the proposed standards.

I also believe that the standards are made so complicated that it will be difficult for the average person to understand them or even follow the same. The procedure to protect neglected children must be written, not only for the legal expert, but for the persons who provide the services.

The limitations placed on coercive intervention fail to recognize that many cases of neglect can be solved when there is an authority able to order someone to cease and desist.

I believe there can be a basis for intervention other than physical harm sufficient to lead to an eventual termination of parental rights.

Children find home situations which are intolerable and they need some support in correcting those situations. The proposed standards

---

*These statements were prepared with reference to the standards in the tentative draft, but they are relevant to the revised standards in principle, although details may differ.

allow battering and abusing children as long as it does no severe permanent damage and I believe this is wrong. I quote from the commentary,

> The proposed definitions seek to distinguish between cases of physical discipline which even if they result in minor bruises, pose no threat of severe or permanent damage and cases which do pose such a threat. This does not imply acceptance of corporal punishment as a means of discipline. Rather it reflects the judgment that even in cases of physical injury, unless the actual or potential injury is serious, the detriment from coercive intervention is likely to be greater than the benefit.

I submit that a child has a right to proper care. This country has made some progress against the theory that children are chattels. If the state is not going to speak for neglected children, someone will have to speak out for them. If the state cannot assume this protective role, perhaps this country will need to again ask private organizations such as the "Society for Prevention of Cruelty to Animals" to establish such societies in every community and broaden their jurisdiction to include children.

If the law of negligence can establish a degree of care that the reasonable prudent person owes to strangers with whom he has contact, certainly the law can establish a standard of care that the reasonable prudent parent of a particular culture owes to his children.

I dissent to Standard 3.3 which requires court approval of investigations by agencies who receive complaints of neglected or abused children. There is nothing wrong with the present procedure. The idea that only a court can perform this function is not correct. I know of no abuse of the present method of investigation and I see no reason to place the court in this position. The court does have a role in enjoining improper investigations but that authority presently exists. Nor should the court determine whether a petition should be authorized as provided in Standards 4.3 A. and 5.2 A. and B.

I object to Standard 4.1 which calls for an emergency caretaker to enter a home where a child has been left unattended but provides no protection for that caretaker or immunity to the caretaker. No one will know whether it will be safe for a caretaker who is found in the home when the parent eventually returns. There may be some cases where this will work but it should not be a standard.

I object to 5.3E. requiring a jury trial in what really amounts to an equity action where the rights of the child and the parent are the issues. The jury trial provision will make it impossible to meet the time limitations as required by other standards. To also require the decision of the jury to be unanimous, clearly indicates that the proceeding is not one which considers the rights of a child as a party but treats a neglect proceeding synonymous with a criminal prosecution.

The standard of proof as set forth in 6.4 C. 1. is a preponderance of the evidence that the child cannot be protected in the case of physical abuse but Section 6.4 C. 2. requires clear and convincing evidence that the child cannot be protected from further harm in the case of emotional neglect. In an area where proof is difficult the standard makes proof practically impossible.

Standard 6.4 C. 4. sets forth a standard that states that a child cannot be removed from the home even if the child is threatened with death if the condition is due to environmental factors beyond the control of the parents. If the choice is between death and removal, I vote for removal and I object to the standard.

I believe that the standards on termination of parental rights are unconstitutional under "due process" and "equal protection." To make the length of time that a child is in a foster home the determinative factor as is shown by the following commentary is wrong.

> The standards require that parental rights be terminated, in most cases, after the child has been in placement for a specific period of time, even if this means terminating the rights of some parents who would regain custody if given more time and help. They do not require any showing of parental "unfitness" other than unfitness to resume custody without endangering the child. It is recognized that many of the parents who will lose their children have suffered from the grave inequalities in our social and economic system, as well as from discriminatory practices in the delivery of social services.

I believe that Standard 8.5 which says that a child shall not be removed from a foster home if the foster parents are unwilling or unable to adopt a child, but are willing to provide and are capable of providing the child with a permanent home assumes that when a foster parent states that they will provide a permanent home, that the statement is an accomplished fact. As a matter of fact, many foster homes start out to be permanent foster homes but circumstances change resulting in foster parents changing their mind. It will be no solution to the problem to have the foster parents utter the magic words that they wish to be "a permanent foster home," but more serious is the fact that the adoption of such a standard would mean that foster parents would take the position that they were willing to provide a permanent foster home thereby bringing more uncertainty into the life of that child. Subsidized adoption would be an answer to the problem but allowing a foster parent to bring uncertainty into the life of the child by stating that they are willing to provide a permanent home would open a "Pandora's box." To recommend this position as a standard only illustrates how easy it is to call an "innovative idea" a "criterion of excellence."

In conclusion, the writer of this dissent acknowledges the fault of any dissent not having the benefit of group discussion to correct and clarify the ideas expressed.

Statement of Commissioner Justine Wise Polier

This important IJA-ABA volume proposes a new model for dealing with the problems of children subject to court intervention by reason of neglect, abuse, abandonment or destitution. Its first general principle is the safeguarding of family autonomy, and it abandons the goal of seeking the best interests of a child on an individual basis. It assumes that all juvenile court action is "coercive," bad, and to be avoided, except in extreme situations, and that juvenile courts are not and cannot become constructive instruments for help to vulnerable families.

In support of the new model, the volume reports on wrongful over-intervention by courts, the niggardly resources provided by legislative appropriations, and the limited knowledge on what is best for children. It records the harms done to children placed by families or courts in the endless limbo of foster care. There is, however, a lack of hard data on the consequences of leaving children in as contrasted with removing children from, harmful and seriously inadequate family situations.

The major standards presented can be broken down in three parts:

First, the standards propose needed procedural protections for families and children subject to court intervention under present laws. There is, however, a leap from the proposed due process recommendations to the assumption that rules laid down by state legislatures to restrict judicial action will lead to greater justice and services to children, or achieve "quality decisions." Whether this position is based on greater confidence in state legislatures than in the courts or is only a strategy to restrict the jurisdiction and discretion of the courts is not clear.

Second, the standards would eliminate neglect, abuse, abandonment or destitution as grounds for juvenile court jurisdiction. They would be replaced by a single category—"endangerment." Endangerment is defined as primarily limited to serious physical harm. Serious emotional harm is excluded unless there is also clear and convincing evidence of the child showing symptoms of severe anxiety, depression, withdrawal, or untoward aggressive behavior, *and* of the parents being unwilling to provide treatment. This position is also taken in regard to cases involving family incest.

The proposed standards assume that children subject to physical harm are at greatest risk, and that, therefore, the limited resources available should be reserved for them. This assumption is not supported by data. More important, it fails to consider the experience of those who have worked with neglected children. Crippling harms including delinquent behavior have been found to result when children suffer neglect by reason of the mental or emotional disabilities of parents who cannot cope with parenthood.

The standards propose that more services made available to parents on a truly voluntary basis should replace coercive intervention by the courts. However, services that can be secured voluntarily are at least as, if not more, scarce than the resources available to the juvenile courts. In addition, parents of many neglected and abused children are unwilling or unable to either seek or accept services voluntarily.

Third, in striking contrast with the major principle of support for family autonomy, the standards move to almost exclusive concern for the "best interests" of a child after removal from home. Here, it is acknowledged that many children who enter foster care cannot be returned to their biological parents. For those who are unable to return home, swifter termination of parental rights is recommended to achieve permanent homes, hopefully through adoption. However, the recognition that all biological parents cannot act as parents, and that children are entitled to growing up in homes that will provide permanence and continuity, is limited to those children who have been placed in foster care voluntarily or following a finding of "endangerment".

Time tables for court action to terminate parental rights are proposed for this group of children. Whether they are adequate or too rigid raises questions that can only be answered by further study of the constitutional issues and more experience of what actually happens to children.

In conclusion, this volume challenges many of the wrongs perpetrated against children who are neglected by their families and the community. Unfortunately it was prepared during a decade when disillusionment, frustration, and increasing avoidance of concern for human problems dominated the ethos. The response is too largely one of lowering goals required to protect children. At this time, despite past failures, standards for the future should require more rigorous assessment of children's needs, effective monitoring of services, research on the results of different ways of providing services, and expansion of services to all children in accordance with their needs.

The denigration of state or court action by appending the adjective "coercive" does not solve the problems of neglected children in American society. Benign neglect is no more valid as an answer to the needs of children than it is to continuing racism in this country. The word "coercive" is not appended to legislative decisions, administrative decisions, to denials or discrimination by voluntary services, or to conditions imposed by parents on their children. While maintaining that deference to family autonomy is most likely to be helpful to most children, the question of which children will be helped and which hurt by such deference is never faced. Finally, inaction to meet the needs of children is not recognized as coercive.

Bibliography

BAR PUBLICATIONS, COMMISSION AND LEGISLATIVE REPORTS, MODEL LAWS

American Public Welfare Association, "Standards for Foster Family Services System" (1975).

Child Welfare League of America, "Standards for Child Protective Services" (1973).

Education Commission of the States, "Child Abuse and Neglect: Alternatives for State Legislation" (1973).

Joint Commission on Mental Health of Children, "Crisis in Child Mental Health: Challenge for the 1970's" (1969).

"Report of the New York Select Committee on Child Abuse" (1972).

U.S. Children's Bureau, "Legislative Guides for the Termination of Parental Rights and Responsibilities and the Adoption of Children" (1961).

BOOKS, MONOGRAPHS, AND REPORTS

B. Bernstein, D. Snider, and W. Meezan, "A Preliminary Report: Foster Care Needs and Alternatives for Placement" (1975).

A. Billingsley and J. Giovannoni, *Children of the Storm* (1972).

J. Bowlby, *Child Care and the Growth of Love* (2d ed. 1965).

G. Brown, ed., *The Multi-Problem Dilemma: A Social Research Demonstration with Multi-Problem Families* (1968).

Children's Defense Fund, *Children Without Homes* (1978).

E. Davenstedt, *The Drifters* (1971).

P. DeCourcy and J. DeCourcy, *A Silent Tragedy* (1973).

V. DeFrancis, *Child Abuse Legislation in the 1970's* (rev. ed. 1973).

C. Devereaux, A. Fagerstron, and G. Kerr, "Adoptions and Foster Care Study Report" (Calif. Dept. of Health 1973).

D. Fanshel and E. Shinn, *Dollars and Sense in the Foster Care of Children: A Look at Cost Factors* (1972).

D. Fanshel and E.B. Shinn, *Children in Foster Care: A Longitudal Investigation* (1978).

B. Fraser, *Legislative Approaches to Child Abuse: A Statutory Compilation* (1973).

203

B. Fraser, "The Guardian Ad Litem, the Abused Child and the Colorado Law" (1974).

D. Gil, *Violence Against Children* (1973).

J. Goldstein, A. Freud, and A. Solnit, *Beyond the Best Interests of the Child* (1973).

A. Gruber, "Foster Home Care in Massachusetts" (1973).

R.E. Helfer and C.H. Kempe, *The Battered Child* (1968).

S. Jenkins and S. Norman, *Filial Deprivation and Foster Care* (1972).

S. Jenkins and M. Sauber, *Paths to Child Placement* (1966).

M. Jones, R. Neuman, and A. Shyne, "A Second Chance for Families: Evaluation of a Program to Reduce Foster Care" (1976).

A. Kadushin, *Child Welfare Services* (2d ed. 1974).

S. Katz, *When Parents Fail* (1971).

J. Koshel, *Deinstitutionalization—Dependent and Neglected Children* (1973).

N. Littner, *Some Traumatic Effects of Separation and Placement* (1956).

H. Maas and R.E. Engler, Jr., *Children in Need of Parents* (1959).

M. Paul, *Criteria for Foster Placement and Alternatives to Foster Care* (1975).

M. Phillips, A. Shyne, E. Sherman, and D. Haring, *Factors Associated with Placement Decisions in Child Welfare* (1971).

N. Polansky, R. Borgman, and C. DeSaix, *Roots of Futility* (1972).

N. Polansky, C. DeSaix, and S. Sharlin, *Child Neglect: Understanding and Reaching the Parent* (1972).

N. Polansky, C. Hally, and N. Polansky, *State Knowledge of Child Neglect* (1974).

Regional Research Institute for Human Services, Portland State University School of Social Work, "Barriers to Planning for Children in Foster Care: A Summary" (1976).

M. Rutter, *Maternal Deprivation Reassessed* (1972).

D. Shapiro, *Agencies and Foster Children* (1976).

E. Sherman, R. Neuman, and A. Shyne, *Children Adrift in Foster Care* (1973).

B. Steele, *Working with Abusive Parents from a Psychiatric Point of View* (1975).

H. Stone, *Reflections on Foster Care* (1969).

A. Sussman and S. Cohen, *Reporting Child Abuse and Neglect: Guidelines for Legislation* (1975).

Y. Tormes, *Child Victims of Incest* (1968).

S. Vasaly, *Foster Care in Five States: A Synthesis and Analysis of Studies from Arizona, California, Iowa, Massachusetts and Vermont* (H.E.W. 1978).

E. Weinstein, *The Self-Image of the Foster Child* (1960).

S. White, *Federal Programs for Young Children: Review and Recommendations* (1973).

ARTICLES, NOTES, AND COMMENT

Areen, "Intervention Between Parent and Child: A Reappraisal of the State's Role in Child Neglect and Abuse Cases," 63 *Geo. L. Rev.* 887 (1975).

Becker, "Due Process and Child Protection Proceedings: State Intervention in Family Relations on Behalf of Neglected Children," 2 *Cumb.-San. L. Rev.* 247 (1971).

Bourne and Newberger, "'Family Autonomy' or 'Coercive Intervention'? Ambiguity and Conflict in the Proposed Standards for Child Abuse and Neglect" 57 *B.U.L. Rev.* 670 (1977).

Briar, "Clinical Judgment in Foster Care Placement," 42 *Child Welfare* 161 (1963).

Burt, "Developing Constitutional Rights Of, In and For Children," 39 *Law & Contemp. Prob.* 118 (1975).

Burt, "Forcing Protection on Children and Their Parents: The Impact of *Wyman v. James*," 69 *Mich. L. Rev.* 1259 (1971).

Burt and Balyeat, "A New System for Improving the Care of Neglected and Abused Children," 53 *Child Welfare* 167 (1974).

Campbell, "The Neglected Child: His and His Family's Treatment Under Massachusetts Law and Practice and Their Rights Under the Due Process Clause," 4 *Suffolk L. Rev.* 631 (1970).

Chappell, "Organizing Periodic Review in Foster Care: The South Carolina Story," 54 *Child Welfare* 477 (1975).

Council of Judges of the National Council on Crime and Delinquency, "Guides to the Judge in Medical Orders Affecting Children," 14 *Crime & Delinq.* 107 (1968).

Daly, "Willful Child Abuse and State Reporting Statute," 23 *U. Miami L. Rev.* 283 (1969).

DeFrancis, "Protecting the Child Victim of Sex Crimes Committed by Adults," 35 *Fed. Prob.* 15 (1971).

Dembitz, "Child Abuse and the Law," 24 *Record* 613 (1969).

Dembitz, "Welfare Home Visits: Child Versus Parent," 57 *A.B.A.J.* 871 (1971).

Dobson, "The Juvenile Court and Parental Right," 4 *Fam. L.Q.* 393 (1970).

Eads, "Observations on the Establishment of a Child Protective Services System in California," 21 *Stan. L. Rev.* 1129 (1969).

Fanshel, "Parental Visiting of Children in Foster Care: Key to Discharge?" 49 *Soc. Serv. Rev.* 493 (1975).

Fanshel, "Status Changes of Children in Foster Care: Final Results of the Columbia University Longitudinal Study," 55 *Child Welfare* 143 (1976).

Festinger, "The New York Court Review of Children in Foster Care," 54 *Child Welfare* 211 (1975).

Fischer, "Is Casework Effective? A Review," 18 *Social Work* 5 (Jan. 1973).

Forer, "Child and the Courts," 53 *Women's L.J.* 43 (1967).

Forer, "Rights of Children: The Legal Vacuum," 55 *A.B.A.J.* 1151 (1969).

Foster and Freed, "A Bill of Rights for Children," 6 *Fam. L.Q.* 343 (1972).

Franklin, "An Exception to Use of the Physician-Patient Privilege in Child Abuse Cases," 42 *U. Det. L.J.* 88 (1964).

Gambrill and Wiltse, "Foster Care: Prescriptions for Change," 32 *Pub. Welfare* 39 (Summer 1974).

Gil, "Institutions for Children" in *Children and Decent People* (A. Schorr ed. 1974).

Gill, "The Legal Nature of Neglect," 6 *N.P.P.A.J.* 1 (1960).

Goldstein, "Medical Care for the Child at Risk: On State Supervention of Parental Autonomy," 86 *L.J.* 645 (1977).

Goldstein, "Why Foster Care—For Whom, For How Long?" 30 *Psychoanalytic Study of the Child* 647 (1975).

Gordon, "Terminal Placements of Children and Permanent Termination of Parental Rights," 46 *St. John's L. Rev.* 215 (1971).

Grumet, "The Plaintive Plaintiffs: Victims of the Battered Child Syndrome," 4 *Fam. L.Q.* 296 (1970).

Handler, "The Juvenile Court and the Adversary System: Problems of Function and Form," 1965 *Wis. L. Rev.* 7.

Hansen, "Child Abuse Legislation and the Interdisciplinary Approach," 52 *A.B.A.J.* 734 (1966).

Kaplan, "Domestic Relations—Appointment of Counsel for the Abused Child," 58 *Cornell L. Rev.* 177 (1972).

Katz, "Freeing Children for Permanent Placement Through a Model Act," 12 *Fam. L.Q.* 203 (1978).

Katz, Howe, and McGrath, "Child Neglect Laws in America," 9 *Fam. L.Q.* 1 (1975).

Ketchum and Babcock, "Statutory Grounds for the Involuntary Termination of Parental Rights," 29 *Rutgers L. Rev.* 530 (1976).

Levine, "Caveat Parens: A Demystification of the Child Protection System," 35 *U. Pitt. L. Rev.* 1 (1973).

Levine, "Foundations for Drafting a Model Statute to Terminate Parental Rights: A Selected Bibliography," 26 *Juv. Justice* 42 (1975).

Libai, "Protection of Child Victims of a Sexual Offense in the Criminal Justice System," 15 *Wayne L. Rev.* 977 (1969).

Light, "Abused and Neglected Children in America: A Study of Alternative Policies," 43 *Harv. Ed. Rev.* 556 (1973).

Lincoln, "Model Statute for Termination of Parental Rights," 27 *Juv. Justice* 3 (November 1976).

Littner, "The Importance of the Natural Parent to the Child in Placement," 54 *Child Welfare* 175 (1975).

Maas, "Children in Long-Term Foster Care," 48 *Child Welfare* 321 (1969).

Maccoby and Masters, "Attachment and Dependency," in 2 *Manual of Child Psychology* 159–260 (P. Mussen ed., 3d ed. 1970).

McCathren, "Accountability in the Child Protection System: A Defense of the Proposed Standards Relating to Abuse and Neglect," 57 *B.U.L. Rev.* 707 (1977).

McCord, "The Battered Child and Other Assaults Upon the Family," 50 *Minn. L. Rev.* 1 (1965).

Mnookin, "Foster Care—In Whose Best Interest?" 43 *Harv. Ed. Rev.* 599 (1973).

Mnookin, "Child Custody Adjudication: Judicial Functions in the Face of Indeterminacy," 39 *L. & Contemp. Prob.* 226 (1976).

Note, "Acting 'In Loco Parentis' as a Defense to Assault and Battery," 16 *Clev.-Mar. L. Rev.* 39 (1967).

Note, "Appointment of a Counsel for the Abused Child: Statutory Schemes and the New York Approach," 58 *Cornell L. Rev.* 177 (1972).

Note, "Child Beating: Recent Legislation Requiring Reporting of Physical Abuse," 45 *Ore. L. Rev.* 114 (1966).

Note, "Child Neglect: Due Process for the Parent," 70 *Colum. L. Rev.* 465 (1970).

Note, "Court Ordered Non-Emergency Medical Care for Infants," 18 *Clev.- Mar. L. Rev.* 296 (1969).

Note, "The Custody Question and Child Neglect Rehearings," 35 *U. Chi. L. Rev.* 478 (1968).

Note, "Evidentiary Problems in Criminal Child Abuse Proceedings," 63 *Geo. L.J.* 241 (1975).

Note, "The Fundamental Right to Family Integrity and Its Role in New York Foster Care Adjudication," 44 *Brooklyn L. Rev.* 63 (1977).

Note, "*Palmer v. State; Craig v. State*: Criminal Liability of Parent for Omission Causing Death of Child," 21 *Md. L. Rev.* 262 (1961).

Note, "Privileged Communication—Abrogation of the Physician-Patient Privilege to Protect the Battered Child," 15 *DePaul L. Rev.* 453 (1966).

Note, "Representation in Child Neglect Cases: Are Parents Neglected?" 4 *Colum. J.L. & Soc. Probs.* 230 (1968).

Note, "State Intrusion into Family Affairs: Justifications and Limitations," 26 *Stan. L. Rev.* 1383 (1974).

Note, "*State v. McMaster*: Due Process in Termination of Parental Rights," 8 *Willamette L.J.* 284 (1972).

Note, "Termination of Parental Rights and the Lesser Restrictive Alternative Doctrine," 12 *Tulsa L.J.* 528 (1977).

Note, "Termination of Parental Rights Statutes and the Void for Vagueness Doctrine," 16 *J. Fam. L.* 213 (1977–78).

Note, "Termination of Parental Rights—Suggested Reforms and Responses," 16 *J. Fam. L.* 239 (1977–78).

Paulsen, "Child Abuse Reporting Laws: The Shape of the Legislation," 67 *Colum. L. Rev.* 1 (1967).

Paulsen, "The Legal Framework for Child Protection," 66 *Colum. L. Rev.* 679 (1966).

Paulsen, Parker, and Adelman, "Child Abuse Reporting Laws—Some Legislative History," 34 *Geo. Wash. L. Rev.* 482 (1966).

Pavenstedt, "An Intervention Program for Infants from High Risk Homes," 63 *Am. J. Pub. Health* 393 (1973).

Robertson and Robertson, "Young Children in Brief Separations," 26 *Psychoanalytic Study of the Child* 264 (1971).

Shepherd, "The Abused Child and the Law," 22 *Wash. & Lee L. Rev.* 182 (1965).

Sullivan, "Child Neglect: The Environmental Aspects," 29 *Ohio St. L.J.* 85 (1968).

Swanson, "Role of the Police in the Protection of Children from Neglect and Abuse," 25 *Fed. Prob.* 43 (1961).

Symposium, "The Relationship Between Promise and Performance in State Intervention in Family Life," 9 *Colum. J.L. & Soc. Probs.* 28 (1972).

Tamilia, "Neglect Proceedings and the Conflict Between Law and Society," 9 *Duquesne L. Rev.* 579 (1973).

Wald, "State Intervention on Behalf of 'Neglected' Children: A Search for Realistic Standards," 27 *Stan. L. Rev.* 985 (1975).

Wald, "State Intervention on Behalf of 'Neglected' Children: A Search for Standards for Placement of Children from Their Homes, Monitoring the Status of Children in Foster Care, and Termination of Parental Rights," 28 *Stan. L. Rev.* 626 (1976).

Wiltse and Gambrill, "Foster Care, 1973: A Reappraisal," 32 *Pub. Welfare* 7 (1974).